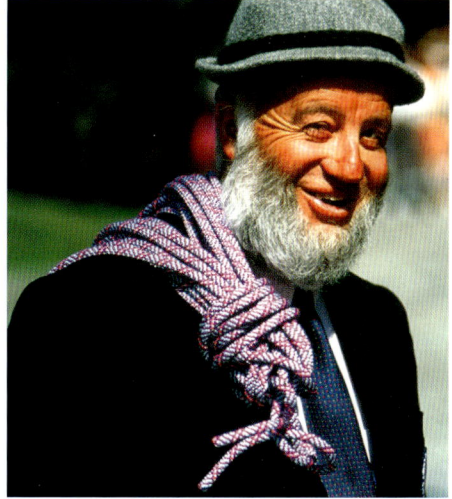

For JP Devouassoux
who was the first
to believe in this book
and who opened up
so many doors to me...

THE COMPAGNIE DES GUIDES DE CHAMONIX

A HISTORY

Mario Colonel

Roger Frison-Roche
in 1996
with his grand-daughter
Béatrice Mugnier,
also a member of the
Compagnie des Guides.

PREFACE

1930 was a good year for me!

I got married and I was admitted to the Compagnie des Guides de Chamonix.

I was the first 'foreigner' to join their close-knit fraternity, testament to the friendship of those who were prepared to propose me!

My sponsors included Alfred Couttet Champion, Ravanel Le Rouge – with whom I made the first descent from Mont Blanc via the Miage glacier and the Kennedy Route on the Italian side of the massif – as well as Armand and Georges Charlet from Argentière and not forgetting Camille à Pic (Devouassoux). In those days we would regularly train at the end of the season in the Aiguilles Rouges: on Persévérance and the Doigt de Mesure (which has since collapsed). These climbs among friends ended up with Armand Charlet making the first winter ascent of the Aiguille de Bionnassay from Saint Gervais!

Later on, as 'adults', we would do route after route: in the Dolomites with Couttet Champion, on the Grands Gendarmes next to the Aiguille du Chardonnet, winter ascents, and skiing in the mountains. My one and only victory in a downhill ski race was an extremely rapid descent from the Col Supérieur du Tour Noir down to the Argentière plateau.

I started off as a porter with Ravanel Le Rouge, and continued doing routes with André Devouassoux and, more often, Marcel Burnet, the greatest guide of his generation.

The story of our Compagnie des Guides is a great and yet a very human one, filled with success, failure and grief.

I am proud to have kept the promises I made on that day in 1930, when I was admitted as an active member of this doyen of professional guiding associations, that is high-mountain guide associations.

I respectfully salute those who stand out among the great mountain guides – Michel Croz, Alfred Couttet, Argentière's Ravanel brothers – and all the past, present and future members of our esteemed Compagnie.

May it long continue!
Chamonix, 5 May 1997

Roger Frison-Roche

This preface was written for the first edition of this book, published in 1997.
Roger Frison-Roche, author, journalist, mountaineer and guide passed away on 17 December 1999, the eve of the 21st century. He will be remembered by Chamoniards and all those who love the mountains.

CONTENTS

SHADOWS AND LIGHT

Nothing but a legend, you say?
You want nothing but facts?
Facts are perishable, believe me, only legends remain, like the soul after the body, or
perfume in the wake of a woman.
ROCK OF TANIOS. AMIN MAALOUF

This is just a story, a history. This is a narrative of those 900 men who for two cen-
turies have devoted themselves to the mountains. Whether anonymous or illustrious,
they have woven through their dreams, their technical ability and their humanity the
fabric of Chamonix's Compagnie des Guides. A seal of quality of sorts, which since its
inception has exerted a kind of unquestioning fascination or total disdain; either way
it is difficult to have no opinion.

Strange as it may sound, this company par excellence has always had a curiously
ambiguous existence, one of shadow and light.

That is the shadow of the guides who carry out their work with style; the light of
those others whose fine first ascents and exploits have left their mark on the pillars of
Mont Blanc and elsewhere. It is also the story of community and individualism, of a
community defending its rights and privileges, fellow members and a way of life; the
individualism of men with a passion for freedom. Finally, it is also a tale of personal
ambition and selflessness; of those driven by a desire for fame and others devoting their
lives to the service of others. Seen from outside, this ambivalence has been magnified
and distorted. A small number of often top-class and remarkable guides have acted for
some time, whether voluntarily or not, as ambassadors for this mass of men who are
passionate about their work. And the Compagnie has been reduced to a Michel Croz,
an Armand Charlet or a Roger Frison-Roche. Yet can a man be reduced to a simple
calculation or the letters of a chemical formula?

I would have been tempted to say that guides, like contented couples, have no story.
However, a glance at their decades of work shows that none of them deserves to be
forgotten.

This book represents a journey, with its merits and its faults. It makes no literary or
historical pretensions; it is simply a track following a mountain path. It is as though
modern-day Chamonix needed to rediscover its roots and learn once again about the
personalities that have in a way fashioned the region in their own image...

Mario Colonel

BIRTH
OF
A LEGEND

IT WOULD TAKE NEARLY SEVENTY YEARS
FOR THIS GREAT INSTITUTION TO TRULY FIND ITS FEET.
FROM THE CONQUEST OF MONT BLANC
AND THE EARLY SCIENTIFIC EXPEDITIONS
TO THE FIRST TRAGEDIES AND GREAT DISPUTES,
THE COMPAGNIE WOULD PLAY A PIVOTAL ROLE
IN THE HISTORY OF MOUNTAINEERING...

It all starts with, and comes back to, Mont Blanc, and it is no coincidence that mountain guiding as a profession was born on its slopes.

Its shattered geology has all the ingredients for a truly exceptional adventure. The range is packed with handsome peaks, icy north faces on intimate terms with their warm south-facing cousins, a summit revealed to be the highest in Western Europe, great rock with its high quality gneiss, and last and not least, the men. With their thickset frames, faces tanned like old sailors and hands etched by a lifetime of work and adventure, Chamonix's menfolk were continually casting worried yet excited glances above them.

And like the mountains, they were destined for epic existences. A tour of the hamlets, houses huddled round a church or chapel, in Les Mouilles, La Frasse, Taconnaz or Les Pélerins would always find a montagnard – mountain-dweller – ready to put in a track, plough his way through drifts of fresh snow, to find a way through fields and mountain pastures for livestock and people.

And if demons continued to inhabit the lofty peaks and send down avalanches, floods and other great misfortunes, the day would come when a Chamoniard would gaze at the mountains with something other than a sense of dread and foreboding.

Chamonix had the good fortune to be visited by a number of inspiring travellers who would help in this change of opinion.

The Englishmen Windham and Pococke started the fashion for all things glacial in 1741. Then there came Horace-Bénédict De Saussure from Geneva.

He would make the third ascent of Mont Blanc and give Chamonix a reason to start exploring the mountains. By putting up a handsome reward for the person who could find a route up Mont Blanc, he threw the spotlight onto all those who had, for the preceding decades, been climbing the couloirs and surveying the summits in complete anonymity.

The Montenvers Hotel at the start of the 19th century.

Extract from the book 'Huit jours au pas de charge en Savoie et en Suisse' (An eight-day charge through Savoy and Switzerland), by Paul de Quick.

Mountaineering history was at last starting to be written. The Droites and the Courtes had already been climbed by crystal hunters, but until now they had been wary of talking about their discoveries.

The crystal and chamois hunters – no doubt the same people who took it upon themselves to open up lines of communication between the hamlets and villages when the winter and bad weather came – were the masters of these high lands. They were already set apart from the rest of the valley's inhabitants.

De Saussure described the chamois hunters as *"wild-looking with something of the haggard and fierce about them that makes them stand out from the crowd"*. They would be the first to challenge superstition but always within limits, they were afraid to sleep up high, especially on the glaciers. So, they would rush up the mountains, extract the crystals and get them down to the valley as quickly as possible. If they were benighted they would find shelter in the rocks, dozing against a wall of rock or curled up in a gap in the boulders like a marmot. But they never fell asleep on a glacier. No montagnard wanted to tempt fate and risk freezing to death. The superstitions ran deep indeed…

Hunting chamois and crystals – smoky quartz, fluorite, morion quartz – were what first pushed the valley's inhabitants to explore the mountains.

Previous page :

From the first explorations of the Mer de Glace, it would take the Chamoniards almost 100 years to establish a network of huts, such as this one at the Pierre Pointue, in the range.

*Paccard and Balmat
immortalised
by L.A.G. Bacler d'Albe
in 1788.*

THE LEGEND LOSES ITS LUSTRE: BALMAT AND PACCARD

Pierre Simond had climbed to the Col du Géant and Jean-Marie Couttet and Cuidet had ventured as far as the Dôme du Goûter but dared not go any further, they had to be back on terra firma before dusk.

Thus Mont Blanc, an icy domain par excellence, remained too distant and committing an objective.

Men tried in vain for the next 20 years to find a way around the mountain via the Mer de Glace or the Col du Géant. This choice of itinerary was not entirely down to chance. The crystal hunters and shepherds had always used it as a means of accessing the mountains. But the Combe Maudite ('Accursed Coomb') and the Envers du Mont-Blanc (the 'Other Side of Mont Blanc') quickly brought them up short.

The Massif's vast southern wall wasn't ready to be subdued and attempts were few and far between. It should be noted that the explorers of the day were not really rushing to meet the challenge. The most experienced among them preferred to guide the growing number of tourists wishing to visit the Mer de Glace.

By 1783 Chamonix already had three inns and received about 1500 visitors per year, providing extra work for some of the locals. These were the same men who could have had a go at climbing Mont Blanc, but then why would they want to give up work that paid well for a dangerous and uncertain objective?

They bided their time, reconnoitred the area, starting in the main from the rocks that stuck out of the snow. And the Montagne de la Côte, Grands Mulets and Rochers de l'Heureux Retour became waypoints.

But who would dare to go further and higher, to venture into the very heart of the glaciers?

Other precursors joined the initial group and Michel and François Paccard, Jean-Nicolas Couterand and Victor Tissay, from Lombardy and known as the 'Grand Jorasse', tried in vain to approach the giant. Of Jorasse, De Saussure said, *"his delicate and sentimental soul contrasted the enormity of his face and simplicity of his manners"*. They all tested the ground, used each other's routes and made discoveries, but not one of them dared take the final step.

Until Jacques Balmat entered the fray. An odd fellow, this crystal hunter, and like most montagnards of the day, he had a filthy temper. But is it hardly surprising given the exceptional lives they were expected to eke out of extreme circumstances? As a hunter, Balmat was used to exploring the mountains on his own.

When he met François Paccard and Joseph Carrier

De Saussure, the godfather of alpinism, during an expedition to the Col du Géant.
He would have to wait 20 years to see his dream come true.
Below: Marc-Théodore Bourrit (seen here in a painting by Saint-Ours), the instigator of the plot against Paccard.

at the foot of the Montagne de la Côte on 7 June 1786, he knew they were setting off to climb Mont Blanc and he wanted to be part of the attempt. The two men begrudgingly let him join them. Balmat accompanied them at a distance. When they reached the Grand Plateau he was in front of them, alone, as was his habit.

On the Dôme du Goûter the two Chamoniards met Pierre Balmat and Jean-Marie Couttet, who had come up from the village of Saint Gervais on the other side. The plateau was filled with fog. The group decided to go back down.

By this time Balmat was far in front. *"Well"*, they thought, *"he's a bear of man, he'll just have to look after himself"*. Finely balanced on the crest of the ridge, he carried on, oblivious to the departure of the others. All of a sudden he saw four tiny specks down below, on the Grand Plateau. "The scoundrels, they've abandoned me!" he exclaimed. But there was no way out. Like great figures of mountaineering history to come after him, he felt he was forcing the hand of destiny. He was stranded at over 4000m and, to make matters worse, dusk was falling.

He had to bivouac, and fight off the cold and the mountain's evil spirits. The bivouac was freezing and he spent the whole night banging his feet together and moving his hands to keep them warm. The following morning, 9 June 1786, he found he was numb but alive. And he knew that to conquer Mont Blanc he would have to spend another night at altitude.

He took the time to study the mountain's north face and was convinced there was a way up it. All he had to do now was find a partner to share the risks of the ascent with him.

He met Michel-Gabriel Paccard at his daughter Judith's bedside. Paccard was young, only 29, and had just finished studying medicine in Turin and Paris. He was an educated man with a passion for the natural sciences.

Since 1783 he had made several attempts to climb Mont Blanc. He climbed up the Vallée Blanche first before trying a route via the Aiguille du Goûter.

Paccard was the very image of the passionate amateur and right from the start, it was clear that he was deeply motivated by a desire to succeed. He was a scientist and it was his ardent wish to be the first man to conduct experiments on the summit. However, it never occurred to him to take any glory in the achievement. Jacques Balmat, on the other

The third ascent of Mont Blanc, 2 August 1787, sees De Saussure finally reaching the summit. He is accompanied by 18 guides and porters as well as his trusty valet.

hand, was a pragmatist interested in the prize and he saw the potential rewards of such a partnership. Paccard persuaded Balmat to go with him by promising him his share of De Saussure's prize.

On 7 August 1786 they discretely set off for the Montagne de la Côte. They had neither crampons nor rope. Their equipment, such as it was, included iron-tipped staffs, a blanket and the doctor's scientific instruments.

They set off early on 8 August and headed off just above the Rochers Rouges ('Red Rocks'), right in the middle of the north face of Mont Blanc. It was a good choice. On the snowy summit slopes Paccard went straight, while Balmat made a detour to the left and had to run to catch up with his companion. They reached the summit at 6.23pm precisely.

They got back to the Montagne de la Côte by the light of the full moon and in one go. There they had a comfortable bivouac and it was Jacques Balmat who guided Paccard back to Chamonix. The doctor had lost his hat while on the mountain and was suffering from snow blindness. The official history ends there and Balmat had become the first mountain guide in history. He made second and third ascents the following year.

The latter, on 2 August 1787 to be precise, with De Saussure brought an end to 20 years of failed attempts. The human side of the story, however,

was to spiral precipitously out of control.

Marc-Théodore Bourrit, cantor at Geneva Cathedral and a decidedly mediocre mountaineer, pitted Balmat against Paccard. The affair quickly reached disastrous proportions. Balmat was made out to be Paccard's guide and the man who had taken all the risks. Pretty much right from the start, on 10 August, Paccard had seen fit to draw up a signed affidavit detailing his account of the ascent. But it was to no avail, the myth of Balmat had been born.

By the following year, the situation degenerated further still when a simple conversation between the two men came to blows. From that moment on, Paccard chose to cloak himself in a dignified silence. He explained his choice in a letter in 1823: *"I could have sought financial reparation in the courts, in view of the fact that I had the means. Yet I had been told that it is better for the soul to endure such insults rather than seek to crush them and have them punished, and that greater glory and merit is to be found in enduring such slanders and not seeking to avenge them"*.

As for Balmat, he was quick to reap his rewards, and became the darling of those wishing to make an attempt on the summit. It went without saying that it was he who guided De Saussure. And the King of Sardinia even accorded him the

right to call himself 'Mont-Blanc' and made him Chamonix's official tax collector for life.

Novelists also seized on his life's story, and Alexandre Dumas – author of the Three Musketeers – was one of the first to transform the man from the mountains into a modern-day hero.

History also omitted to record that 8 August 1787 was also the day Judith Balmat died, while her father was seeking glory on the slopes of Mont Blanc with her doctor...

Strange though it may seem, the Balmat-Paccard duo represented not just a guide and his client but rather the professional and the amateur. This very first encounter proved to be catastrophic and there would remain a wall of incomprehension between the two areas of climbing for a long time to come.

Jacques Balmat's career had its highs and lows. The winnings, he had gone to Geneva to claim, were stolen from him early on and although he did become rich and famous, it was not to last. So, he set off in search of pots of gold.

The north face of Mont Blanc.

One can quite clearly see the three routes, starting from the Grands Mulets, used by the guides over the years.

———— *Historic route,*
used up until Doctor Hamel's accident
(1820)

———— *The Corridor route*
was used until 1870.

———— *The normal route,*
that climbs up the Bosses ridge, only became
the standard route up the mountain after 1870.

A writer called Magnard wrote, in 1814, of how he and his companions "*... had very little hope of meeting him [Balmat]. This very singular man, during his wanderings in the mountains, never follows the beaten track and moves as the crow flies, from rock to rock, wherever his fancy takes him, on his search for the rarest minerals. This man has an iron constitution, he has abused it greatly but he cannot seem to destroy it*".

In 1834 Balmat was 72 years old and a rumour, that was probably false, led him to believe that there was a seam of gold near Mont Ruan, not far from Chamonix. He set off with Pache, a hunter from Vallorcine in a neighbouring valley. The impressive rock walls of the Fer à Cheval ('Horse-shoe') rise up at the end of the valley of Sixt, and the two men set about climbing them. A narrowing ledge blocked their route and Pache turned round. Balmat continued. He may have slipped or a hold broke off in his hand, nobody knows. Suffice to say, Balmat fell, into nothingness, alone and with no witnesses. He was never seen again and his body was never found...

HESITANT FIRST STEPS

As to Mont Blanc, although De Saussure lost no time in making the third ascent of the mountain, he was soon to be forgotten. The French Revolution was in full swing. The arrival of Bonaparte and the Empire vaguely reignited the craze.

Yet between 1802 and 1820, only seven 'caravans' of climbers made their way up the north face. One of them even broke new ground, in an odd sort of way...

In August 1818, a young Polish aristocrat, Count Antoni Malczewski, went to Chamonix anxious to climb Mont Blanc. Unlike the other tourists, however, he dreamed of climbing Mont Blanc via the Aiguille du Midi.

A slightly extravagant project, which he described thus: "*I devoted all my attention to this Aiguille, even though my first thoughts were preoccupied by the King of Mountains [Mont Blanc]. To reconcile all these things, I conceived of a project that was even larger in its scope; that was nothing less than traversing over to Mont Blanc having reached the Aiguille [du Midi] and then returning by the usual route.*"

Thus, he recruited six guides, walked up the Mer de Glace and came up against the Piton Nord (north summit) of the Midi and its mighty wall of granite. By dint of obstinacy, the team reached the summit but the young count was thoroughly dispirited. It seemed impossible to go from this

point to the summit of Mont Blanc. The troupe went back down to Chamonix and into virtual anonymity. They had failed to climb Mont Blanc. And, moreover, this major exploit in the history of mountaineering, the principles of which would not be reclaimed until some 40 years later (once again on the Aiguille du Midi and by another count, Fernand de Bouillé...) would fall into complete obscurity.

Mention was scarcely made of it in the records of the Compagnie du Mont Blanc and even the guides had forgotten it only a few decades later. It was, nevertheless, the first ascent made in the Chamonix Aiguilles or 'needles'.

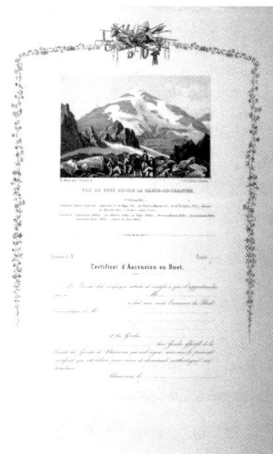

Certificate of ascent
of Mont Buet. 3094m high
and known as
the 'Ladies' Mont Blanc',
the Buet was for a long time
considered an essential route
for those wanting
to become guides.

Doctor Hamel's accident, as portrayed by Gabriel Charton. This was the first time the question of who, the guide or the client, was responsible for the team arose during an ascent of Mont Blanc. The only destination of any note for climbers at this time was Mont Blanc and most of the other mountains would have to wait almost one hundred years to be climbed.

Below:
Joseph-Marie Couttet was the first great Mont Blanc guide with thirteen ascents to his name. He was the lead guide for Doctor Hamel's caravan of climbers.

THE HAMEL ACCIDENT
MONT BLANC'S FIRST TRAGEDY

Let us return now to a more conventional expedition, that of Doctor Hamel. Like most of the would-be ascensionists, Doctor Hamel was first and foremost a scientist.

Born in Saint Petersburg, he was a prominent figure in the Russian court and an advisor to Czar Alexander I. After a first attempt made from Saint Gervais via the Aiguille du Goûter, he fell back on to the historic first route.

It was to be the ninth caravan of mountaineers to try for the summit. It seems slightly incredible that thirty-four years since the first ascent had been made there had been so few subsequent attempts, but the French Revolution had meant that between 1788 and 1802 there had not even been a request to climb it.

In short, climbing Mont Blanc was still quite an exploit. On 16 August 1820, accompanied by two English tourists, Dornford and Henderson, Doctor Hamel left Chamonix with twelve guides. They stopped, as was the custom, at the rocky outcrop known as the Grands Mulets. The following the day the weather was atrocious. The group members could not make up their minds about what to do, equivocated,

discussed, argued and finally put off the decision until the following day. But sometimes the mountains can be cruel. Another day of bad weather meant the group had decided to turn back when all of a sudden the clouds cleared and Mont Blanc appeared. Hamel, who wanted to be the fifteenth visitor to stand on its snowy dome, insisted they carried on.

The guides grumbled. They knew all too well that the gusts of wind, snow-filled coombs, and sudden cold risked making the push to the top difficult and dangerous. They were torn between the desire to turn around and go back down to the valley and the lure of money.

Hamel made the most of their hesitation, tempers frayed and he accused them of cowardice.

The montagnards were trapped. The gauntlet had been thrown down. The Chevalier Bourdet, a French aristocrat who had joined the group, decided to go back down with two guides. Joseph-Marie Couttet gave the order to leave, and watching the men set off, he muttered *"let's go, at least then we won't all break our necks up there…"* The group struggled its way across the Petit

Plateau. The ten men acting as guides had to take turns at going in front, battling their way through deep snow. They finally reached the Grand Plateau and, with some difficulty, the bottom of the north face, just above the Rochers Rouges. Then, as they crossed a slope, a huge mass of snow started to move. They had just cut through an enormous section of wind slab.

Five guides were dragged towards the gaping hole of a crevasse just below them. By some kind of miracle, two of them, Jean-Marie Couttet and Julien Devouassoux, were spared at the last minute, as the barometer in the bag they were carrying became wedged between two walls of ice. But Pierre-Joseph Balmat, Jean-Marie Auguste Tairraz and Pierre Carrier were gone, swallowed up in a cavern of ice.

This was to be the first in a long line of tragedies on the slopes of Mont Blanc. In Chamonix, where there was an ever-present fear of the Monts Maudits or 'Accursed Mountains', news of the disaster was met with consternation, even despondency. Collections were made, the Sardinian government, under whose administration the valley fell, was informed and the King of Sardinia ordered pensions to be given to the grieving families.

Ascent of Mont Blanc in the 1840s.
Little by little ropes were starting to be used
(although they wouldn't be a permanent fixture until around 1850)
yet crampons were hardly used at all.
Guides preferred instead to cut hundreds of steps into the ice
with wide axes that were easily over 1.30m long.

THE BIRTH OF THE COMPAGNIE DES GUIDES

The affair illustrated the need to define the notion of responsibility in a party. Was it the guide or the client who should make the crucial decisions? It also provided the pretext for a kind of tidying up of sorts in a valley where glorious disorder reigned.

Women, selling refreshments and dairy products, would assail travellers on the way up to the Montenvers (one of the mountains that overlooks the Mer de Glace).

For a while, those who had taken a few head of cattle up to their 'alpages' or high summer pastures called themselves guides and would have no compunction in going as far as Bonneville (some 50 or so kilometres away) to offer their services to the travellers there. The Intendant, or regional administrator, of Faucigny (which included Bonneville) even went so far as to say, in a letter to the Minister of the Interior, that, *"the guides, innkeepers, and cart drivers squabble over foreigners with outrageous indecency, as if over prey!"* It was time to organise the activities of the guides in the Chamonix valley and give them some kind of structure, especially as tourism was becoming a lucrative source of income.

The Vice-Intendant of Faucigny, Gaspard-Sébastien Brunet, a lawyer by training, submitted a draft set of rules concerning the activities of the guides to the municipal council. The die was cast.

On 24 July 1821, the municipal council approved the first statutes and the first stone in the edifice of Chamonix's Compagnie des Guides was laid.

Although it was still in an embryonic stage, the Compagnie's eleven articles provided the framework for an organisation which, nearly 200 years later, functions along the same lines. Curious though it may seem, the men responsible for the idea of the Compagnie were actually ahead of their time.

The articles included the famous tour de rôle ('taking of turns'), a head guide (still known as a commis or clerk), the obligation to wear a distinctive professional insignia, fines for failure to respect the rules and the payment of professional tax allowing the payee to officially work as a guide.

The names of thirty-four guides and twelve deputy guides appeared on this first list.

Two years later, on 9 May 1823, the Sardinian state represented by the Royal Chamber of Counts approved the final model for the

The climbing caravans that made their way up Mont Blanc were veritable expeditionary forces. Would-be climbers would generally set off in large groups, and it wasn't unusual in those days for over 20 people to find themselves on the summit together. Now of course, this figure seems small.

enterprise as well as the 53 articles clearly defining the areas of activity and prerogatives of the Chamonix guides. In a broader sense, the model for the Compagnie added a social dimension to these new rules, which, for its time, was visionary. The fines were reduced and, moreover, while they used to be paid directly to the commune, they would from now on finance a benefit fund (caisse de secours), a forerunner of modern relief funds. In this way, the monies collected, together with subscriptions, the masses, were intended to assist all of the families, guides in need and to even pay the head guide's salary.

The number of guides was increased and two categories were established: in the first were guides who already had alpine experience, while in the second were the less experienced guides who were to be employed as porters. The number of full guides rose to 40 and the number of porters went up to 24.

Sixty-four locals were allowed to look after travellers, who in 1820 undertook 1200 routes and excursions in the valley. This limit meant that each guide could lead roughly 30 excursions (mostly trips up to the Montenvers) each guiding season. Two kinds of excursions were defined: 'extraordinary' and 'ordinary'.

The first included trips to:

1) the summit of Mont Blanc,
2) the Jardin du Talèfre known as the 'Garden',
3) the glaciers (except those that descended into the Chamonix valley) and those sections of these lower glaciers above the tree line,
4) the Le Buet glaciers.

The 'ordinary' routes covered all those not mentioned on the list above.

A few other rules merit attention here, such as the article setting the minimum age at 18, later raised to 23. The upper age limit was set at 60.

The prices for each route and excursion were also set out in writing: 40 'livres' for Mont Blanc and the client was obliged to hire four guides. This did not include the cost of the porters, food and refreshments... The client could also choose his own guide, circumventing the famous system of turns, but this would cost him an extra two livres.

A colourful detail comes in article 34 of the rules. It decreed that a guide was not allowed to set off on a route on a Sunday or a religious holiday before having heard mass. The curé, therefore, was required to schedule the first mass of the day at five in the morning.

Finally, even though article 4 stated that admittance was open to all, *"the inhabitants of Chamonix*

*Le Buet and
the Jardin de Talèfre were,
at the start of the 19th century,
important and prized routes
and from the summit of Le Buet
the visitor is afforded stunning
panoramic views of the entire
Mont Blanc chain.
Women, as shown
in the engraving, would happily
climb in full-length dresses...
Stoutly aided by two guides.*

and the rest of the valley can be admitted without distinction, so long as they have the required qualities."

As it happened, the Argentéraux (men from Argentière, at the top of the valley) were excluded from this first list. There were two reasons for this: firstly, there was significant rivalry between the two villages and secondly, and more importantly, the distance between them placed the Argentéraux at a distinct disadvantage.

It took them between an hour and an hour and a half walking along the tracks to get to Chamonix. It was difficult, therefore, to always be present when one's turn came. Nevertheless, after much protest the men from Argentière were allowed to join the collective.

Looking at this first list we find a number of the same names that appear on it today, names such as Tairraz, Balmat, Couttet, Payot, Cachat and Devouassoud.

From 1828 onwards, the Compagnie played a huge financial role in the valley. Thus, in that year alone, after having paid the head guide's salary, the Compagnie earned 634 livres from the excursions, 732 livres on the mules and 235 in fines. That was the equivalent of more than a thousand working days for a labourer, destined for only a handful of individuals.

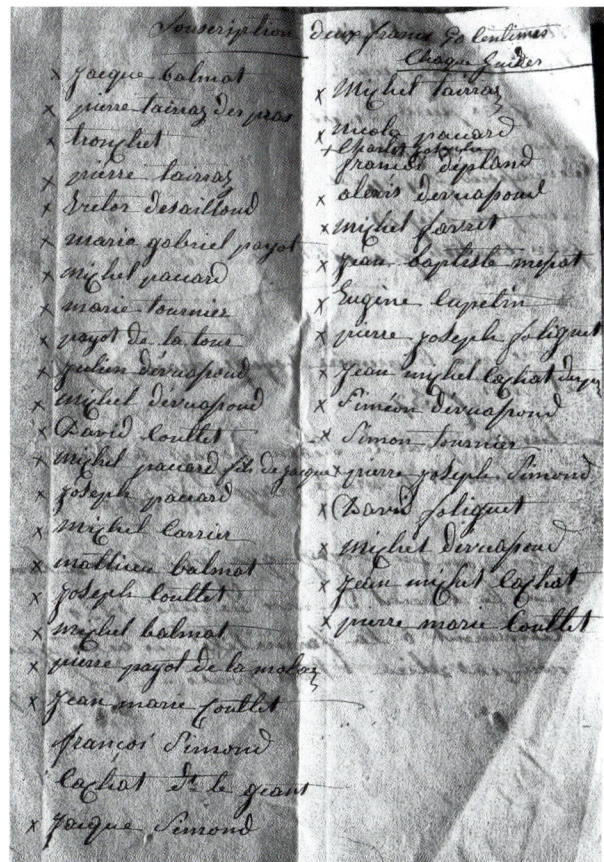

*A rare document:
a list of the first guides, members of the Compagnie,
preserved as part of deeds.*

The first woman to climb Mont Blanc was Marie Paradis, a servant from Chamonix who was carried, pushed and cajoled to the summit. The first true woman alpinist was, however, Henriette d'Angeville, who had 21 alpine ascents to her name (including Mont Blanc) and who considered Mont Blanc her 'icy lover'... From a lithograph by Baumann.

Henriette d'Angeville in her climbing clothes,
which were especially designed for her ascent of Mont Blanc.

A WOMAN ALPINIST AMONG THE FIRST GUIDES

All the Chamoniards, who benefited from this monopoly, had to do was exploit and maintain their goldmine. The ascent of Mont Blanc by Henriette d'Angeville would bring Chamonix into the limelight once and for all.

It was September 1838 and Henriette, a young aristocrat, dreamed of climbing. Up until then, only one woman had dared venture onto the mountain. She was a maid from Chamonix called Marie Paradis. Carried, dragged and cajoled up the mountain by her guide friends, Marie Paradis was not really strictly speaking an alpinist.

It was, however, Henriette d'Angeville's ambition to be one. And although she was advised against such an undertaking, she meticulously prepared for the climb. She followed her doctor's advice down to the letter: "… *Do not drink any wine, but drink good hot tea, [or] water mixed with barley water. If it is bitingly cold and your fatigue great, take a teaspoon or two of excellent brandy in a glass of sweetened water. If your breathing becomes difficult, slow your pace, do not say a single word and stop frequently, and do not make any unnecessary movements. Finally, if a tightness [in the chest] brings on strong spitting of blood, then, you would have to abandon the enterprise*". At that time Mont Blanc was certainly no trifling matter and Henriette d'Angeville's preparations included the smallest

details, studying everything on the subject, starting with the dozen or so works already dedicated to it. She made her own clothes, a kind of skirt with baggy trousers in the Zouave style (Zouaves were Algerian troops in the French army who traditionally had their own rather exotic uniform). And she chose her guides and porters.

In her memoirs, d'Angeville paints written portraits of her guides. Hers is a particularly interesting account, for her group in 1838 was made up of men who were part of the generation of guides that created the Compagnie.

She wrote:
"Joseph-Marie Couttet, the head-guide of my caravan, forty-five years old, small of stature, quick and intelligent face. He is one of the most renowned Chamonix guides and he deserves this reputation, for he possesses a varied knowledge and makes the dispensing of it to travellers as pleasant as it is useful. First and foremost is his knowledge of the area, for there is not a single corner of land, plateau or aiguille of which he cannot give the name; not a piece of information he cannot furnish. He is at once mineralogist, botanist and tradesman.

Anselme Tronchet: fifty-two years old, quite a distinguished air, due as much to his great height as to the gravity with which he presents himself and speaks. He is the senior member of our caravan and although he

Henriette d'Angeville's guides about whom she wrote detailed descriptions in her account of the ascent.

has only been once to Mont Blanc, he has a reputation as an excellent guide. He is at once a miller, carpenter, mason, pickman on the roads and stone cutter...

Jacques Simond: fifty years old, medium stature, open face. He excels at hunting chamois...

Pierre Joseph Simond, my first guide in Chamonix: forty-seven years old, tall, greying hair, a good and honest face if there ever was one!... As good on his legs in the middle of the glaciers as if he were on a wide, open road. He has already taken part in three ascents, and even though he had promised himself he had turned his back on it all, he accepted this [invitation to join a] fourth one out of courtesy to a lady he had already taken to the Garden...

Michel Favret: forty-two years old, serious and agreeable appearance, very attentive towards the travellers he accompanies [...] Favret has such high regard for his region that it is he who is charged with carrying out trusted missions for the administration [he would become head guide from 1842 to 1852].

François Desplan: thirty-nine years old, a little taller than average, excellent expression in a face that shows openness and cheerfulness. Legs of a chamois, jumping crevasses like one in a single bound. As valiant walking as he is in front of a bottle at rest stops..."

This gallery of portraits would not be complete without a description of the porter, Jean Mugnier, who was so efficient on the ascent that afterwards he would be known as 'Henriette d'Angeville's guide': *"Thirty-one years old, small, high, wide and bulging forehead revealing intelligence; but a pale, thin, and shy-looking face gives no sign of the energy he possesses..."* Henriette d'Angeville would even go so far in her eulogy as to say *"I predict that this brave young man will become the valley's [new] Balmat, not in the sense of new discoveries but in the sense of the deserved trust and esteem that Chamonix's hero enjoyed".*

That Monday morning, 4 September, she finally set off. 'Mont Blanc's fiancée' was motivated solely by her project. She was roundly teased and mocked with cruel jibes such as *"Madame d'Angeville is a mad old woman and an insufferable prankster".* She felt entrusted with a mission, to be *"the first woman on the summit to be able, in spirit at least, to be passionately in love with an icy lover..."*

They reached the Grands Mulets and all was going as it should. At dawn, despite an icy cold night, she felt in good form. There were two other caravans on their way up. Henriette's team caught up with Mr Stoppan's caravan, crossed the crevasses and cut a quite incredible number of steps in the ice. *"Monsieur Stoppan had counted the number of steps in our 'staircase' up the Mur de la Côte and informed me we had climbed 354 of them..."* wrote d'Angeville. She was starting to feel the altitude,

her heart was thumping wildly and she had to stop every 10 steps.

She fell asleep, drunk with the altitude and the guides began to curse their bad luck. With a burst of pride, she opened her eyes and begged the guides, *"if I die before reaching the top, promise me you will carrying my body to the summit and bury me there!"* A few more steps and the summit was in sight. All of the sudden the palpitations and nausea eased.

She was carried to the summit by her guides, so as to be higher than Mont Blanc. Mademoiselle d'Angeville had become history's first female alpinist. She had opened the way for future climbers such as Miss Breevort, Isabella Straton and Catherine Destivelle...

Top:
one of the oldest surviving photos of the Compagnie des Guides, dating from 1855. On the far right is Jean Mugnier who earned his spurs as a guide on Henriette d'Angeville's expedition. There are two other guides in the picture: on the far left is Ambroise Ducroz and on the right, kneeling, is Michel Bellin.

Right:
three axes from the 19th century. We can clearly see how the axes changed with time, from the early hatchet-like design on the right to Michel Payot's more modern-looking axe on the left.

This sketch by James Forbes shows a slab of rock supported by a column of ice on the Mer de Glace. Several scientific expeditions visited the glacier, which at that time was still growing.

MOUNTAINEERING WITH A SCIENTIFIC PURPOSE

As comical as it may sound, Henriette d'Angeville's ascent of Mont Blanc is surprising in one way. Most ascensionists, even in the middle of the 1840s, were scientists, following on from the Geneva botanist De Saussure.

Each ascent gave rise to absurd situations, such as C. Martins' 1844 expedition, during which an unusual experiment was carried out on the summit of Mont Blanc.

The three guides – Michel Couttet, Alexandre Simond and Jean Mugnier – were invited to get undressed so that each one's 'lower member' could be measured and the effects of atmospheric pressure be recorded. *"To do these measurements we had to stand naked from our belts to our feet for 20 or 25 minutes"*, as one of the guides described the scene later. For some years to come guides would yield to the fads and fancies of the these men, confronting the rigours of altitude with brave poses...

It should be remembered that at this time high altitudes were the seventh continent; they were virtually untouched and everything was still to be invented, starting with the equipment. Ice axes at this time were simple cutting tools, direct descendents of woodcutting hatchets.

The design would not start to evolve until the 1870s with the addition of a horizontal adze for cutting.

Tough fabrics from Valais in Switzerland and Bonneval (from which guides' dress uniforms are still made), wide brimmed hats, skirts for women, various cotton, velvet and woollen garments, even newspaper constituted the basic equipment, with often more psychological than actual technical value.

Curiously, the crampons that had been known about since the sixteenth century and used by the early ascensionists would be forgotten for almost a century. In fact, as their points only covered the heel or the middle of the foot, they proved not to be very reliable on ice slopes. Ailes de mouche (literally 'fly wings' or small metal bars embedded around the edges of the soles of boots) and 'tricounis' (studs in the centre of the soles) were quickly adopted.

But for a long time, guides preferred brute force, cutting thousands of steps into couloirs and slopes, or at least in those they judged climbable...

These four-point crampons, dating from the start of the 19th century, proved to be sadly ineffectual when used.

The first alpinists preferred snow and ice routes and ladders were essential for crossing glaciers. Equipping mountain areas was for a long time the preserve of guides.

THE YEARS OF PLENTY

With or without the help of scientific expeditions, the Compagnie des Guides grew rapidly and became the major economic force in the valley with, for the time, considerable financial resources.

The Compagnie would use its money for good causes such as helping guides in distress. Some of its members gave 200 livres, the equivalent of 130 days' work, a subsidy that was sometimes repaid. Letters preserved by the Compagnie reflect its concerns and the size of the donations that were sometimes made, not only to its members but also to their contemporaries. Documents written by the Compagnie and sent to the Intendant de Faucigny (who supervised the Compagnie's finances) make for interesting reading. Jean Michel Devouassoux in 1836 related the story of a man who *"said that this last 29 August he was charged, as a guide, with taking travellers to the Garden [Jardin de Talèfre]. A recent snowfall had just covered the Mer de Glace and the suppliant, having done this excursion several times before, was walking as he would normally. While crossing a crevasse he did not know about and which was covered in snow, he fell in to a depth of thirty feet. Taking fright, the traveller ran off abandoning the man as he lay between life and death. To his good fortune, he kept his head and although he was badly injured, his body covered in injuries and blood, he took out his knife* and cut steps into the ice in order to save himself, and after two hours' work he got back to the surface. Nevertheless, today he is bedridden, incapable of working as a guide..."* He was eventually awarded the sum of 200 livres.

Other letters have a whiff of medical embellishment about them, as all requests of support were sent with letters from doctors as evidence. One such report reads: *"We hereby certify, to whom it may concern, that as of the first of December last as Doctors we have treated Paccard, Joseph, born in Chamonix, who was struck down by necrosis of the lower part of the tibia in the right leg. A disease he contracted while, and was aggravated by, the frequent and laborious excursions he had made in the exercise of his profession throughout the summer and from which he has not perfectly recovered. The disease produced several extremely painful fistulous abscesses, which necessitated two months' absolute rest in bed, a diet and remedies appropriate to his condition. Among these were different surgical operations that we performed upon him and for which we expressly went up to Chamonix three times..."* This man also received a tidy sum.

One or two guides every year were the beneficiaries of these generous grants. Earnings exceeded expenditure in the three decades that followed the creation of the Compagnie and pensions were

Jean Payot, the ancestor of a long line of Compagnie guides going back seven generations.

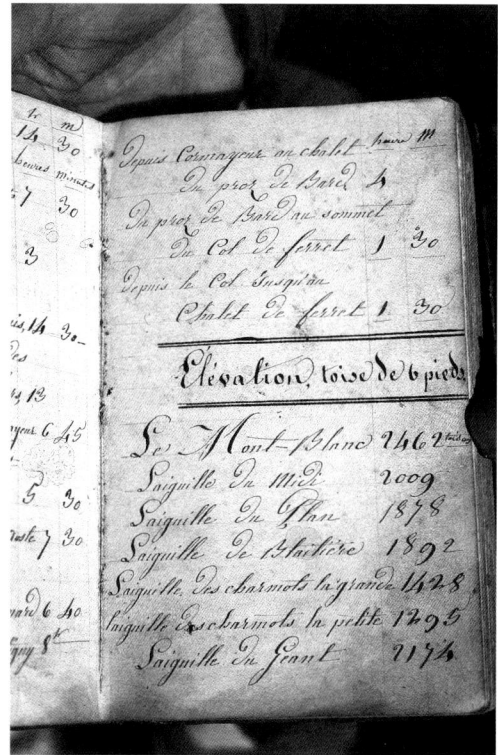

It is surprising to find that he noted the heights of the mountains in 'toise' or fathoms (the equivalent of six feet) in his guide's logbook.

given to guides too old to work. The Compagnie's esprit de corps and social security benefits were revolutionary for their time and were applied to other fields.

The Compagnie was so well off that on 28 November 1838 it made an interest-free loan of 520 livres to the municipal authorities of Chamonix for the construction of a new building at the Montenvers.

Joseph-Marie Couttet, known as 'The Chamois', took the initiative in putting a road in up to the Montenvers. The Compagnie paid him 90 livres in 1839 for the work already done.

As they had to attend mass on Sundays and some of them had three hours' walk to the first service, the guides paid the salary of a priest who was to work solely for them.

The Compagnie was heavily involved in the entire life of the valley and handed over the sum of 1500 livres for the altar screen in Chamonix church, which is still there.

The Compagnie's actions and influence exceeded its professional sphere and large payments, of more than 400 livres, were regularly made to the syndic (the local administrative body) to help the destitute. A further sum of 400 livres was given away by the Compagnie on 19 July 1840, after fires had destroyed parts of the nearby town of

Sallanches. A guide was even despatched to Turin to buy blankets.

Guides at this time accompanied all the major crowned heads of Europe. And Jean Payot, when he was not being employed in Switzerland and Italy by Rodolph Toppfer (author of Voyages en Zigzag), guided the Prince de Polignac (Prime Minister of France under Charles X), Prince Eugène of Savoy and the Emperor of Brazil.

Jean Mugnier guided the Comte d'Aubigny, the Prince de Solnes, Baron de Buddenbrock and a young Prussian officer called Bismarck.

At the start of the 1840s, when the Compagnie was working at full capacity, one of its most emblematic figures seems to have been Auguste Balmat. Balmat was a guide unlike the others. The high-mountain environment was seen solely as a means of making money and guides were mindful of declaring something of a penchant, indeed a passion for climbing. Balmat, however, having spent time with the great men of letters shared their excessive thirst for the sciences.

With no proper training, he had a passion for the nascent disciplines. Perhaps intrigued by the work of Doctors Forbes, Wills and Tyndall, whom he supported on the ground, he was smitten. He made observations of the evolution of the glaciers and reported his measurements to scientists of the

day, took them to the sites of particular interest and equipped the crossing from the Montenvers to Le Chapeau on the other side of the Mer de Glace. As Stephen d'Arve reports in his book Les Fastes du Mont Blanc ('The Splendours of Mont Blanc'), *"... better than anyone he could discuss the rarity of a mineral sample, all the various families of alpine flora, the atmospheric phenomena of the mountains and glaciers..."*

Without a thought for his own personal gain, caught in a whirlwind of learning, he sometimes forgot to charge clients a decent rate for his work. He was recognized for his very human qualities and daily received letters from the across the world. For a time he represented Chamonix's syndic, was then head-guide, and it was he who led the Empress Eugénie (wife of the Emperor Napoléon III) across the Mer de Glace. Auguste Balmat, through his thirst for knowledge, was without doubt one of the first guides to resist the lure of money and he died in absolute poverty. In an indirect way and before the arrival of the notion of climbing for sport, he was one of the first Chamoniards to give a meaning to the mountains.

Another character is worth a mention here. Joseph-Marie Couttet, known as 'Le Moutelet', was stubborn and courageous with a colourful and engaging personality. He would remain centre stage for sixty years, often thanks to his eccentri-

cities. He was quite a character. He guided for De Saussure who called him 'The Chamois', no doubt because of his agility. The locals preferred the nickname Moutelet or La Belette ('the weasel').

He was not kept on when the Compagnie was founded. He was 59 years old and not a little deaf but the mountains were his life. A crystal hunter and visionary, he toiled away for a year and a half to improve the track up to the Montenvers. He dug the path, cleared away dead trees and those blown down in storms, and cleared it with mines without asking anything from anyone.

He was still going into the mountains, especially Mont Blanc, when he was 70. When he was with a caravan he tried to persuade the young guides to use a new route up Mont Blanc, his route.

The guides no longer went straight up the north face, after the accident involving Doctor Hamel's group. But the Chamonix guides persisted in continuing to use the Corridor, a section that is exposed at the top.

Couttet had found a way up via the Bosses du Dromadaire ('The Dromadary's Humps'), which seemed shorter and safer, nobody took any notice of the old man. Nevertheless, he persevered and one day he learned that a caravan of 64 people was leaving for Mont Blanc. He was 78 by this time and it was as good an opportunity as any to prove

the validity of his theory. He set off for the Grands Mulets dressed in cut-off woollen socks as gaiters, thoroughly unsuitable shoes and a high hat.

Up on the mountain there were stares as the other climbers wondered where the old man that stank of pine-sap and did not even have a walking stick had sprung from. *"How could he climb up here without a stick?"* they asked. With a cracked voice and a mischievous glint in his eye, he replied *"I did have one but a crevasse licked it clean out of my hands"*. The groups tried to get some sleep. An Englishman lying next to Couttet awoke with a start and exclaimed, *"my God, there's cholera here!"* In fact, Moutelet had opened a bottle containing an elixir of his own devising...

The next morning he decided to accompany the group. He argued with the climbers and both guides and clients thought he was nothing more than a mad old man. He set off to prove he still had all his faculties. He left the group and climbed the obvious ridge with its humps, arriving on the summit before everyone else. Just for fun, he even went back down towards the group, which had just got to the Petits Mulets, and they reached the summit together.

Yet still nobody wanted to put his route to the test, not even on the way down. So, he set off on his own again and rejoined them at the Grand Plateau.

It was only 23 years after his death, and after another accident, that the Compagnie des Guides adopted his access route.

The old man, who died at the age of 84, had been right all along and his was to become the normal route up Mont Blanc...

The summit of Mont Blanc
has not changed a great deal in the past two centuries
and the views are just as breathtaking as they were then.
They include Switzerland's Valais ranges,
Italy's Gran Paradiso, France's own Ecrins range and,
on a clear day, you can even make out the 'Jet d'Eau',
or water-jet, in Geneva.

The town had three inns in the 18th century and at the beginning of the 19th century the Tairraz brothers built the Hotel d'Angleterre and Hotel de Londres. From a painting by Muller.

THE REBELLION OF THE HOTELIERS

For the first part of the century these 60 men were without contest one of the most influential groups of people in Haute-Savoie. Jealousies quickly sprung up and the Compagnie passed to within a whisker of disappearing altogether.

In the space of three decades the Compagnie had grown very wealthy, so wealthy that grudges had started to surface even in the valley itself. The hoteliers were undoubtedly its most virulent opponents. They wanted to counteract the power of the Compagnie, as farmers and guides, often the same people, ran the town. Of course, they did not share the same points of view.

Moreover, recruitment to the Compagnie had hardly changed at all since its creation. Ninety men (60 guides and 30 aspirants) managed what was in effect a monopoly. This number soon became the centre of a local controversy.

In Chamonix itself several young men, who had not been taken on by the Compagnie, considered forming their own bureau. The hoteliers were looking to wrest power from the guides and they realized it was in their interest to support the rebellion. One of them offered the use of his horses. Others grew rich by offering travellers a service including mules and guides.

By 1848 and the start of the Second Republic in France, there was quite a mess and it would only get worse in the four years that followed. Three hoteliers – Ferdinand Eisenkrämer, Edouard Tairraz and Michel Simond – stoked the fires of the rebellion.

The head guide, Michel Favret, referred the matter to the Intendant of Faucigny but the Sardinian authorities seemed to have other more pressing matters to which they had to attend. There was procrastination, negotiations and even a few raised voices, but nobody seemed to want to take the matter in hand.

There was virtually a civil war in Chamonix. A petition was circulated and more than 200 people demanded the disbanding of the Compagnie! It was a complete shambles. Guides got work directly from innkeepers.

In 1850, the Compagnie reported a negative balance. The year 1851 started just as badly and it was only the interest from investments that saved the situation for the Compagnie. Finally, in May 1852, the King of Sardinia, Cyprus and Jerusalem put the association in order and removed the limit on the number of guides in the Compagnie. The situation turned around almost immediately. The masses brought in by the new guides set the whole operation in motion once more and a language school (English and German) was even set up in 1854. The Compagnie was ready for a new adventure...

ROUTE DU MONT-BLANC

LITH. BRUMM-KNECHT, GENÈVE

ITINÉRAIRE

Distances : De Chamonix à Pierre Pointue 3 h. – aux Grands Mulets 7 h. – au Grand Plateau 11 h. – au sommet du Mont-Blanc 16 h. –

Hauteurs : Mont-Blanc 4810 m. – Mont-Maudit 4771 m. – Aiguille de Bionnassay 4061 m. – Dôme du Goûté 4331 m. – Grand Plateau 3932 m. – Aiguille du Midi 3843 m. – Grands Mulets 3050 m. – Pierre à l'Échelle 2411 m. – Pierre Pointue 2049 m. –

Ascension N° 540   Année 1874

CERTIFICAT D'ASCENSION AU MONT-BLANC

Le Guide-Chef soussigné atteste et certifie à qui il appartiendra que le 21 Août 1874 Monsieur Charles E. Wild a fait avec succès l'ascension du Mont-Blanc, accompagné de M et des guides Simond Joseph, Simond Hubert, Payot Jean Pierre tous guides effectifs de la Société des guides de Chamonix, qui ont signé avec moi le présent certificat qui est délivré pour servir de document authentique au titulaire.

Payot Jean Pierre
Simond Joseph
H. Simone

Chamonix, le 5 Août 1874
Le Guide-Chef :
Payot Frédéric

Certificates first started to be given to people who had climbed Mont Blanc in the second half of the 19th century and at that time they testified to their owner's great exploit.
Each certificate was numbered and recorded, and the owner of this one had number 540.

GRANDEUR AND DECADENCE

IT WAS NOT UNTIL THE YEARS BETWEEN 1850 AND 1880
THAT CLIMBERS TURNED THEIR ATTENTIONS TO MOUNTAINS
OTHER THAN MONT BLANC AND THE CHAMONIX GUIDES TOOK PART
IN SOME OF THE GREATEST CHALLENGES IN THE ALPS.

AT THE SAME TIME THE MONOPOLY OF THE COMPAGNIE WAS STARTING
TO BE CONTESTED BY A WHOLE GENERATION OF ALPINISTS
WHO NO LONGER TOLERATED ITS PRIVILEGED POSITION.

The crisis with the hoteliers had been resolved and the guides turned their attentions back to high-altitude matters.

At the start of the 1850s, Mont Blanc still exerted the same sway over people. When Albert Smith's caravan set off in 1851 it was, in complete keeping with the standards of the day, heavily laden to say the least. Quite apart from the 16 guides and 18 porters engaged for four clients, it included 103 bottles of which seven were of lemonade and raspberry syrup and the rest were more alcoholic in nature. There were also 20 loaves, 10 small cheeses, 6 packets of chocolate, 6 packs of sugar, 4 of prunes, 4 of raisins, 2 of salt, 4 candles, 6 lemons, 4 legs of mutton, 4 shoulders of mutton, 6 pieces of veal, 1 piece of beef, 11 large fowls and 35 chickens.

The ascent of Mont Blanc was laborious, as was the digestion of all the food... The return, however, was triumphant, as Albert Smith described. *"First went the chiefs of the party [...] then we came on our mules; after us walked the body of the guides, with such of their families as had come to meet them, and little boys and girls, so proud to carry their batons and appear to belong to the procession; and, finally, the porters and volunteers with the knapsacks brought up the rear. [...] As we entered the village we were greeted with a tremendous round of Alpine artillery from the roof of the new Hotel Royal. [...] The whole population was in the streets. [...] When we got into the court-yard of our hotel, M. Edouard Tairraz had dressed a little table with some beautiful bouquets and wax candles, until it looked uncommonly like an altar, but for the half-dozen of champagne that formed a portion of its ornaments; and here we were invited to drink with him, and be gazed at, and have our hands shaken by everybody."*

As extravagant as this may sound, climbing Mont Blanc was at this time still celebrated as a major feat, close to 70 years after its conquest. It obviously came at a price and Smith was the first to recognise the fact. He wrote: *"The sunset, the glaciers,*

It was common for climbers,
having reached the summit of Mont Blanc, to crack open a bottle of champagne.
The custom died out in the 20ᵗʰ century.

and the Mur de la Côte have come down to a matter of 'little bills'". It was a prohibitive amount, the trip coming in at 584 francs per tourist (the equivalent of around 3000 Euros today). This figure included guides, porters, meals, drinks and accommodation in Chamonix. Just for the record, the caravan spent only one franc and 50 centimes on milk.

Albert Smith would become a kind of ambassador for the Chamonix valley. Upon his return to Britain, he took it upon himself to publish an account of his trip, give lectures, organise a show, and invent a game of snakes and ladders with a Mont Blanc theme. The success of the expedition was so unexpected that he invited his guide François Favret to London, begging him to bring some dogs from the Grand Saint Bernard pass with him, two of which were for the Prince of Wales himself.

Smith's spectacle about his ascent of Mont Blanc was becoming one of the most prized attractions in London and was not perhaps unconnected to the growing craze that was prompting Britons in increasingly greater numbers to visit the Mont Blanc Massif.

Possibly as a result of this publicity, the year 1854 saw 14 caravans on the summit of Mont Blanc. This was an exceptionally high figure as the average since 1786 was a mere two or three ascents per year.

Since that time Mont Blanc had become a kind of business, made all the more easy to manage by the fact that the Chamoniards had the exclusive rights to it.

However, demand was rising steadily and certain travellers, some rash, others inquisitive, were starting to eye up other mountains. Mont Blanc was no longer enough. In the space of 20 years, alpinists had set about trying to tackle all the peaks large or small. This revolution had rather curious beginnings in Chamonix, as it was all down to a political gesture...

Previous page:
these two engravings by the British artist Baxter
were inspired by Albert Smith's expedition.
The images toured the world and were undoubtedly
a factor in the growing craze for all things Mont Blanc,
including its guides...

*The ascent
of the Aiguille du Midi
by members of Count
Fernand de Bouillé's
expedition marked
an important turning point
in mountaineering.
It was the first time a team
had deliberately set out
to climb a mountain
other than Mont Blanc
and it proved quite a challenge
for the Chamonix guides.*

THE AIGUILLE DU MIDI, AN UNUSUAL FIRST ASCENT

Count Fernand de Bouillé was an odd kind of mountaineer. After having successfully climbed Mont Blanc via the classic route, he dreamed of scaling the Aiguille du Midi. Like all his contemporaries, he was convinced it was an unclimbed peak, even though a young Pole, Count Malczewski, accompanied by six Chamonix guides, had made a successful attempt on the north summit in 1818. Bouillé got his team together and Chamonix said its touching goodbyes to them. *"A large number of travellers came to shake my hand and to wish me success in a venture in which no-one believed; as to the guides, they shook their heads as we passed saying 'try not to let anyone kill themselves; but none of you will ever make it'"*, he reported in the magazine l'Abeille de Chamonix in August 1856.

Thus it was a veritable expedition that set off up the Mer de Glace and along the foot of the east face of the Mont Blanc du Tacul, picking its way over the glaciers and along vertiginous ridges before even getting to the Aiguille du Midi. They stuck to the same old style of mountaineering and it was becoming a bit staid. The troupe bivouacked on the glacier. Protected by a blanket, they tried to sleep. Under the silent sweep of stars, the night was short and icy. At three thirty in the morning the Count gave the order to move out and they reached the foot of a 300-metre high wall

of rock. Using staffs and ladders they got to 24 metres below the summit. Bouillé knew that the difficulties to come would be beyond his abilities. Alexandre Devouassoud and the Simond brothers were chosen to overcome the final difficult sections. They were back an hour later. Devouassoud had the following words for the Count: *"Sir, your flag flies up there, the ascent has been made. But I would not repeat our walk along the ridge we have just climbed for all the riches in the world. I'll not go up there again, it's over."*

The intrepid 11 returned to Chamonix and were given a standing ovation by more than fifteen hundred people. Bouillé, the fervent royalist, could admire his Fleur de Lys flag in the knowledge that he had made a fine first ascent and had cocked a snook at the Second Empire.

Despite his rather special motives, Bouillé's ascent opened the way for a new kind of mountaineering. From now on, attempts on unclimbed peaks for sport were seen as interesting and laudable. The days of pseudo-scientific experiments and excuses for climbing up to the gateways to the heavens were gone. Climbers finally dared to admit to having a penchant for these pointless walls of rock, a trend that was confirmed in the years that followed.

The Aiguille du Midi, with its north and south 'pitons' or summits, photographed at daybreak.
Fernand de Bouillé, who financed the first ascent, said afterwards "I doubt there shall be a second."
A century and a half later and on a busy day, 4000-5000 people will reach the mountain's summit thanks to the Midi cable car...

As a brief aside, which would nevertheless fuel quarrels between guides and amateurs for nearly a century, is the story of the 1855 English ascent of Mont Blanc.

Messrs Kennedy, Hudson, Ainslie and the Smyth brothers, foregoing the professional help of guides, found a route from Saint Gervais and made the first unguided ascent of Mont Blanc. Yet it was an isolated case and even though it represented a new trend in mountaineering, they remained the exception and not the rule.

A young 'returner' takes his mules back to the setting-off point. For over a century, one of the guides' principal activities was providing mules for trips and excursions above the valley.

MULES,
A MUST FOR TRIPS INTO THE MOUNTAINS

The majority of the 5000 visitors to Chamonix in the middle of the nineteenth century were happy to go for rides on mules.

There were more than 300 mules in the valley and almost as many guides-muletiers, guide-mule drivers. In fact, it was the Compagnie's most important activity.

Gathered on the square in front of the church, the mules were described by the l'Abeille de Chamonix in 1865 as *"...waiting for the tourists who will honour their rumps with their more or less gracious poses."*

The caravan had to be led by a guide. He was assisted by a youngster, aged between 15 and 20 years old, going on his first excursions with the possibility of becoming a porter and then a guide in his own right.

Among the classic outings were the Montenvers, Croix de la Flégère and Brévent. For the latter, the caravans went as far as the Bellachat from where the tourists would reach the summit on foot. As they did this, a mule driver would lead the mules beneath the Brévent and along what used to be a well-worn path by the foot of the granite spires of the Lames du Brévent, and which has now disappeared, to meet the clients at Planpraz. All that was left to do was go back down to Chamonix, some 1000 metres below. A trip up to the Montenvers or the Brévent cost six francs.

The hire of a chair and porters was another amusement for travellers and the price was not dependent on the weight of the load. *"Once again it fell to me and my mates to carry a fat woman up to the Pierre à Pointue, and from there across the Mer de Glace, up to Le Chapeau and then return to Chamonix via the village of Les Tines. A long day for twelve francs and the lady never once got down from her seat. From this amount we had to deduct the cost of hiring the chair and the meal at the Plan de l'Aiguille. I do have fond memories of it all the same, as the straps holding the chair broke on the way and the lady was pitched into the stones without sustaining too much damage, luckily. She complained to the head-guide as soon as she got back..."* As one guide recorded dryly.

The Compagnie had evolved very little and even if a new set of rules tried, in 1859, to shake it up a little, it still required two guides to go to the summit of Mont Blanc (article 37) and guides could carry no more than seven kilos per route (article 35). Nevertheless, the management of the Compagnie also tried to instil in the guides a sense of responsibility. Article 34 is interesting reading regarding this last point, as it states that, *"unless he is surprised by a storm, a guide who loses his way will be stripped of his privileges and his duties, and*

Client being carried up to the Jardin de Talèfre on a sedan chair.
Accompanying tourists with these kinds of apparatus was quite an exploit and,
thankfully for the guides, this rather special clientele soon disappeared.

The Mer de Glace glacier was so large in the 19th century
that the village of Les Bois almost had to be evacuated.
A walk up to it was one of the most popular outings for tourists.

cannot regain them until he has taken another test. A repeat of the offence and he will be dismissed."

But this new set of rules, passed by the Sardinian administration, was too restrictive for the Chamoniards and was quickly forgotten as the valley became part of France in 1860. The Compagnie was sufficiently powerful to be able to amend

Setting off for Montenvers via the old Chamonix road.
At this time there were almost 300 mules in Chamonix.

Mont Blanc seen from Plan-Praz.
Rides on mules in this area carried on up to 1928 and the building of the Brévent lifts.
The guide-muleteers quickly disappeared from Chamonix after this time.

rules set out by the government.
Participating in the equipping of routes in the mountains, the guides had the strong feeling that they were protecting their interests and beware any from the neighbouring Swiss canton of Valais or the Aosta Valley who sought to break this taboo. They would find themselves pitted against a lively and sometimes brawny opposition...

Napoléon III's visit to Chamonix.
No less than 60 guides led the Emperor and his entourage up to the edge of the Mer de Glace. From the Illustré magazine.

The Empress takes a few steps on the Mer de Glace.
Just behind her stands Auguste Balmat.

THE CHAMONIARDS BECOME FRENCH

It was a military alliance between France and the Kingdom of Piedmont-Sardinia that allowed the Chamoniards to choose their own destiny.

Chamonix, on 22 and 23 April 1860, voted with an overwhelming majority together with the rest of Savoy to join France with the creation of a zone franche, or free trade zone. The figures spoke for themselves. Of the 620 votes cast, there were 11 abstentions, one spoilt paper, one yes and 601 'yes with zone'. Soon afterwards, guides climbed up Mont Blanc and planted the French tricolour on its summit.

Napoléon III and his court visited the valley in the autumn. The Emperor didn't climb Mont Blanc but did take a ride up on the back of a mule to the Montenvers with the Empress Eugènie. No less than 60 guides accompanied them and Auguste Balmat had the honour of holding the Empress's hand on the Mer de Glace.

Beyond the event itself, indeed its impact on the press was rather limited, a happy consequence of the visit was that the Emperor himself made it a personal undertaking to see that the road to Chamonix be improved. One year before the opening of the new road, Chamonix was starting to feel the effects of the improvement and from 1865 it was receiving more than 12,000 visitors a year.

In 1866 the Route National 506, or main road linking Sallanches and Chamonix, was finally inaugurated. The days of the horrors of the Montées Pelissier, a particularly perilous section on the climb up to Chamonix outside Servoz, were gone and Chamonix was more accessible. The tourists swept in. This same decade saw the creation of a proper tourist infrastructure through the whole valley, including the middle and high mountain areas.

In 1853 the Compagnie, whose primary concern it was, had taken charge of the construction of a permanent cabin at the Grands Mulets, the first mountain hut in the Mont Blanc Massif. At the same time the municipal authorities had a number of pavillons, cabins or huts, built between the Montenvers and the Couvercle, at the Brévent and between Les Bossons and the Grands

The Grands Mulets hut, built in 1853.
Apart from the Temple de la Nature,
opened at the Montenvers in 1795, the Mont Blanc range
had been until then free from man-made structures.

Mulets. These included: a cabin at Le Chapeau (1854); the Pierre Pointue (1862); the Mont Blanc du Tacul hut (1863); the Caillet cabin and one at the Plan de l'Aiguille (1864); Chablettes, Les Bossons and Le Tour (1865); at the Brévent (1866); and the Pierre à Béranger hut (1867).

In addition to the accounts and illustrations of the area, the new discipline of photography made an even greater contribution to Chamonix's development. Photographers, guides or not, now entered the fray...

On 25 July 1861, the Bisson brothers set out from the Hôtel Royal (the modern-day casino) on what they thought was the first photographic expedition to Mont Blanc. It was an imposing caravan and included 25 guides. Porters carried up a Daguerre lantern, easels, tripods, flasks of cyanide and collodion, mattresses, provisions, ropes and axes.

On the summit Louis Auguste and Auguste-Rosalie, after having melted some snow, battled with the cold to take a sum total of three photographs. Their Herculean efforts had been rewarded. They could go back down to Chamonix, convinced they had pulled off a great first.

An article in the paper Le Figaro, dated 15 September 1861, related an encounter between the Bisson brothers and the photographer and guide Joseph Tairraz. The guide told how one of the brothers, official photographer to Napoléon III, described himself as *"glowing after having been able to take three shots on the summit of Mont Blanc, from which he would not be parted for 80 thousand francs, but when he saw my shots he was embarrassed to ask a hundred francs..."* The year before, Tairraz had performed the same feat of alchemy and Mont Blanc had had its portrait taken. Whatever their provenance, the first images of Mont Blanc would only serve to increase the public's infatuation with the mountain. Whether it was from his study in Paris or his club in London, the alpinist now had a precise idea of what Mont Blanc and the massif as a whole looked like.

Does this explain why the practice of alpinism would change dramatically during this period? Apart from the benefit of technical detail, this is obviously not the case. Although alpinism at this time was rather boring, with climbers happy to knowingly repeat ascents of Mont Blanc via the normal route, it was in fact changing. Practically none of the surrounding peaks, except of course the Aiguille du Midi, had been climbed and most of the faces were unknown. Thus the small world of mountaineering, mainly composed of intrepid British climbers, would throw itself head long

*Three moments from the first photgraphic expedition to Mont Blanc.
Led by Charles Bisson and carrying food and photographic equipment,
the porters set out from the Hôtel Royal (what is now the casino).*

*We see the same expedition among the seracs and crevasses
of the Jonction and beneath the Petit Plateau.
These images, together with those taken by Joseph Tairraz,
would make a huge contribution to the mountain's fame.*

into this world of new challenges. From this point onwards the teams, which until now had been composed of occasional climbers, would give way to those made up of full-time alpinists, employing guides for more than just a single route, for a series of challenges spread over several years. This would later be known as the Golden Age and gave rise to legendary climbing partnerships. The Chamonix guides would play an active role in this turning point in the history of mountaineering.

Presented to 'The Society of Guides'
by C. D. Cunningham.
1 July 1887.

François Devouassoud
is photographed here by C.D. Cunningham, the author of one of the first books about the guides, Pioneers of the Alps.

François Devouassoud in the Caucasus.
He is second from right, standing with the local guides.
His client, Douglas Freshfield, is seated in the centre.

INDESTRUCTIBLE FRIENDSHIPS

François Devouassoud,
THE FIRST GREAT TRAVELLER

François Devouassoud was without doubt one of the first guides to form a real climbing partnership. He left an indelible mark on Chamonix yet most people pass by him without even noticing. The gravestone to the right of the entrance to Chamonix church reminds us of how great a figure he was. These days his epitaph engraved in Latin is not really very inspiring. It does, however, provide an excellent summary of the character traits of such an extraordinary personality. The translation reads as follows: *"To an upright and honest man, to a much missed pleasant friend and companion, to an astute and indomitable guide that we have known for over forty years; of whose virtue neither our memories nor the example will be lost; a few of his friends, whom he had oft taken over Alpine cols and through the snows of the Caucasus, took care to have this stone erected."*

Unusually modern in his outlook and cultivated (he was teacher in Chamonix for 14 years), he embarked on a long list of adventures that would include no less than 50 first ascents, starting in 1852.

These first ascents were gleaned not sim-

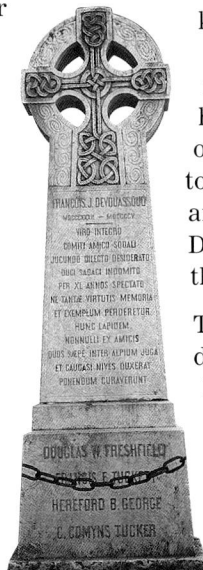

ply from the Mont Blanc Massif but from the four corners of the globe and include the Sasso Major and the East Face of the Rosengarten Spitze in the Dolomites.

Charming and lively, he was one of the first guides to be associated for life to a single climber, in this case Douglas W. Freshfield. He went on a sort of Jules Verne-style world tour with Freshfield, smoking a pipe with Cossacks, taking tea with the Armenian Patriarch of Echmiatsin, serving coffee to a Turkish pasha in Jerusalem and paying his respects to the Archbishop of Canterbury on the way. One of his greatest journeys was to the Caucasus, and in 1868 Freshfield, Moore and Tucker, accompanied by the indispensable Devouassoud, conquered Kasbek (5043m) and the east summit of Elbrus (5593m).

Theirs was a genuine friendship and as he was dying, Freshfield called for François, his lifelong friend, to bring him his climbing boots so that they might set off on a route together...

Devouassoud's grave,
a last vestige of the original cemetery.
His gravestone, by the right-hand corner
of the church entrance, was paid for by his clients.

*Michel Croz
is considered by many
to be the greatest guide
in the history of mountaineering.
In the space of just a few years,
he conquered some of
the greatest peaks in the Alps.
Whymper, not known
for his compliments,
declared that "without Croz
I would probably not have climbed
the Matterhorn."*

MICHEL CROZ, FRIEND OF WHYMPER

This exemplary friendship, another first in the history of alpinism, proved that sincere friendships could exist between a guide and his client. At practically the same time and on the same basis, two other guides from the Compagnie became associated with British mountaineers.

But first let us discuss Michel Croz. *"I know what my friend meant. Croz was happiest when he was employing his powers to the utmost [...] and it was only when he got above the range of ordinary mortals, and was required to employ his magnificent strength, and to draw upon his unsurpassed knowledge of ice and snow, that he could be said to be really and truly happy. Of all the guides with whom I travelled, Michel Croz was the man who was most after my own heart."* This tribute to Croz from Edward Whymper, who was always quite hard on the Chamonix guides, was made after the accident on the Matterhorn and summarized the feelings that bound him to this exceptional guide. For, even if Croz's alpine career was in the end rather short, it was nevertheless dazzling. Curiously, he started rather late. Until the age of 29 he was happy to climb Mont Blanc, to go up to the Jardin de Talèfre and onto the glaciers of Le Buet. The real change came in 1860.

Accompanying Mathews, Bonney and Hawkins, and then Tuckett, Moore, Adams-Reilly and most of all Edward Whymper, he would be part of the fabulous period in climbing history when every summit presented a possible first ascent.

Croz cut steps, discovered routes on Mont Viso and Mont Pourri (1861), crossed the Col des Ecrins, Col du Sélé and the Col du Glacier Blanc in 1862. 1863 saw him on the Grandes Rousses and the following year he was part of the team that pulled off the first traverse of the Brèche de la Meije, and first ascents of the Barre des Ecrins and the Col de la Pilatte. Incredibly, he also shared this virtuosity with the other great guide of the period, Christian Almer, from the Bernese Oberland. There was neither jealousy nor the slightest rivalry between the two of them, both exceptional men. *"The combination of Croz and Almer was a perfect one"*, declared Whymper. The union of the two men was so perfect that, on the first ascent of the Barre des Ecrins, Whymper recounted how *"Almer was a few feet in front, and he, with characteristic modesty, hesitated to step on the highest point, and drew back to allow us to pass. A cry was raised for Croz, who had done the chief part of the work, but he declined the honour, and we marched on to the top simultaneously."*

The team forged ahead with ascents of Mont Dolent, the Aiguille d'Argentière, and then the south face of the Grandes Jorasses. Exceptionally, on the first ascent of the Moine ridge on the Aiguille

Whymper was greatly affected by the accident and it marked the end of his Alpine climbing career. He famously later wrote "Climb if you will, but remember that courage and strength are nought without prudence, and that a momentary negligence may destroy the happiness of a lifetime."

Verte, Croz climbed without Whymper and instead accompanied Hudson, Kennedy and Hodgkinson, just six days after Whymper had made the first ascent of the Verte with Almer and Biner.

Croz was at the height of his fame and was, at this time, a central figure in the Compagnie. This was not just because he was one of its technically strongest climbers but also because he was one of the most open and tolerant of the Compagnie guides. He was sharply critical of those Chamonix guides who, in a fit of pique and with a somewhat blinkered view, took against Whymper and his Swiss guides after their first ascent of the Verte.

Like all alpinists active at this time, he dreamed of conquering the Matterhorn, one of the most powerfully symbolic peaks in the Alps. On the morning of 14 July 1865, he was ready and eager to climb the mountain's east face. The rock was steep, the protection precarious and the climbing exposed. Moreover, the glimpses they were afforded of the north face showed it to be particularly daunting. Croz had been hired by the Reverend Charles Hudson, and Whymper, for whom this would be the eighth attempt, had accepted the invitation to join the team. Guided by the Taugwalders, father and son guides from Zermatt, Whymper was keen to share the risks and hopes of such an ascent when he knew Croz would be there. In spite of black ice and vertical towers that were continually in front of them, Croz searched and felt his way up, picking a fine logical line. A final section of

snow, a few steps, a final obstacle and they finally reached the summit.

They were the first to conquer the Matterhorn, but only just. Carrel a guide from the Aosta Valley, was a mere stone's throw away from them, on the Lion Ridge. There were cries of joy at their victory and the team watched the fabulous sweep of the clouds and the vague outline of the horizon. Now they had to descend via the same route. Croz weighed up and recalled in his mind the sections they had crossed and the difficulties they had encountered. It was better if he went in front so that he could spot any potential difficulties. Whymper, on the same rope, followed with the Zermatt guides. All of a sudden the young Hadow, a total beginner on ice, slipped and fell into Croz, knocking him off his feet. By a terrible yet fortuitous twist of fate the rope snapped, saving Whymper and his guides. In shock they cried out *"Chamonix, what will Chamonix say!"*

After a long silence it was time to face facts. Four members of the team had fallen down the north face. There was no hope for them. The bodies of the hapless climbers were found at the bottom of the face and the town of Zermatt buried and honoured a princely figure of mountaineering. Whymper, scarred by a moment of carelessness that had destroyed a lifetime's happiness, vowed never again to climb in the Alps. He was profoundly troubled by the death of a loyal companion who, over the years, had become his best friend...

Michel Payot,
one of the great guiding names
of the Golden Age of mountaineering.
He made first ascents of some of
the best routes in the Mont Blanc range.

Together with his brother Alphonse (below)
and James Eccles, he made
the first exploratory climbs
on Mont Blanc's southerly Brouillard face.

MICHEL PAYOT
AND THE QUEST FOR A NEW WORLD

Michel Croz was dead and it was one of the young guides that he had trained who took up where he had left off.

Michel like his brothers, Alphonse and Frédéric, was the son of a well-known guide. Jean Payot was the first in a long line of guides that are still active in the profession today.

Michel started his alpine career properly speaking at the age of 18 when he accompanied Auguste Balmat and Professor John Tyndall to the summit of Mont Blanc.

In 1863, at the age of 23, he was made a member of the Compagnie. The following year he was employed by the cartographer Anthony Adams-Reilly, who was working on a map of the Massif.

His trips with Whymper and Adams-Reilly allowed him to observe at first hand the high-level technical skills of Michel Croz, and he was happy to assist the great guide on his ascents of Mont Dolent, the Aiguille de Trélatête and the Aiguille d'Argentière.

"He is still young, but he certainly has a great future ahead of him", went an entry in his guide's assessment diary for the same year.

The death of Michel Croz on the Matterhorn propelled him into the ranks of the top Chamonix guides. Then, in 1869, his meeting with Eccles would carry him still further along in the competition to make big first ascents. The partnership of Michel Payot and James Eccles was more than just a simple sporting partnership as it lasted over 40 years and took the Chamoniard far beyond the confines of his native mountains.

Associated exclusively, from this point on, with the British climber Eccles, he and Eccles would actively participate in the final stages of the Golden Age of alpinism. In 1871 he made the first ascent of the Aiguille du Plan, then a year later he traversed the Aiguille de Rochefort from Mont Mallet down to Courmayeur, opening up in reverse a route that today remains a classic. In 1877 they explored the south face of Mont Blanc and the Frêney glacier, climbing part of the Peuterey ridge on the way.

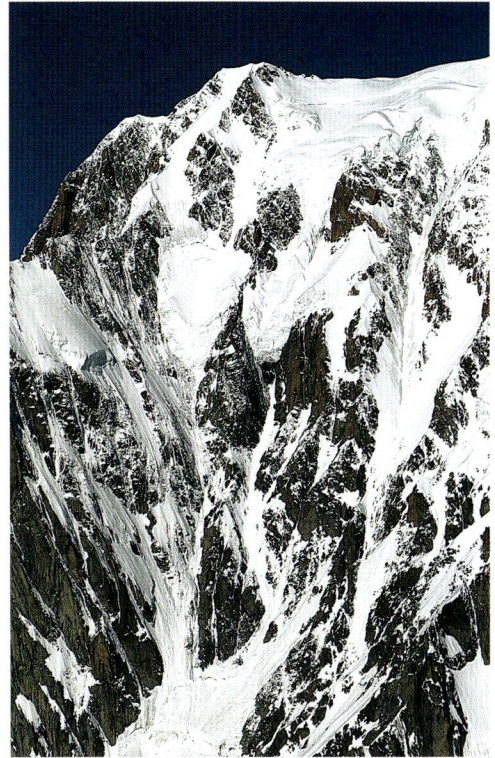

Below:
A forty-year friendship.
James Eccles and Michel Payot
(in the front row)
with two porters.

His brother Alphonse accompanied them on the trip, and it was he who cut steps for over eight hours on a ridge so narrow that Michel was unable to move to the front. Eccles saluted the performance of the two brothers, explaining that *"the major part of the ridge was hard ice and it was necessary to cut deep steps into it. The work was very hard but he carried on right to the end without a single break and as gaily and imperturbably as if cutting steps in blue ice was all he had ever done in life."*

It has to be said that alpinism at that time was very different from today. Climbers in those days had simple nails under their boots for crampons, equipment that was little suited to conditions in the mountains, no pitons or ice screws and ropes that were heavy and difficult to handle. The guides literally had the weight of the group on their shoulders and in their hands. Moreover, step cutting would remain the preserve of the professionals for a long time to come. It was only after the arrival of 10-point crampons and, later on, front-point crampons that these methods, more akin to the techniques used by woodcutters than modern mountaineers, would fall out of use. In short, the guides at this time were immensely tough with the constitution and strength of farmers and stockmen, which, when they weren't guiding, is

what they were. The Payot brothers were no different.

Yet the rustic nature of the guides did not stop Eccles developing a bond with Michel Payot and inviting him on a great adventure: an expedition to the Rockies at the height of the Indian Wars. The Sioux had massacred Custer and his regiment just two years earlier and Michel Payot was entitled to be worried. Truth be told, the trip was not a resounding success and, with the exception of a second ascent of Mount Fremont, the team did not manage any big first ascents as it had done in the Alps. Michel Payot, only the second Chamoniard to properly leave the valley, came back with a "mortal dread" of American Indians that would stay with him for the rest of his life.

James Eccles was very attached to this open and interesting guide, and invited him on several occasions to join him hunting in Scotland. Thus, as well as a chamois specialist, Payot also became an expert grouse hunter. Eccles died in 1915 and the alert Payot now in his 70s continued to wander through the mountains as he had always done before. A year before his death, at the age of 81, he completed yet another half tour of Mont Blanc and was incensed when a band of over-zealous customs officials confiscated his mules at the Col de la Seigne...

Tragedy on Mont Blanc:
one of the greatest dramas to happen on the mountain. It captured the popular imagination
(no doubt thanks to Dr Bean's letters) and the French magazine Le Petit Journal
published an artist's impression of the discovery of the bodies by the rescue party.

Previous pages:
Rochefort Ridge.
Michel Payot and James Eccles climbed the ridge on 14 August 1873.

TRAGEDY ON MONT BLANC

Even if there were a few outstanding guides and if ascents of Mont Blanc had by now become almost commonplace, the mountain still didn't pull its punches. And although the guides had a great deal of experience (some had over 40 ascents to their name) and were better equipped, they were still only men, strangely fragile in the face a mother nature that could lash out savagely.

The summer of 1870 was calamitous. Storms, snow, miserable weather and leaden grey skies had made it a disastrous season and an English team had almost died on the summit of Mont Blanc when it got lost in the clouds.

Yet an American in his fifties, Mr Randall, still dreamed of climbing Mont Blanc. Thanks to his extensive reading on the subject, he knew all the mountain's glaciers without ever having set foot on a single one of them. He even managed to convince a fellow American, Dr J.B. Bean of Baltimore, and a Scot, the Reverend George McCorkindale, to have a crack at the adventure with him. None of the three had any alpine experience. On 5 September, led by three guides and five porters, they nevertheless headed off in the direction of the Grands Mulets. None was seen alive again. The following morning, and after a brief respite that encouraged them to continue, a storm came in from the west and descended upon the range. The wind blew like a tornado and huge amounts of snow fell.

The sky remained obstinately socked in and it wasn't until 14 September that observers below with binoculars could hope to spot the group on the mountain.

Finally, on the 15 September, a clear spell seemed to be setting in. Sylvain Couttet, a guide from the Compagnie, hurried up to Plan Praz. He was able to make out black dots left of the Petits Mulets, which had not been there before.

A rescue team of 23 guides was finally able to set off the following day. It reached the Mur de la Côte on 17 September and found the bodies of McCorkindale and those of two porters, Auguste Couttet and Ferdinand Tairraz. One hundred metres higher up lay the body of Bean, his head resting on one hand and his elbow leaning on a bag, and higher still lay Auguste Cachat. Frozen by the cold and fatigue they looked asleep. Neither Randall nor the three guides and two remaining porters were ever found; they had no doubt been swept away by an avalanche and buried in a crevasse.

In one of Bean's pockets was a notebook. Very quickly the whole of Chamonix knew about the tragedy. *"Tuesday Sept. 6th, temperature 34. At 2 am. ascended to the top of Mont Blanc with ten*

other men, eight guides and porters and Rev. Mr. McCorkindale and Mr. R. Arrived at summit at 2½ o'clock when immediately I was enveloped in an awful snow-storm at some 15,000 ft. Dug a grotto and spent the night very uncomfortably – was very sick all night" wrote Bean.

His account continued in the same pitiful tone, "Mont Blanc, Sept. 7th. If anyone shall see this, they will please send it, this book to Mrs. H. M. Bean, Jonesboro', E. Tennessee, United States of America.

My Darling Hessie: We have been on Mont Blanc in two days of awful snow-storm, we have lost our way, are in a grotto hewn in the snow 15,000 ft. above the sea. I do not think we will ever get down. If we do not, this may be found in some way and sent to you. Let Robert Hunter see it and have it published in the Baltimore papers. Have Robert close up the business. I hope he will do it right. We have no provisions and my feet are already frozen and I am quite exhausted. I have just strength to write these few words.

Tell Chapin [Bean's son] I have left means for his education, and you must apply it properly. I will die in good faith in Jesus Christ and with many thoughts of you and Chapin. If I perish I bid you good bye and hope we will meet in heaven."

They spent another hellish night out, arms and leg starting to freeze. His handwriting very shaky, Bean found, in a final burst of energy, the strength to write these last few lines: "Sept. 7th. Morn still very cold and snowing hard – much trouble with the men. Please write to Dr. A. H. Balderston, Poste Restante, Paris, tell him of the accident and that my effects are on my body, at the Hotel de Mont Blanc, and two Portmanteaus sent by Post, Schweizerhof, Geneva, Suisse, and pay bills at the Hotel, etc. You will be remembered in heaven for your kindness."

Mont Blanc, which had been climbed for nearly a century and observed from every possible angle, had just claimed 11 victims, eight of which were members of the Compagnie. This was one of the heaviest tolls the Compagnie had paid in the mountains.

A rescue team at the Jonction,
on the route to Mont Blanc, in 1865.
The guides were in charge of rescues and,
as after the 1870 tragedy, they made it a point of honour
to bring back victims' bodies to their families.

*The guides' office
at the time of the Compagnie's dissolution.
It would not change premises
for almost 150 years.
Drawing by Edward Whymper.*

MONT BLANC AT THE HEART OF THE FIRST DISPUTES

Even if the tragedies that we have just discussed curbed the mood of general euphoria, the Compagnie still lived and breathed Mont Blanc and the adventures of a Payot or a Devouassoud were the exception not the rule. Demand essentially focused on this one route or those ordinary routes that today have more in common with hiking than mountaineering.

The Compagnie was resting on its laurels and the 1874 season, with its 24,000 outings and 44 Mont Blanc trips, was excellent. The Chamoniards clung to a range of privileges that were starting to be seriously questioned. Discontent had been growing for over 10 years. A Miss Grove, who had it in mind to climb the Aiguille de Bionnassay, wrote in 1865 that *"I made our projects known to our guides [...] I cannot say that they fully subscribed to our idea. [...] The Chamonix guides are conservative. They cling to their prices and are happy to follow in Jacques Balmat's footsteps."*

Possibly too sure of themselves, fixated on their privileges, the Chamoniards were going to cede ground. Even the French were starting to find the Chamonix guides a little cantankerous. V. Opperman wrote that there were *"more than two hundred guides in Chamonix: of this number, I am pleased to admit, forty or fifty are top class, the others are mediocre."* Yet some of their middle and upper class clients could not acknowledge the fact that these tough men from the mountains had character faults of their own. They praised their admirable qualities – technical skills, courage, composure – and passed swiftly over their faults. Ignoring the alpine valleys they came from and the difficulties, and moral and social pressures of such a world, as they did.

The Alpine Club was their most scathing critic. In 1874 it printed a manifesto that was particularly hard on the Chamoniards, reproaching them for, among other things, their ignorance, their system of recruitment, the tyrannical power of the head-guide, and finally their pricing structure that it considered prohibitively expensive. Article 33 of the 1872 rules still stipulates that, *"for the ascent of Mont Blanc, a traveller must take three guides and one porter. Two travellers, four guides or even three guides and two porters with an extra guide for every addition of two travellers."* The Chamoniards were unaware of the evolution in the world of mountaineering. Clubs were growing up in every country, which were redefining the practice of mountaineering. Most importantly, their members could not accept being compared to mere tourists with no alpine experience. With incredible obstinacy, the Chamoniards refused to give an inch and little by little British mountaineers opted for Swiss guides. Some of the most well known ones included Almer, Burgener and Anderegg, who were perhaps more biddable and prepared to accede to the demands of the English lords...

The inscription reads:
"Souvenir of ascent of Mont Blanc. First ascent of the year 1881, made on 29 June by Mr Léon Lochet,
notary in Chamonix, accompanied by the guides Messrs Alfred Comte and Edouard Cupelin. L. Lochet"

Edouard Cupelin,
Mont Blanc specialist.
He was known to his peers
as 'the captain of Mont Blanc',
with 90 ascents to his name.
He was the second guide
in the Compagnie to be granted this title,
which at the time was considered
extremely prestigious.

EDOUARD CUPELIN,
A GUIDE IN A GREAT TRADITION

If the Chamonix community suffered from what was essentially justified criticism, some guides did an honest job, even on Mont Blanc. Edouard Cupelin was one of these lesser-known guides. Although he did not have a glittering career, one of his clients did not hesitate to compare him to the Bernese Oberland guides, *"in many of his manners he had the cut and temperament more akin to an Oberlander than a Chamoniard..."* This was quite a compliment for, given his nickname, 'the captain of Mont Blanc', was a rather traditional-style guide.

In addition to his 54 ascents of Mont Blanc, he also managed to notch up a number of winter ascents including the Aiguille du Midi (first winter ascent), the Col du Chardonnet, the Fenêtre de Saleinaz and the Col du Tacul. He visited the Canary Islands with a Dr Marat and, while he was there, climbed the 'Pic Ténériffe' (Pico del Teide, 3718m). He also picked up a few other first ascents such as the Col des Grandes Jorasses in 1864, the Schwartzhorn in 1873 and Mont Mallet via a new route in 1882.

He wore the number 162 in the Compagnie and was accepted into it on 5 July 1865. However, his career changed forever on 12 August 1884. He was leading a group with François Simond and an American, Ramssler.

The Whymper couloir was in the shade and he was climbing up the Talèfre face of the Grande Rocheuse as it was coming into the sun, the Aiguille Verte somewhere above them. They had nearly finished the route, another half an hour and they would be on the summit slopes. Simond described the scene that followed *"I was finishing off the steps ten metres from where we had had our last meal when Cupelin set off. Just at that moment a rock broke away. Cupelin fell and broke his leg. Fortunately, he was still attached to the rope. We got him down to the Couvercle [hut] that evening. But he has been crippled since then."*

He carried on for a few more years, mostly on Mont Blanc, but was now disabled and unable to do the bigger routes. Like many former guides he went on to run some of the local mountain huts. First the Pierre Pointue, on the right bank of the Bossons glacier, on the route up to Mont Blanc (all that remains of it today are the foundations), and following that the Grands Mulets Hut. He died in 1906 at the age of 66.

Mont Blanc in the heart of winter, seen from the Col des Grands Montets.
Covered in fresh snow from December to February,
it looks even more dazzling and no doubt inviting.

Jean Charlet and Isabella Straton.
One of the legendary mountain couples. Seen here on the right of the picture.

First Winter Ascent of Mont Blanc

Everything revolved around and ultimately came back to Mont Blanc. The best climbing partnerships had abandoned it in search of other challenges, yet the first winter ascent remained a major prize, a challenge that any guide would eagerly accept.

In the winter of 1875-6 there was very little snow on its slopes. A curious paradox when one considers the fact that in Le Tour, at the other end of the valley, there were snow drifts 10 metres high. This had never been seen before in the valley and Mont Blanc appeared to be in excellent condition. Large numbers of tourists arranged to meet up at the end of December with a sole objective in mind: to be the first to greet the winter from the mountain's summit. Miss Breevort, the Reverend Coolidge, James Eccles, Gabriel Loppé, the crème de la crème of the mountaineering world tried in vain, their assaults repelled by strong winds, powder snow and biting cold. Another group set off at the end of January.

Miss Isabella Straton, who already had a number of first ascents under her belt including the Pointe Isabella and the Aiguille du Moine, set off with her appointed guide, Jean-Esteril Charlet. She was by no means a beginner and a first attempt took them as far as the Bosses ridge. However, an accident involving a porter obliged them to retrace their steps and the team stopped at the Grands Mulets. They set off from here the following morning, 31 January, at 3:40am. It was bitterly cold and the brave mountaineer knew that the tips of her fingers were frozen. Nevertheless, she persevered and, together with Jean-Esteril Charlet, Sylvain Couttet and the porter, Michel Balmat, she reached the summit's dome poking out of the clouds, standing over the surrounding peaks. She had just made the first winter ascent of Mont Blanc. In her short account of the event, she said that *"the thermometer read –24°c, the view was beautiful beyond description. I had made the ascent three times in the summer but until now I had never perfectly contemplated the spectacle. The immense quantity of snow that had accumulated on the Italian side added a great deal to the grandeur of the scene."*

The story might have ended there, and once again it might have been the client who took the glory with no mention of her guide, but chance would decide otherwise. Having shared the same trials, dangers, exhaustion and joy, the guide and his client had become united by a profound sense of affection. This final trial on Mont Blanc would cement the extraordinary bond between the couple and on 29 November 1876 Jean-Esteril Charlet married Isabella Straton in the church in Argentière. In the context of the time, when guides were considered excellent followers of instructions but certainly not their clients' equals, this was to cause a small revolution. One of Chamonix's own had questioned his station in life and took responsibility for the sporting ambitions of the mountaineers in his charge, products of the upper middle class and the aristocracy...

The Drus the day after a storm,
seen from the valley bottom and the village of Les Praz. Jutting up against the Verte,
they quickly became the emblematic mountain for the guides and still adorn the guides' badges today.

One of the first
reportage-style photos
taken by Joseph Tairraz
showing the victorious
Drus team.
From left to right:
Prosper Payot,
Jean Charlet-Straton
and Frédéric Folliguet.

Below:
Charlet-Straton
at the beginning
of the 20th century.
He was by this time
a huge figure among
the Chamonix guides.

Charlet Straton
DOES IT AGAIN ON THE DRUS

As sometimes happens, Chamonix had produced a guide unlike the others. Even the community itself sometimes had trouble understanding and reining in Jean-Esteril Charlet-Straton. Yet powerful figures such as Charlet-Straton, often stifled and held back within a group, have a hugely important role to play, as it is they who challenge old ideas and breathe new life into crumbling institutions.

Charlet-Straton quickly set about putting his ideas into practice. And he had the means to do it, as he was not only one of the best guides in Chamonix but was now also a wealthy man thanks to his marriage.

He had been thinking about the Drus for some years. The Drus, together with the Verte, symbolized for the people of Les Frasserands, Charlet-Straton's home village, a vertical world. It became his main challenge. On 13 July 1877 he set off on his own for the Petit Dru, saying to his friends *"if I'm not back by the day after tomorrow, it means I've taken my last tumble."* He started up the route, that was still given grade IV, with an ice-axe, a rope and a stick to plant a flag on the summit. But he came up against a steep chimney. He retreated from the climb thanks to the rope, inventing as he did a technique that is still used today: the rappel or abseil. Charlet-Straton refused to give in, realizing that for this route he would need a climbing partner.

He was shaken by the news that C. Dent, on his eighteenth attempt, had just conquered the Grand Dru with the Swiss guide Burgener.

But he did not admit defeat and still dreamed of conquering the Petit Dru, very different from the Grand Dru and dreadfully difficult. He set off again on 28 August. The skies were clear as he headed up the Le Chapeau path. This time he was with two other guides, Prosper Payot and Frédéric Folliguet, and was amply equipped; between the three of them they were carrying three 100-metre ropes!

After bivouacking on 29 August at the bottom of the wall, they set off. He recounted the details of the ascent in

The Drus and Verte,
two peaks closely linked to the history and legend of the guides.

the 1879 French Alpine Club (CAF) yearbook. His account is made more interesting by the fact that very few of the guides wrote about their adventures, as for the most part they let their clients do the talking. He wrote that *"the rock became smooth and uniform, the features and protrusions that we might have held on to were rarer and rarer. I climbed up onto my companions' shoulders and looked for cracks in the rock with room enough for me to put either my hands or my feet. Once I had found a slot, my feet would leave the shoulders of the guides so I could move myself onto an axe that was raised to the point where I thought I could reach. Once there, I fixed my rope to a protrusion of rock, holding it carefully in my hands, and the two guides got to me by holding on the rope. When the shafts of the axes were no longer long enough, we were obliged to give up and look for other holds, slots for which we eagerly scoured the terrain. We were gripped by our desire to climb, our feet were wedged into the sharp rock. We were, exactly as Folliguet put it, 'stuck to the rock like leeches'."*

They were hardly worried about style, the principal aim was to make progress upwards. Finally, after eight hours of effort, they reached the summit. Canon fire in Chamonix saluted the success of some of its own. The flag planted and a cairn built, there was nothing left to do but to descend down the Charpoua glacier, making 14 rappels.

Somewhere along the line, Charlet-Straton had anticipated a change in mountaineering that would lead alpinists towards a more athletic and acrobatic form of climbing. This was especially true on rock routes where grades would be pushed higher and higher. Enter Mummery. Had the Chamoniards met their match?

You needed quite a store of courage (or perhaps to be blithely unaware of what you were getting yourself into...) to set off up the grade IV and V routes, which marked a new stage in the history of alpinism, with nailed boots, a hemp rope tied around your waist and no pitons...

Most guides at the beginning of the 1880s were content to carry out the main part of their job,
which consisted in guiding tourists on the Mer de Glace.
The arrival of Mummery would shake up old habits.

THE COMPAGNIE IN THE DOLDRUMS?

IN 1880 A YOUNG ENGLISHMAN, ALFRED MUMMERY, DEFIED CONVENTION
AND SET OFF TO CONQUER THE GRANDS CHARMOZ AND GRÉPON,
IN THE AIGUILLES HIGH ABOVE CHAMONIX. HE BROUGHT THE NEW SPORT
OF ROCK CLIMBING TO THE HIGH MOUNTAINS.
HOW DID THE GUIDES REACT? THEY QUITE SIMPLY BESIEGED THE CHAMONIX
AIGUILLES AND THREW THEMSELVES, PIONEER-LIKE, INTO SKIING.
BUT THE GAME HAD GONE INTERNATIONAL AND THE CHAMONIARDS
WERE NO LONGER THE ONLY PLAYERS IN THE ALPS…

Did Charlet-Straton pave the way for the arrival of those devilish Britishers? It's impossible to tell. But a year after Charlet-Straton's amazing feat, a young man named Alfred Frederick Mummery turned up in Chamonix.

Mummery was well-mannered, keenly intelligent and had a caustic sense of humour. Scientifically-minded and hard-working, rational and experienced, Mummery was an economist by training and decided to take up climbing as a sport. Gangly and short-sighted, he also had a deformity in his back that meant he was unable to carry heavy loads.

He climbed with Burgener, the brutish bear-like guide from the Swiss canton of Valais with a giant's hands and a peasant's stamina who would hack away at the mountain when the pace wasn't to his liking.

The duo started on the Grands Charmoz and the following year Mummery set to work on the Grépon.

Bottles of champagne in their rucksacks and a tot of Cognac as a pick-me-up, the pair set off with a joker up their sleeves, a certain Venetz, an impish little fellow who almost ran up cracks in the rock.

The trio knew that the peak was still unconquered. One of the sections, the famous C.P. terrace – named after Pierre Charlet and Prosper Payot – had been climbed to within a few metres of the summit, where the pair had had to admit defeat.

On 5 August 1880, the trio made rapid progress up to the north summit from where they joined the Grand Gendarme and then a wide ledge, the 'vire à bicyclette'. The highest point was now only a few metres away. A bottle was opened and, with champagne bubbles in his beard, Venetz climbed onto Burgener's ice axe, held out at arm's length, with nothing but 800m of space between him and the ground below. The mood was buoyant and Venetz the acrobat pushed himself up onto the summit block.

The Grépon had been conquered. A canon was fired in Chamonix to salute the men's efforts.

A new chapter in mountaineering

Three guides
from the golden age
of mountaineering.
Joseph Cachat, Frédéric Payot
and Joseph Simond
photographed in 1877.

history had been opened and a new style of climbing had come into being, one that the Aosta guide Guido Rey would name 'alpinisme acrobatique' or gymnastic alpinism.

And this time it was no coincidence that the Chamoniards were no longer the sole players in the evolution of mountaineering. If the conquest of Mont Blanc had their initials on it, from now on they would have to contend with the Swiss, Italians and the English, who had taken it upon themselves to sweep away the old habits.

Mummery was so sure of himself, so sure that the Chamoniards were completely out of their depth,

that he made a wager. He offered *"1000 gold francs to the first man to bring me back the ice axe I left on the summit!"* The guides simply had to rise to the challenge and a client called Henri Dunod had the talent to meet it. He had already been part of the team that made the first ascent of the Grands Charmoz and wasn't intimidated by the Grépon. The team, which also included François Simond, Gaspard Simond and Auguste Tairraz, made a series of attempts over four years.

Then, on 2 September 1885, the Chamoniards and their client stood on top of the Grépon's exposed summit crest.

On the summit of the Dent du Géant. Equipped right from the start with fixed ropes, this proud needle of rock would quickly become a much sought-after route for mountaineers.

François Simond gave a marvellous account of their route that day. *"One morning I said to Dunod, 'let's go up it, today I do or die!'*

Up we went again and there we were! I would have trouble telling you how I did it... With my feet, my hands, a knee, my nails, I held on where I could, in cracks, in holes, on lumps...

Since then people have asked me which route I followed, but I couldn't tell you... I am sure that an hour later I was holding Mummery's ice axe in my hand. I didn't even know at the time that Mummery had offered a prize. Someone said to me 'François, you've won 1000 francs.'

And then they told me about it. But I'm not as pleased about the money as I am about the axe itself... And in any case I never got a penny of it, as when we told Mummery about our adventure he declared that his bet was only valid for the year 1881!"

Yet the Chamonix Aiguilles would have to wait a little longer for their Pygmalion.

The routes here remain outstanding classics, the work of inspired mountaineers climbing steep and difficult ground.

The north side of the Chamonix Aiguilles
after a fall of snow.

Great new exploits would take place on these granite arrows,
from the Aiguille de la République on the left to the Aiguille du Midi with Mont Blanc behind it.

The two protagonists in the 'war of the observatories'.
Joseph Vallot camping on the summit of Mont Blanc with his two guides
and regular companions Frédéric Payot and Michel Savioz. And Janssen on his return from his epic ascent
of Mont Blanc (he was carried, winched and dragged up it) surrounded by his team of guides.

The Janssen observatory on Mont Blanc in around 1900. The building quickly became covered in snow and ice and by 1910 it had fallen into disuse. Its turret was rescued and brought back down to the valley where it is housed in the Alpine Museum.

THE WAR OF THE OBSERVATORIES

And if a few mavericks chose the Chamonix Aiguilles as their playground, the masses only had eyes for Mont Blanc. The grand old dame of the Alps was a little bit worn at the edges but she had lost none of her pride and her reign was far from over. Moreover, the greatest event of the 1890s in Chamonix, which naturally took place on Mont Blanc, was the epic achievement of Joseph Vallot. Joseph Vallot was a curious figure.

A wealthy and self-educated man, Vallot was devoted to the cult of all things high-altitude. He had already spent three days, during which time he carried out his first altitude experiments, on the dome of Mont Blanc in 1887 in the company of his guides, Michel Savioz and Alphonse Payot.

But this was not enough and he dreamed of constructing a proper hut-observatory at the foot of the same giant dome of ice. He was quite a character and could be very persuasive. He managed to bring the town's authorities, the guides and his family around to his way of thinking. He used all his powers of persuasion to present the project to the Compagnie des Guides in a letter. And he was thinking big. He wanted to set up his observatory on one of the final rocky outcrops below the ridge, the Arête des Bosses. He thought that this would be a safe spot and a catastrophe, such as that which befell Dr Bean's party in 1870, would be

virtually impossible. As, thanks to its position, the hut could serve as a fallback point for climbers in case of bad weather. The project unleashed a storm of wildly differing views and opinions. And woe betide anyone who mentioned the scoundrel Vallot's name in the local taverns. But he was a pragmatist and, with the support of his cousin, Henri Vallot (creator of the Vallot climbing guides), he stood his ground.

And in 1890 the first loads were finally transported up to the observatory's construction site.

Three guides – Frédéric Payot, Alphonse Payot and Jules Bossoney – were charged with overseeing the project. The wood was supplied by the commune and the owners of eight mules together with 110 guides and porters were to each carry up, virtually for free, 15kg loads to the Arête des Bosses. After five days of intense and extremely hard work, from 25 to 29 July, the observatory had been built. It was five metres long by three metres wide and three metres high and had two separate rooms, one for Vallot and the other given over to the Chamonix municipal authorities.

The hut was quickly extended with six rooms being built after 1892 and Vallot soon had to built a second hut on a neighbouring rock.

The famous man of letters, Jules Janssen, soon

Entrance to the Vallot observatory. It was run by the Chamonix guides and was a crucial fall back point when in bad weather. A duralumin shelter was added to the Vallot observatory in 1937, which is used these days as a hut. The primitive cabin structure was reserved for scientists. Adolphe Balmat is on the extreme right-hand side.

paid the observatory a visit and he too envisaged building an observatory, but this time on the actual summit of Mont Blanc. The men didn't take to each other. The guides, amused onlookers, were able count the points of difference between the two, as it was they who were to make the projects happen.

Janssen was the antithesis of Vallot. One was 35 years old, had a limited amount of university education, a cast iron constitution and an insatiable appetite for everything mountain-related.

The other man, Janssen, was 70 years old, had a scientific background (he was responsible for the construction of, among other things, the observatory in Meudon, Paris) and was in failing health. Carried on a chair by porters (one of the last of its kind) and then dragged up on a sledge, Janssen got to the summit of Mont Blanc in 1893 for the inauguration of his observatory.

The war of the observatories was in full swing. Yet, as Vallot had predicted, Janssen's observatory soon started to subside, swallowed up by the movement of the summit ice slopes.

For 16 years, the structure like some kind of submarine set adrift, was the perfect waypoint for those climbing Mont Blanc. Its turret, its architect's (a certain Gustave Eiffel) pride and joy, was finally recovered and the remaining seven tonnes of timber used as firewood in Vallot's observatory...

An entire infrastructure was now in place on Mont Blanc's north face and the scientists' battle had allowed a bivouac hut to be built, perfect for the ascent of Mont Blanc. And the Chamonix guides had taken part in both project.

The 'envers' or other side of the Chamonix Aiguilles. The Aiguille du Plan, south face of the Fou and the Grépon are all clearly visible. At the turn of the 20th century, Ravanel Le Rouge and Emile Fontaine would make them their high-altitude playground.

A QUARTET ON THE AIGUILLES

Barely a decade after his coup on the Grépon, Mummery was back in Chamonix to notch up the first traverses of the Grépon and Dent du Requin, and without guides.

The stakes were high between the Chamoniards and the rest of world up on the Chamonix Aiguilles, and the French seemed rather reluctant to take up the gauntlet.

Apart from De Bouillé's ascent of the Aiguille du Midi and Dunod's climb to the north summit of the Grépon, they held back and hesitated when it came to the athletic rock climbs that were nothing like the traditional normal routes.

Some peaks, however, were worth a visit, starting with the Fou ('Madman'), so named by Michel Savioz. Whilst out taking topographical measurements with Joseph Vallot, Savioz studied the mountain's rock face and exclaimed *"If a madman asked me to climb that aiguille, that's the way I'd go."* Thus, peak 3502 became the Aiguille du Fou.

And the madman was a monchu, or foreigner, Emile Fontaine. (It must be remembered that the Chamoniard term 'monchu', meaning 'monsieur' in patois, does not merely refer to people from other lands but includes all those not born in the valley…).

Every time he came to Chamonix to climb, Fontaine always stayed in the hotel at the Montenvers. Not because he disliked Chamonix, for he made the return trip to the valley for training purposes on his rest days. What he did dislike was bivouacs and he found the hotel an ideal base camp from where he could, depending on the project, get an early start on big routes. He was a modest man and was happy to put the guides first, naming peaks after them and shunning all forms of publicity.

He was, moreover, the man who 'discovered' the Ravanels. That's Ravanels plural, for there was Ravanel Le Rouge ('The Red'), Camille and the youngest, Jean. That's not forgetting Léon Tournier, a burly man 5 feet 9 inches tall. In fact, Emile Fontaine was to awaken the curiosity of an entire generation and turn its attention to highly technical and difficult routes.

Let us start with Joseph Ravanel, known as Le Rouge. He had a robust character and was the son of peasants from Argentière and the eldest of a family that included four guides. He is also one of the heroes of Roger Frison-Roche's celebrated novel Premier de Cordée (published in English as "First on the Rope"), and appears as Ravanat.

Frison-Roche didn't have to look very hard for inspiration, the book's plot, power, and the charac-

The famous Joseph Ravanel with his brother Jean on the summit of the Aiguille des Drus.
It is 23 August 1901 and they have just done the first aid-free traverse from the Petit to the Grand Dru
with Emile Fontaine (behind the camera).

ters' backgrounds all have an authentic feel and sense of the heat of the moment. If, over 70 years after his death, Ravanel Le Rouge's career is just as pertinent as it was then, he owes this interest in great part to his insatiable curiosity that took him back time and time again to the mountains and new adventures. He established himself, at the start of the twentieth century, as the best guide in the Compagnie. His career was punctuated by remarkable first ascents, unusual accidents and strange experiences. Hewn out of rock and iron, the Aiguilles de Chamonix and the Talèfre basin were his favourite rock climbing areas and his suffered his fair share of accidents. While climbing the Petit Dru in 1899 a small rock hit him square in the face, knocking him senseless for a few seconds and breaking three teeth. But it didn't stop him finishing the climb... He also has a peak named after him in the Mont Blanc Massif, the Aiguille Ravanel, just along from the Courtes and for evermore associated with Mummery.

Le Rouge had just completed the first ascent with Emile Fontaine and Léon Tournier and, as was the custom, he suggested naming the mountain after the client. *"You see that trickle of water that comes straight off the aiguille? Doesn't it make you think of your name? I think we should call it the Aiguille Fontaine [fontaine meaning 'fountain']"*, said Ravanel. *"Let's talk about it this evening Le Rouge"*,

replied his client. That evening Fontaine raised a glass of champagne as a toast to the Aiguille Ravanel, and there was nothing more to be said...

Le Rouge, so named because of his red hair, had quite a collection of first ascents including the north summit of the Blaitière, the Aiguille du Fou, the first traverse of the Grands Charmoz, the Dent du Crocodile, Aiguille des Pélerins, the Dent du Caïman, Aiguille du Peigne and the Ciseaux, not forgetting the first traverse of the Drus without aid, and the traverse of the Aiguille Sans Nom to the Verte.

He also had a collection of exceptional clients, and in addition to Emile Fontaine there was a Mr Lefebure, with whom he climbed the Aiguille de l'M. In the evening one of his friends said to him, *"I know your tourist, he's a general I saw during the war, he was decorating someone for something"*.

In fact, the fellow was none other than Albert 1st, King of the Belgians. Together they would scour the massif for routes, climbing the Grands Charmoz, the Grépon and the Drus.

A sincere friendship developed between the great guide and his distinguished climbing partner, and the king of guides became the guide of kings. He was a typical-looking guide with his imposing stature and had an almost superhuman sureness of himself in the mountains. The following account

Ravanel Le Rouge looks out over the heart of the Mont Blanc Massif from the summit of the Drus.
Photo taken from the Revue Alpine.
Below: Léon Tournier, the third guide to join the partnership of Emile Fontaine and Jean Ravanel.

of a meeting with him, taken from his biography that appeared in 1932 in French Club Alpin's review, La Montagne, perfectly encapsulates his mountain skills. The narrator, M.P., recounts how *"in 1917 I was climbing the Tour Noir with my son. [...] I was traversing when I saw a guide with a client who was very unsure of himself coming the other way and underneath me, on the 'Javelle' ledge. 'Ah, it's Le Rouge', I said, 'Good morning Ravanel'. 'Good morning', he said, 'It's you. Here again.' He smiled broadly. I was above him and while I waited a moment I was able to watch him at work. It was a pleasure to behold. He could not belay the man from a distance, across the slope, so he was right behind him, holding the rope tight the second he saw the slightest hesitation or slip of the foot. I admired him, for not for a minute on this delicate section was he ever less than in complete control of the situation."*

Le Rouge was the major figure at the start of the century and remained so for the following three decades. He took part in the first Chamonix-Zermatt 'haute route' on skis, in the 1920s he was part of the teams that carried the statues of the Madonna to the summits of the Drus and the Grépon, and became the warden of the Couvercle Hut.

Following in his wake, there came other guides eager to be part of the epic first ascents made at the beginning of the century. To start with there was his brother Jean, known as Le Bon Diandian. Quieter and smaller than Le Rouge, Diandian admirably complemented his brother. Emile Fontaine, through force of circumstance and thanks to the contact he had with them, is our chronicler of the period and recounts the first ascent of the Aiguille du Caïman in 1905. The climbing was going well and they had reached the huge monolith with a lasso-like throw of the rope, free-climbing having yet to have made its mark on the climbers of the period.

In short, Jean Ravanel, Léon Tournier and their client, Emile Fontaine, were perched on the Caïman's summit. Now they had to get back down and it was Tournier who set off first and disappeared behind a spur of rock. Jean followed him. It was now Fontaine's turn to grab hold of the rope. That is grab the rope and not to wrap it around oneself as on a rappel, at this time one descended a rope by holding on to it with no kind of belay device or even wrapping it around the body. Our alpinist was now two-thirds of the way down when, *"I suddenly felt my muscles tense up and I let go"*. He fell and crashed

Emile Fontaine (front) was one of the few 'monchus' to rival the British climbers of the period. Here he is with usual climbing partners, the guides Joseph Ravanel (sitting) and Jean Ravanel (standing).

into Jean Ravanel on his way down, knocking him off his feet, while Fontaine started to *"pirouette and roll down a very steep slab..."* He light-heartedly described the scene that followed: *"the wide open space that opened up beneath the somersaulter gave him an excellent view of one the most spectacular plunges that an alpinist might experience."*

In short, he was preparing himself for his final leap when he came to an abrupt halt. Jean Ravanel had managed at the last minute to grab his fellow traveller while holding on to a pillar of rock with other hand. His client's only thoughts were for *"his final plunge"*.

A fatal accident had been avoided. Jean Ravanel, like most of the guides of the time, had fists of iron and if they couldn't hold them, well, they were in God's hands...

Léon Tournier, the third member of this group of alpine virtuosos, was also quite a force of nature who *"when he talked of a hold being 'as small as my finger' was describing what was, in reality, a crack wide enough for a normal person's hand!"*

Unsurprising really, as these colossal men had scoured the Chamonix Aiguilles for routes and were built to tackle Alpine granite...

The north face of the Grands Charmoz with the Aiguille de la République on its left edge. This slender and airy needle of rock still gives high class climbing.

Joseph Simond and his crossbow, which allowed him to reach the summit of the Aiguille de la République. Now considered absolutely out of the question, the use of crossbows was not uncommon up until the 1920s.

AN UNUSUAL FIRST ASCENT, THE AIGUILLE DE LA REPUBLIQUE

And thus the route had been established and even if it was not regularly used, other guides would take it upon themselves to look after it, to pass on the itinerary and tips to others so that these slabs of mountain would become their territory.

Little by little, the Chamonix Aiguilles would fall into the hands of the guides. They knew how to look for and pick out the best lines and sometimes they even got the chance to make the first ascents of them. Their technique was not necessarily very purist but they made do as best they could without pitons, harnesses, indeed without even reliable ropes. The guides, like a great number of the montagnards of the time, always had a solution up their sleeves, a bit of DIY that would get them round the problem of a tricky section. The first ascent of the Aiguille de la République was made in a rather unusual manner.

The client, H.E Beaujard, told the story in La Montagne, in 1905: *"Everyone's heart was beating fast, mine too when the crossbow released its bolt high into the air; by a remarkable stroke of luck the silk cord was taken up to exactly the right place, in a notch that seemed to have been made to hold it fast. It remained for the porter to move round to the other side of the arête to act as a counterweight. At around 5 o'clock, after a series of manoeuvres during* which he risked his life more than twenty times, Louis announced he was solidly ensconced and was ready to play his role. Off we set! Not without a great deal of excitement, I watched Joseph take off his jacket and anything else that might weigh him down, except his shoes, and step onto Alfred's shoulder and cross the first few metres that were overhanging. I soon lost him from sight [and] only the sound of the nails [of his boots] scraping the granite filtered down to me. A few interminable minutes went by. Then, all of sudden, there came an extraordinary cry, the sound of which will not leave my memory with any great speed, to let us know that he had happily reached the top..."*

Yes, as well as bottles of champagne, they also managed to find room for crossbows in their backpacks!

Camille Ravanel on the summit of the Grépon and a fitting celebration of the ascent with his client.

The Lames du Brévent at the start of the 20ᵗʰ century.
Immortalised by the Gaston Rébuffat photo, the Lames were a popular climb among the guides in 1900.

The guides' bureau at the start of the 20th century. The small office under the mairie was an essential point of call for those wishing to go into the mountains.

THE COMPAGNIE IS UNIONIZED

Back down in the valley, the Compagnie, although it had been restructured, remained at the centre of controversy. The hoteliers continued to contest its power. The foreign guides and in particular the Swiss guides from Valais no longer tolerated the Compagnie's monopoly over the massif, and the various alpine clubs were grumbling about recruitment and the fact that they were not allowed to choose their own guides.

There was also the recruitment policy that excluded men from the neighbouring villages, who were forced to make do with working as porters like the 'Chirves' from Servoz and the Vallorcine men. This atmosphere of dissatisfaction had encouraged the Compagnie's cabal-like reign for years. Except that the context had now changed. The monarchy and Second Empire had given way to a republic, which was busy defining its values. Recruitment was still only open to Chamoniards, the entrance exam, the co-option system (only open to existing members of the Compagnie); these admission requirements were hardly designed to put candidates on an equal footing.

The government decided to act once and for all in the matter and, on 30 December 1892, the Compagnie was dissolved. It caused a revolution. The system of privileges having been abolished, now, in theory at least, any French citizen could become a guide in Chamonix. Once the brouhaha had passed, however, a union was created that used passive resistance to stop foreigners coming to the valley. The system was in place right up until 1930 when the first 'foreigner', Roger Frison-Roche, was accepted into the valley and the guides' company.

Certificates of ascents. From the beginning of the 20th century the Compagnie offered certificates for all routes in the massif.

Alfred Simond and client in 1909
at the Col des Grands Montets.
At that time, before the building
of the cable car,
the Grands Montets was remote
and difficult to access.

17 January 1903.
The pioneers of the winter Haute Route take a break on the Saleina glacier, under the north face of the Aiguille d'Argentière.

The winter Haute Route, which links two of Europe's great centres of mountaineering, has not changed very much since the first time it was skied and remains a must for many ski tourers.

THE HAUTE ROUTE IN WINTER

The Chamoniards went back to the mountains. This time it was the powder-filled winter slopes that attracted their attentions and first on their list was the most well-know route of them all, the Haute Route.

A British group had already done the route in summer, and by the 1860s Chamonix-Zermatt had become an alpine classic. With the discovery of skiing, brought to France from Scandinavia by Henri Duhamel, new possibilities opened up.

It began in 1897, when Wilhelm Paulke and a group of guides crossed the great glaciers of the Swiss Oberland.

And in the Chamonix valley it was Doctor Payot who first dared to venture out with planks of wood strapped to his feet. From 1900 onwards he visited the various hamlets in the valley on skis and was able to visit his patients no matter the conditions. After a few attempts, he crossed the Col du Géant, high up in the heart of the massif, with a group of friends. Why not try to go from one of the capitals of the Alps to another, from Chamonix to Zermatt?

The conditions in January 1903 were excellent as it had snowed the whole of the preceding month and the thick layer of snow seemed stable. Payot got a group of men together, which included Joseph Ravanel, Joseph Couttet and Alfred Simond. As well as these three guides, considered among the best in the Compagnie at that time, the team also included three porters charged with carrying the food and a camera weighing 19kg (roughly 42lb)!

All the equipment was scrupulously prepared and each skier had a pair of 2m (6ft 5in) skis, a pole made of ash that was 1.80m (5ft 9in) long with a basket on the bottom, and a 10kg (22lb) backpack.

The caravan set off from Argentière, heading for the Lognan chalets, on 16 January. That night was cold and starry and a temperature of –10°c led them to be believe that the weather would remain stable. They started on their way up the Argentière glacier at 2 o'clock in the morning, guided by the stars.

Payot described the crossing of the Chardonnet glacier in the September 1903 issue of the French Club Alpin's review. *"The snow bridges appeared suspect. We moved forward cautiously, the rope tight. All of a sudden there was a shout! A snow bridge had collapsed under Simond who was testing its solidity. The rope held him on the edge of the chasm, which on further inspection was large enough to accommodate all of us until spring time."* They finally made it to the Col du Chardonnet without any further mishap. They crossed the Fenêtre de Saleina and reached the Orny cabin or mountain hut. Here

Two sections of the first Chamonix-Zermatt Haute Route were recorded in photographs, which was very unusual for the time. Crossing the Trient plateau.

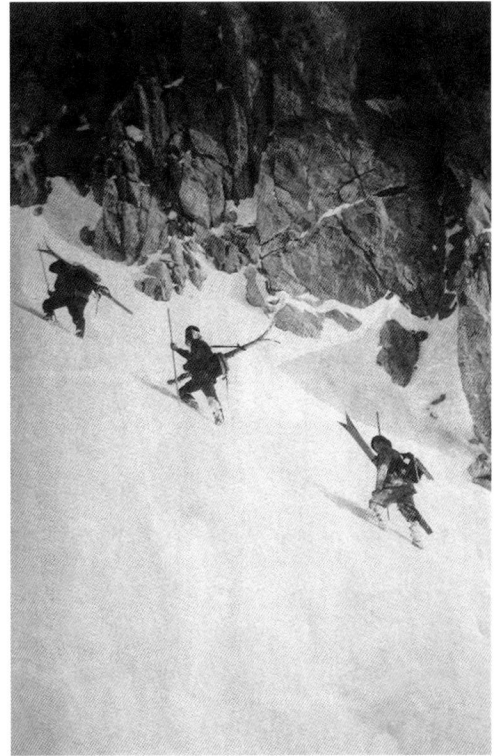

The climb up to the Fenêtre de Saleina.

These shots were taken from the album kept by Alfred Simond, who joined Doctor Payot, Joseph Couttet and Joseph Ravanel and three porters in the adventure.

the repast was a short affair as the roast beef and wine was frozen... They next descended to the village of Orsières from where they were driven to Le Châble.

The following day, the 18 January, after transferring by horse-drawn sleigh, they started their climb up to the Chanrion hut at 7 in the morning. After nightfall, and taking every rock for the hut, they finally reached it.

On 19 January the weather quickly got worse and they were forced to turn around after having tried to get to the Col de l'Evêque.

Tuesday 20 January and supplies were short, they went back down to Martigny and ate among other things a raclette. Finally the fine weather returned. The troupe set off again and picked up their route almost exactly where they had been forced to stop. Now they took the train to Sion, a carriage up to Evolène and on Thursday 22 they finally made their way up the Ferpècle glacier that had a thick covering of powder snow. Ravanel Le Rouge seemed very pleased with his new toys and exclaimed: *"My word, these planks are good! I'm never taking them off again, not even to sleep!"*

They finally reached the Col d'Hérens at four in the afternoon and finished their journey by lamplight, once again walking with a tight rope between them all. They reached Zermatt at midnight. The town was asleep and, knocking at a door, they were taken for drunks...

In the end the local priest helped them and they found their way to Zermatt's only hotel. The route was modified and improved in the years that followed, notably by Joseph Ravanel himself, who returned to it in 1908 and did the Chanrion-Zermatt section in one go, a marathon 18 and a half hour non-stop effort!

Nevertheless, Payot and his group had established the basic itinerary and it would provide the motivation for an entire generation of skier-climbers to launch themselves into the winter mountain environment.

Payot succinctly summarized his achievement thus: *"What have we gained from this long but wonderful crossing? Many will say nothing... but unprecedented fatigue and all kinds of suffering. We do not bother ourselves with the opinions of the uninitiated. We maintain the ardent desire to continue with our marvellous winter excursions. We now appreciate the value of skis as a means of transport: we know that ascents may be made quite quickly only in the right season; that if the descent of a mountain is, in summer as tiring and is the climb up it, it is nothing but a delicious pleasure on skis in winter..."*

It would be another 50 years before this great route would become an alpine classic, but the seed had been sown and in the decades that followed,

Camille Ravanel, known as 'à la Zitte', was a forerunner of modern ski tourers. He was a porter on the first Chamonix-Zermatt Haute Route and continued to explore the best slopes in the massif long afterwards.

Alfred Couttet, photographed here before the First World War, was the first civilian winner of the French Ski Championships. He was charismatic and generous and founded the first ski school in the Chamonix valley.

guides would continue to explore the massifs on skis to find new areas for their clients but also for the pleasure of visiting them. Other Chamoniards were quick to explore the possibilities.

First there was Camille Ravanel, know as à la Zitte, who was a porter on the first skied Chamonix-Zermatt crossing. He too went on to become a great guide and he made first ascents with clients of the Brenva Spur and the Aiguille Verte via the Sans Nom ridge with his cousin Alfred Léon Ravanel, and the north face of the Dent d'Oche in the Chablais massif (south of Lake Geneva). Yet like many Argentéraux he would become a fine skier. Was it perhaps his older brother's love of his skis that guided him in his choice? It's difficult to say, but he too would explore the mountains with very rudimentary equipment. It was he who first did the tour in 1908 that crosses from Mont Joly to Bourg Saint Maurice via Hauteluce, with his client Madame Bailly.

A jovial figure and less rugged that his brothers, Camille was still to be found with seals skins on his skis two decades later, this time touring around Mont Tondu and the Dômes de Miage.

The inhabitants of this alpine valley had really been bitten by the skiing bug, and it didn't take long for the young Chamoniards to get their teeth into this strange new sport and mode of transport.

The local kids were quick to kit themselves out with cask staves, a pair of galoches (stout leather boots with wooden soles) and a couple of ash poles. So equipped, they would follow in their elders' footsteps... Progress was so rapid that the first race was organised in 1907 and attracted 36 local competitors. Two years later, a Chamoniard was crowned the Champion of France, deposing the previous holder of the title Lieutenant Alloix. Alfred Couttet was the first non-military winner and was given the nickname Couttet Champion. Couttet was invited by the King of Norway himself to rub shoulders and compete with 300 of the best Scandinavian skiers at the legendary Holmenkollen trials. What's more, he finished eleventh! A brilliant performance and the start of what would be a glittering career about which there will be more in the next chapter. He was the first in a long line of skier-guides who made their mark on the history of skiing and he opened the way for James Couttet and Charles Bozon, two future world ski champions. This great sportsman would also, in his own way, steer the young inhabitants of the valley towards the sport. The guides found ski instruction in the winter the ideal accompaniment to their summer work.

The several-time French Champion soon founded a free ski school, which in 1909 had five pupils. In 1914, on the eve of war, it had 96 children.

The French President Armand Fallières visited the town for the opening of the Montenvers railway and is seen here in conversation with a number of guides, pleading their case with the head of state himself.

THE TRAIN TO MONTENVERS, YOUR MONEY OR YOUR LIFE!

Another event was to completely change the life of the valley. If skiing settled into the valley quietly, the Montenvers train was a painful birth.

In 1901, Chamonix had 2,729 inhabitants and more than 300 of them worked as guides in the summer.

In other words, 80 years after it was created, the Compagnie was still the economic driving force for the valley. The guides remained a powerful and influential group, embodying the Chamoniard identity, advocating local autonomy and positioning itself as the main player in the assimilation of the influx of tourists and town folk in relation to the local rural and pastoral society.

It was at this time that the railway project began to take shape.

This project also had the support of the regional administration, to the great displeasure of the Chamoniards. It appeared that the local authorities wanted to shake up the all-encompassing power of the Compagnie des Guides.

A petition quickly went round. Virtually the entire commune signed it. Everyone could sense the guides' disquiet.

How could they accept the competition that the railway would bring to the most profitable route in the valley? One hundred and sixty protests had been received by the spring review in 1906. The protests were making headway and their authors were succinct:

"I protest in the strongest terms against the establishment of the railway line, it is the greatest misfortune that might befall us." Semblanet, François.

"The railway line can only violate the rights of the commune which consist in not taking away from its inhabitants the work which allows them to live. The necessary consequence of [the railway line's] establishment will be to chase away the English, the most serious consequence for the town and oblige the guides to move elsewhere." Cachat, François.

"I protest with all my strength against the proposed railway line, [the Montenvers] being the sole source of income for my family, if this portering work is taken away from me, I shall be reduced to destitution or forced to leave the area." Comte, Armand. Porter.

"I protest against this [railway] line because this lovely two-hour excursion or walk, on a path that is always well kept, gives travellers, who are either

The Fontaine Caillet was a required stopping-off point
for the mule handlers and their clients on the way up to the Montenvers.
Normally run by an old guide, the cabin fell into disuse once the railway line was opened.

on foot or on horseback, enormous enjoyment in all senses, hygiene, beauty, safety and at a fair price. Six francs by mule, return trip." Tairraz, Gustave.

" I, the undersigned, hereby associate myself with all those who are fearful for the interests of their commune and protest energetically against the project." Ravanel, Joseph.

"I cannot accept this damned Montenvers railway line project for the simple reason that we have enough good paths, which are well maintained by the guides and I don't think there is a man in France in favour of taking our means of making our living from us." Claret-Tournier, Jean.

Despite the petitions, protests and demonstrations, nothing could be done and the small cog railway was inaugurated in 1908. By 1911 the Compagnie only had 90 mules and this number fell to 33 by 1920.

The final blow came in 1929, with the construction of the first cable cars, at Le Brévent. By 1929, 'mule handler' had disappeared from the Compagnie's register of activities.

The 'buvette',
cabin serving food and drink,
at Le Chapeau
was more fortunate.
Thanks to climbers and skiers
wanting to cross
the Mer de Glace,
visitor numbers remained
stable until the 1960s.
The glacier's retreat meant
the level of the ice dropped
considerably making crossing
the glacier at this point
very difficult. The cabin,
however, is still there today.

MORAL STANDARDS, NO JOKING MATTER

Despite these massive changes, the internal life of the Compagnie with its system of taking turns and rules for the guides continued as it had done before. The standards of behaviour in the organisation were not to be toyed with and the head-guide was charged with following these rules to the letter.

Thus, the Compagnie's punishment logbook makes interesting reading.

"On 24 August 1907 Edouard Ducroz, set out for the Bossons glacier in the afternoon. The travellers that he had been leading came to me to make the following complaint: that he was drunk and had abandoned them at the last chalet as they left the woods and that they worried for their personal effects that remained in his pockets. And Ducroz declared that he had done nothing of the sort, that he had simply had a Pernod as they left the glacier which had made him unwell and unable to walk any further. It is the Commission's decision on 4 September that he loose a turn as punishment."

"6 September 1912, Arthur Simond, head-guide at the Montenvers came to the office to state that the guides BOZON Léon and BALMAT Gustave arrived later than the appointed time and were both under the influence of drink. Simond forbade them from taking travellers. Bozon did not listen to him and touted for business on the glacier for the descent to Le Chapeau and Balmat spent the whole day playing the fool around the station despite being told not to by the guides' director. Both will lose two turns as punishment for this infraction."

"On the 25 August 1912, Jean Démarchi came in to the office and kicked up a rumpus and gave us a piece of his mind saying that we had got his traveller not to take a porter. He failed to return to the office to inform us that he was going to join a traveller at the Montenvers with the porter Jean Cachat. He merely left us the name of the traveller on a scrap of paper. The decision of the commission on 22 September is the said Démarchi be docked a turn as punishment for insulting the office management and defamation of character."

"On 31 July 1913, the guide DUCROZ François Benjamin committed the following offences at the Montenvers: while descending onto the glacier he held the hand of a lady to help her and while doing the same with the same lady on the way up he asked for 5 francs for his help that she had not solicited and which requires no payment. The travellers in question were most displeased with this obligation and, before witnesses, gave him 4 francs. That afternoon, this same guide was doing a round-trip across the glacier, the fee for which is 6 francs, and he only asked for 5 francs thus contravening the Montenvers pricing structure for the second time. And he only wanted to

Some of the guides working in the massif in the 1880s, photographed in front of the office in 1924.

Front row, seated (l. to r.): François Mugnier known as 'Mugnier le scieur' or 'sawyer',
Alphonse Payot known as 'Alphonse son of Jean Payot', Frédéric Payot known as 'Frédéric son of Jean Payot',
Joseph 'piausse' Cachat, Joseph Claret-Tournier – 'Joseph son of Constance', Adolphe 'the Bourselet Bear' Folliguet,
and François 'the silkworm' Devouassoud from Argentière.

Second row (l. to r.): Alfred 'Bottasson' Tairraz, Joseph 'Batioret' Burnet, Joseph Simond – 'Joseph son of Josan',

Jean Claret-Tournier – 'Jean à Béradit', Alexandre 'Alex from les Tissières' Couttet,
François Pierre Auguste Frasserand, Michel Desailloud - 'Michel son of Philippe', and Joseph Farini.

Back row, standing (l. to r.): François Comte, Paul Cupelin – 'Paul son of Baron', Joseph Demarchi,
Alfred 'the master' Balmat, Alexandre 'Lourgui' Choupin, Edouard 'à la tourche' Ravanel,
Henri 'Lourit des bois' Claret-Tournier, Pierre Devouassoud, Clément Tairraz from les Bois,
Armand Couttet - 'Armand son of Salomon'.

Below:
The first Argentière hut
was opened in 1907.

pay [the Montenvers] 4 francs, claiming that that was the sum he had received. The head guide, having questioned the travellers, stated that the guide wanted to pocket a franc. DUCROZ François loses three turns as punishment for this offence."

The guides were, after all, not superheroes, merely men with their shortcomings and their faults, like the rest of us...

They were like the mountains that surrounded them, rugged, with fault lines running through them, a reflection of the discipline of mountaineering that was progressing by trial and error. The mountains were yet to look the way they do today;

there were no cable cars at this time and barely any mountain huts. The most modern of them was the Grands Mulets Hut which had been fitted with a telephone in 1908. It didn't always work and the sound quality was awful but it didn't matter, the march of progress was making its way to Mont Blanc. Thanks to Doctor Payot, another mountain hut, the Refuge d'Argentière, was built. The original hut had little to do with the structure that we see today. It was a stone and timber construction on the moraine and could accommodate no more than ten people at one time. In the same period, in 1905 to be precise, two other huts were erected: the Charpoua was opened on 17 July and the Couvercle on 7 August.

For most people the mountains remained mysterious. The official guide to Chamonix that appeared in 1897 makes interesting reading, especially in its descriptions of the dangers in the mountains. It starts with mountain sickness, *"which is a sort of summit malady, a peculiar complication of giddiness and gastric inertia."* Avalanches appeared to be just as incomprehensible and obviously had their own rhetorical flourishes: *"The avalanches of the Alps, which are given the name 'lavages', are formed from ice and rock and after detaching themselves from the highest peaks fall with a majestic roar and great whizzing..."* As to storms, they had the *"breath of giants."*

Two figures from this time: Alfred Simond from Les Bois (background, third from r.) had a distinguished career.

Luc Ravanel from Les Grassonets, great grandfather of Roland Ravanel. A branch of the Ravanel family that over seven consecutive generations has produced a guide in each one.

Hygiene was also a popular subject and is worth discussing here. *"In order to be able to confront the beneficial mountain fatigue, one prepares oneself with cold baths, showers and immersions known for their bracing effects and accustoming oneself little by little to climbing and descending. Special care must be taken with boots and Töppfer was right when he said that a toe like stewed fruit may destroy the splendour of a landscape [...] Diet will consist in roast meats and old red wine, abstain from all liqueurs and dishes that are overly spiced [...] While on rest stops, take black coffee, tea, water mixed with absinthe, cognac or Kola and abstain from smoking, tobacco having an unfortunate influence on the respiratory functions [...] One must walk slowly, do not make large gestures and admire [your surroundings] as much as possible... in silence."*

Finally, and in keeping with the rococo style of the period, how can we not bring the Chamonix guides in at this point?

The author Jules Monod described them as *"a strong, primitive and honest race, with austere manners, an agility and bravery in the face of any ordeal, disdainful of danger, they want nothing to do with the pervasive neuroses of civilization..."*

This was the height of the colonial era and one wonders if Chamonix didn't fall under the heading of 'exotic destination'.

AU MONT-BLANC, UNE DESCENTE ÉMOUVANTE
Des guides ramènent à Chamonix le corps d'un de leurs camarades frappé par la foudre

Mountain tragedies would often feature on the front page of Le Petit Journal. In two centuries little has changed...

The Plan-Praz Jumeaux (twins). The climber in this photo is Alfred Couttet.

THE COMPAGNIE OPENS UP

IN THE SPACE OF 20 YEARS
THE COMPAGNIE WAS TO EVOLVE CONSIDERABLY.
MONT BLANC WOULD REMAIN A DEPENDABLE SOURCE OF INCOME
BUT AN ENTIRE GENERATION, LED BY ARMAND CHARLET,
WOULD SET OFF ON FAR GREATER CHALLENGES.

The First World War decimated the ranks of the Compagnie and the guides paid a heavy price: 22 never came back. Then there were the sons of guides; the eldest sons of Joseph Tairraz and the Charlet-Straton family were lost in the mud of the trenches.

There were also those who were forced to abandon their careers as guides: the amputees, gas victims and men irrevocably weakened by their experiences. Only a few survived miraculously unscathed, such as Gédéon Semblanet who spent the whole war in the front line, took part in all the major offensives and who, on Armistice Day, was the sole survivor of his original battalion.

Others would take years to recover their strength, as was the case with Alfred Couttet, the champion skier. And what strength it was!

Before the war he and Joseph Bouchard had made the round trip to the summit of Mont Blanc and back in barely twelve hours, their record remaining unbeaten for 60 years.

Couttet Champion or à la Caulaude, as he was known in Chamonix, showed the way forward for a whole generation for whom he became a kind of older bro

ther figure. With his pipe clamped between his teeth, a Tyrolean-style hat that rarely left his head (he once wore it for eight days solid after having survived a rock fall unhurt), Couttet the high-level athlete started on a second career almost as glittering as the first.

He wandered up and over mountains and crags, crossing the Dentelles de Montmirail (in the Vaucluse), training in Fontainebleau (outside Paris), exploring the Carpathian and Tatra mountains and becoming one of the first Frenchmen to climb in the Dolomites. Italian climbers had just made a first ascent and watched as Couttet followed their new route with such gusto that he completely shattered their time for the ascent. The phrase 'to do a route à la Couttet' was soon used in Cortina d'Ampezzo and Val Gardena, and it meant a fast and stylish ascent.

He was a strong climber, possibly the best of his day, and chalked up more than 40 first ascents in the Mont Blanc Massif, including the 'integrale' traverse of the Grandes Jorasses, the Pic de Roc and the Aiguille des Deux Aigles. And always with clients, after all this was work, not showing off. In his own way he was a pioneer, showing the way

Roger Frison-Roche standing on Alfred Couttet's shoulders.
Although not considered very 'clean', some climbers still use this rather basic method
to solve certain technical problems....

Previous page:
Gédéon Semblanet at the Plan de l'Aiguille (2nd from left).
He was a well respected guide who had survived the First World War.

The guides responsible for opening up the Gaillands climbing area.
Alfred Couttet first had the idea to equip the crag on the road out of Chamonix,
which leads to Les Bossons, in 1927. It became the first 'école d'escalade' or climbing crag in France
and is undoubtedly one of the most popular..

Below:
The reputation of the Chamonix guides was so great that images of them
were used in all kinds of advertisements vaunting
the merits of mountain related products.

for others; and he brought back from Italy the first pitons, carabiners and rope-soled espadrilles, which had never been seen in Chamonix before.

Couttet with the help of a crowbar and a group of guides from the neighbouring village of Les Pélerins – André Clérico, Camille Couttet and Marcel Bozon – cleared away and developed the first dedicated rock climbing site in the valley, Les Gaillands. He was a top-level athlete and introduced the notion of training to the guides. It is not surprising, then, that this generous and charismatic man was named captain of the French team for what was later recognised as the first Winter Olympics, held in Chamonix in 1924.

He injected a new dynamism into the Compagnie and if his true value was not recognized at the time and his projects not acted upon or indeed understood, others would see that they were implemented later on.

Armand Charlet was one of the most talented ice climbers of his generation.
This famous photo of Charlet was taken by Doctor Azéma
while they were on the north-east face of the Col du Dolent.

Armand Charlet with Roger Frison-Roche on the summit of the Droites in 1927. Armand Charlet was instrumental in Frison-Roche's acceptance into the Compagnie.

ARMAND CHARLET

Eleven years Couttet's junior, Armand Charlet was 'as old as the century'. He could well have been one of his pupils, one of the kids taught to ski by Couttet and his friends Jules and Joseph Couttet, Gilbert Ravanel and Doctor Payot. In the mountains Armand applied the older man's principles of training and self-discipline, with perhaps a touch of ambition thrown in too.

Today he is considered by lay observers as the archetypal Chamonix guide. He almost single-handedly restored the reputation of the Compagnie, bringing recognition of its guides' technical abilities. Fame and glory are short-lived and with the departure of Ravanel the Rouge and Charlet-Straton, the man and woman on the street quickly forgot the great exploits of the past.

The arrival of the great unguided parties, the likes of Lagarde and de Ségogne, would tick off the last great mountain bastions, judged unclimbable, leaving the professional climbers speechless in their wake. For a while they were even redundant.

Armand, the son of guiding family in Argentière, was a man of his time. Never without his beret and an inscrutable expression on his face, he represented the very essence of a technical climber and set things straight once and for all... He started out exploring the mountains with his brother Georges, a year younger than him, and together they caused much raising of eyebrows among the old guides. Once, on the Ravanel-Mummery

Traverse on the Courtes, when the brothers were barely even porters, they skirted around a short ladder and climbed up the tricky slab instead. The Compagnie authorities did not appreciate the prank and upon their return the two brothers were reprimanded for their efforts!

Armand Charlet was quick to develop ambitions and during his time in the army, which he left as French ski champion, he had met young middle-class men dreaming of adventure now that the war was over. He adopted their methods and trained when he could.

But how to train when he had to work twelve-hour days in the fields during the best climbing season?

The secret for Armand was to get up even earlier. In his mind it was very simple and he described bitterly his last season as a porter: *"I never left the classic routes and the guides, with whom I would climb, had scarcely any personal ambition."* There, the word had been uttered: ambition.

The concept completely escaped these mountain men for whom each route corresponded to a day's work. For them, ambition and the hazy notion of first ascents were for men and women of leisure, not those who had to work.

What with the livestock, haymaking and the potato crop, there wasn't time to set off on random adventures that didn't bring any money into the home.

Two of the porters
who took part in some
of Armand Charlet's great
first ascents.
Left: Jules Simond
accompanied him
on the first ascent
of the north face
of the Aiguille du Plan
in 1929 and
the Couturier Couloir
on the Verte in 1932.

Right:
Marcel Bozon
was with him
on the Arête Sans Nom
on the Verte in 1926.

This may explain why at the beginning, in the 1920s, the Chamoniards left the 'artists' to it, not wishing to compare themselves to the unguided climbers dreaming of first ascents. These ideas did not belong to their way of life or to their work with clients. Yet, as the technical level of these first ascents rose, the number of people able to repeat them grew smaller. In this austere valley whose inhabitants lived a frugal existence, people found it difficult to understand what compelled men to waste their time, energy and money on flights of fancy in which no-one was interested and which sometimes cost them their lives.

Armand was undoubtedly one of the first people to be torn between these two worlds and he soon chose his camp. He stopped tending the livestock and ceased to be a peasant-guide.

By 1924 he was a qualified guide. *"The exam was purely on theory, which really irked me. [There were] four candidates from Argentière, which included Georges and me. We had to appear before a panel that was made up of the Préfet of Haute Savoie, the Mayor of Chamonix, a magistrate, two representatives from the [French] Alpine Club, plus three guides commissioned by the Compagnie. The examination was on theory alone and that's what really bothered me: you just had to be a good talker, to stay unruffled and get enough points to be admitted, even when no list of routes had been submitted, as was sometimes the case. A list of routes done under the supervision of, and certified by, a guide from the Compagnie had to*

be produced. We had to have ten routes above 3000m, [and] Mont Blanc, Mont Buet and the Three Cols were obligatory." Six of them were accepted into the Compagnie that year but he would learn later on that it was a mere formality and that from 1913 to 1939 no applicant was failed!

He quickly discovered the Verte, his Verte: *"Never again would I feel such intense emotions on the summit of a mountain, not on the Matterhorn, nor the Weisshorn or even on this Aiguille Verte that I have climbed 100 times by at least a dozen different routes."*

The tone had been set, Charlet moved away once and for all from the classic routes on the Grépon and Mont Blanc. He put up great new rock and ice routes, for the most part on and around the Verte, equipped with crampons with no front points and a single ice axe. He became the instigator of a series of projects, for which his companions were mere observers of his style and ability. He was always the leader and without the aid of pitons or carabiners, he led whole pitches without being belayed, climbing hard sections (such as the 'Pas de l'Isolée' on the Aiguilles du Diable), and he even stood in his crampons on Camille Devouassoux's head to reach a hold on the direct route on the Aiguille Sans Non via the Nant Blanc. With each season came whole anthologies of first ascents, generally done with the same group of clients (Mademoiselle de Lonchamp, Platonov and Couturier) or guide friends (his brother Georges, Camille Devouassoux, Roger Frison-Roche).

Whether it was on ice, seen here on the bergschrund on Mont Mallet,

or on first winter ascents, such as on the Grépon, Armand Charlet had his own distinct style and flair. He was the leading climber for an entire generation of guides.

Curiously, just as he was at the height of his powers, the great mountaineer Armand Charlet missed out on some of the most notable climbs of the interwar period. First there was the Croz Spur on the Grandes Jorasses. Despite a valiant effort with Fernand Bellin, he was forced to give up at the upper snow patch. Charlet complained about bivouacking in the middle of the route and perhaps he dreamt of coming back with a client to make the first ascent. The Germans, Peters and Meier, didn't leave him the chance. Then the virtuoso alpinist Pierre Allain plucked the prize of the first ascent of the north face of the Drus from him. The Chamoniards just had to accept the fact that they no longer had the monopoly on the Mont Blanc Massif. As for the first French expedition to the Karakorum, led by Henry de Ségogne, why be away for several months and not even get paid for it?

Nevertheless, climbing with Armand Charlet remained a privilege, as Madame Pighetti, the former Mademoiselle de Lonchamp remembered: *"We would discuss the project and straight away he would weigh up the risks. He would study our chosen face a great deal, noting rock falls and snow slides. He would take very little on long routes: a few prunes, a clove of garlic. Everything was planned in advance. We had thought about doing a direct route on the Nant Blanc face [of the Aiguille Verte] in 1927. I wasn't fit enough [and] Camille took my place. At the foot of the bergschrund they met Lagarde and Ségogne, who were also out to be the first to climb*

the face. Armand warmly invited the two men to join them; he wasn't competitive, he always remained a pioneer. Just for the record, you should know that those two brilliant members of the GHM [Groupe de Haute Montagne, a prestigious body that brings together high-level climbers from across the world] turned back. As for Armand, he drew upon on all his imaginative resources in the icy chimney section."

The years from 1925 to 1935 were his finest years and the guide of guides would pull off some truly great first ascents. His ice routes, on which he excelled, included the Couturier Couloir on the Verte, the north face of the Aiguille du Plan and the Col Armand Charlet. His mixed climbs include the classic route on the Nant Blanc face on the Verte and the direct on the Aiguille Sans Nom; while on rock he climbed the Arête du Jardin, the Aiguilles du Diable, the Carmichael Route on the Aiguille des Pélerins, the north-west ridge on Mont Maudit as well as making winter ascents of the Dent du Requin, the Grépon, Drus and Bionnassay. He could be hard on others and harder still on himself, he would leave his mark on the Compagnie whose ranks had been cut down in their prime during the Great War. So powerful was his reputation, that, whether voluntarily or not, he overshadowed a generation of guides who were also trying to make their mark away from the standard routes of the day.

2 September 1929.
Bradford Washburn (left) proudly poses for a photograph taken by the porter André Devouassoux.
With him are Alfred 'Couttet Champion' (centre) and Georges Charlet (right).
They had just climbed part of the great couloir on the Argentière side of the Verte.
Three years later, Armand Charlet would climb the direct route and name it after his own client,
a certain Mr Couturier.

AN ENTIRE GENERATION OVERSHADOWED

Reading modern accounts of the period, one might be forgiven for thinking that Armand Charlet was the only competent guide of his time.

If that were the case, then Philippe Amiguet's splendid remark would make no sense. *"Of course they are rough, gruff, taciturn, authoritarian when necessary; but when you know them, when they trust you, why, what marvellous companions, what trusty friends they are! What's more, it is with pleasure that each year you return to them. They await you, smoking a pipe; from afar you recognize their thickset frames, the heavy brown cloth of their jackets, their black and green hats with rhododendron flowers and their glacier glasses. As for their boots fitted with powerful nails, they make you want to leave for the mountains without a moment's delay."*

In fact, the Compagnie, which numbered around a hundred guides at that time, actually had some great climbers.

Let us start with Armand Charlet's brother, Georges, a year his junior. A more earthy figure than his brother, he was a strong climber but was less drawn to publicity and was, at one point, the Compagnie's most prodigious earner. His quite extraordinary list of routes doesn't include a single accident and his summer 1926 workload deserves a mention here. With no cable cars to reduce approach times, he managed to notch up a veritable marathon of routes that year:

4 July	Ravanel-Mummery
12 July	Clocher
15 July	Requin
16 July	Aiguille du Plan
17 July	Requin
18 July	Requin
20 July	Aiguille du Grépon from Montenvers
22 July	Doigt de Mesure
23 July	Grépon, roundtrip from Montenvers
24 July	Ravanel-Mummery
25 July	Doigt de Mesure
1 August	Requin
2 August	Requin
3 August	Requin
4 August	Aiguille du Plan/Requin
6 August	Requin
7 August	Traverse of the Courtes
8 August	Rest day
9 August	Aiguillette d'Argentière
10 August	Aiguillette de l'M, Petits Charmoz
12 August	Chamonix face of the Peigne
14 August	Grépon
16 August	Verte (first ascent with Armand)
17 August	Verte by the Arête du Jardin with de Chatellus
18 August	Cheval Rouge (Couvercle Hut)

Georges Charlet was less well known than his brother Armand, yet in his day he was one of the most active guides in the Compagnie. He is seen here on the first ascent of the Arête des Grands Montets in 1928 with P. Dalmats and Paul Mugnier.

On the summit of the Grépon in the same year.

19 August	Ravanel-Mummery
22 August	Mont-Blanc
24 August	Traverse of the Drus with Busk and Armand
25 August	Ravanel-Mummery
26 August	Plan-Requin
27 August	Géant--Rochefort-Mallet
28 August	Charmoz-Grépon-Blaitière
30 August	Traverse of the Drus
31 August	Traverse of the Drus
1 Sept.	Involved in rescue on the Verte
2 Sept.	Traverse of the Courtes up to the Aiguille de Triolett
3 Sept.	Verte via the Grande Rocheuse
5 Sept.	Col de l'Aiguille Verte, looking for Mayendorffs
8 Sept.	Return to the Aiguille Verte, first ascent of the Pointe Eveline

Thirty-nine routes in the space of two months on a series of different peaks. In the same day Georges did a Traverse of the Drus and got back to the Couvercle Hut – quite a performance!

This was the year he discovered the Aiguille Verte. The very next day he took his client, de Chatellus, to it. As with his brother, this peak would play an important role in his career, so large that he quickly developed a ritual with his wife. Germaine remembered it years later: "At that time the huts didn't have telephones. When

Georges was on the Verte and a client was supposed to go up that evening to the Couvercle, we had arranged a signal. I spread out a white sheet in Tréléchamp [the hamlet between the Col des Montets and Argentière]. That meant a client was climbing up to the hut that same night. That way it meant he didn't have to go there and back himself and it happened that I sometimes didn't see him for weeks at a time..."

Alain de Chatellus, with whom he paid his first visit to the Verte as a guide, was Charlet's client for several decades. Seventeen years later, they were once again standing on the summit of the Verte, and de Chatellus wrote: "Georges was right above my head, silhouetted against the sun behind him, the sunlight glistening on the powder snow as he cut through it. A final snow slope and at eleven twenty-five the summit was ours. A square metre of pure untracked snow. Inconceivably steep ridges and couloirs fell away from us on all sides. Georges lit a cigarette whose smoke rose up into the clear air. It was seventeen years to the day since our last visit. We remembered our seventeen campaigns in the Alps, from the Meije to the Jungfrau, as they stood all around us. Dear Georges, so simple and yet so great a man! I shook the hand of my guide who had climbed so many chimney cracks, cut so many steps and had held my rope on the hundred and more routes we had done together in the mountains without incident."

It was Georges who, with his American client

Brad Washburn, Alfred Couttet and a porter, André Devouassoux (also to become a talented guide), did the first ascent of a truly great route, the Couturier Couloir. Rocks were falling straight down the couloir that day, so the group left the central section to tack along the spur that borders the snow slope. Armand Charlet and his client Couturier made the second ascent two years later, following the couloir along its entire length, yet it was merely a variant of Georges's route. Perhaps then it should be known as the Washburn Couloir? Nevertheless, there is no doubt that the skills from one generation had been transferred to the next.

At that time the Compagnie was far from being a single uniform body. Much like Chamonix itself, which beyond the hotels and houses huddled around the church, was still only a fragmented town. It was merely a collection of old Savoyard houses and low, squat farms isolated from each other by islands of greenery and cultivated fields. At that time each hamlet had its own identity, its own way of life and obviously its own guides. When it came down to it, the only time Chamoniards got together was to go to the church and the cemetery.

In Le Lavancher, on the way up to Argentière and the home of the Couttets, there also lived Georges and Ulysse Simond. They were talented climbers, especially Ulysse who although only 1m50 (around 4' 9") tall climbed astoundingly quickly. Thus, one day with a single porter and one client he managed to do the Charmoz-Grépon Traverse, the three summit peaks of the Aiguille de Blaitière, and the Ciseaux and the Aiguille du Fou. By 3pm they were back at the Montenvers...

The Babotche – people from the village of Les Bossons on the way to Les Houches – guides included Armand Couttet and the Tournier brothers, Raymond and Fernand. One brother, Raymond, was as thickset and stocky as the other, Fernand, was slim and slender. Raymond was also one of the masters of the Grépon, a rock climber without rival, who when he looked down on the valley could not help thinking that *"down there they make money doing nothing and us up here with our lanterns, we make peanuts!"* But he wouldn't have changed his peanuts for anything in the world. It was Raymond who rescued Armand Charlet on the Drus when Charlet was hit on the head by a stone, apparently making him more talkative. Climbing the Drus as part of a rescue team or as a guide was still the stuff of legend at that time and his son remembered an old guide pronouncing, in the local patois, *"the kid's on the Drus, now they're lost..."*

Fernand gave his name to a route on the north face of the Droites. Lagarde and Arsandaux had already put up the first route on the same side of the mountain, but the Tournier Spur, which Fernand climbed with Authenac, marked a new level in

Fernand Bellin
could have had
an extraordinary career.
He was a hugely talented
rock climber and came
to within a cat's whisker
of pulling off the first ascent
of the north face
of the Grandes Jorasses
with Armand Charlet.

André Clérico
on the descent
from the Grands Mulets.

Fernand Claret-Tournier
and Firmin Mollier
with Madame Auvert
on 26 August 1937.
They had just done the first
ascent of the north-west ridge
of the Aiguille Ravanel.

Seated (from l. to r.):
André Payot
(priest in Vallorcine),
René Payot,
Fernand Bellin,
Georges Payot.
Standing:
Georges Cachat,
unknown,
Alfred Payot.

Camille Couttet in British Columbia. He and his English clients traversed the province's entire coastal chain of mountains in three months in 1932. Unfortunately, no account of the trip remains.

extremely difficult climbing. Authenac described the climb in the December 1937 issue of the revue Alpinisme. *"Our entire gear consisted in 15 pitons, three carabiners, and one 40m abseil rope for a 1000m wall. [...] We climbed straight up, calmly and patiently following our line. The hours pass quickly during periods of relentless hard work. Under the constant bombardment of ice that my companion generously showered down upon me and against which there was never any kind of shelter, my hands were soon bleeding and my head and shoulders black and blue. This paled into insignificance compared with the virtuosity that my companion displayed. I can attest to his courage, which he combines with modesty and which should serve as an example to others."* Thirty-eight hours later they finally made it to the Couvercle Hut, their exploit somewhat overshadowed by the conquest of the Grandes Jorasses, but significant nonetheless.

In 1942 Fernand Tournier, again with his client Authenac, put up a new route on the dolomitic south-west face of the Aiguille Mummery, which was considered for a long time one of the best climbs in the range.

The two brothers were together on a rescue on the Aiguille de Roc. This time Fernand was in a bad way and had

a broken femur after having been caught in a snow slide. Authenac went back down on his own to get help and it was Raymond who picked up his younger brother in the middle of the storm. He made the following laconic observation about the shafts of lightening: *"We could have read the paper by them..."*

André Clérico, Anatole Bozon, Firmin Mollier, Marcel Bozon and Camille Couttet acted as the leaders of the 'Pélarnis' (Les Pélerins) guides.

Camille Couttet was unusual. Although the guides in the previous century had started the fashion for expeditions with clients to the Caucuses, the Rockies and even to the Canary Islands, the trend had come to an abrupt end, perhaps because of the technical challenges still to be uncovered in the Alps. Armand Charlet, for instance, barely travelled at all.

Couttet, however, was one of the rare guides of the 1930s to have mastered English. He quickly acquired a British clientele passionate about travel and every winter he set off with his hefty expedition backpack from which there always protruded a pair of skis.

One year, with his beret pulled on his head, he boarded a transatlantic liner to reach the starting point of a skiing

Camille Devouassoux (centre), known as 'Camille à Pic', was undoubtedly Armand Charlet's favourite climbing partner and together they climbed a number of new routes including the direct on the Aiguille Sans Nom, a huge achievement. The route would not be repeated until several decades later. He also put up a route on the Migot Spur (north buttress) on the Chardonnet.

Alfred Simond with one the porters he trained, Joseph Tairraz, who like Simond was also from the village of Les Bois.

expedition from the shores of Lake Louise into the heart of the Canadian Rockies. His greatest journey took three months in the spring, during which he carried out the first systematic exploration of the coastal chain of mountains in British Columbia. Having climbed Mount Waddington (4016m), he descended a glacier for over 150km, finishing his journey on the Pacific coast. Of those three months there remain a few photographs but no surviving commentary or texts.

On the Lyret side of town, near the site of the modern-day Aiguille du Midi lift station, lived Fernand Bellin. One could have applied various labels to Fernand and throughout his life he resisted the limelight. Nevertheless, he was a montagnard with incredible instincts and was certainly the guide of miracles and extravagant exploits.

He was a guide of miracles because he came close to death three times and each time he escaped without so much as a scratch. On the Grépon, for instance, both he and his client were caught in a rock fall. After falling a hundred metres they found themselves on the Nantillons glacier, minus their clothes but in one piece. Further south in the Oisans, on Les Rouies, a cornice collapsed and after a 500-metre fall he stood up with barely a look of surprise.

The French author, climber and skier Saint-Loup

jumped on the story and told it in his collection of accounts 'La Montagne n'a pas voulu'. In it, the author describes the astonishing guide, Bellin, who *"is the life and soul on long routes. He loves to thrill his clients with views over vertiginous drops and exposed ridge lines."* A mad-dog figure, he could have had a glittering career and although he made an attempt on the Grandes Jorasses with Armand Charlet, he refused to take part in these first headline-grabbing exploits. He preferred having fun and living in the mountains as he understood them, without owing anything to anyone. He was one of the first people to ski the massif's steep slopes, such as the Bellin Couloir on the Brévent. He also had a penchant for climbing round the outside of the cable car as it carried people over huge drops, much to the annoyance of the tourists. He also took six people to the Grépon and got them all to the summit.

In Les Moussoux, under Le Brévent, there was Alfred Payot and Emile Folliguet who guided, among others, the Belgian royal family and in particular the mother of the current Grand Duke of Luxembourg.

In Les Bois, next to Les Praz, lived Alfred Simond or Alfred Fantien as he was called. Fantien took his regular porter, Joseph Tairraz, with him on every summer trip he made around German-speaking Switzerland.

First Fête des guides in 1924.
Alfred Balmat with Josepht Demarchi to his left is presented the Compagnie's flag by Madame Coty,
the guest of honour.

The first official procession of guides through the streets of Chamonix.
The ceremony of placing flowers at the memorial to the guides who have died in the mountains
still survives today.

The greatest concentration of mountain guides was to be found between Les Mouilles and La Frasse. The clan included the Tourniers (seven guides), Bossonneys, Farinis and Comtes, who knew every corner of the massif.

At the entrance to Argentière is the hamlet of Le Grassonets, which was home to Camille Devouassoux. Small and plump, he was known as a joker and for his good humour. He was also an excellent climber and was famous for the technique he developed climbing on the Aiguillette

Benoît Couttet is presented with the Légion d'Honneur. As President of the Compagnie in the 1930s, he was responsible for organising rescues in the massif. He also represented the Compagnie at the Belgian court for the funeral of Albert 1ᵉʳ.

Another Compagnie man, Jean Ravanel. He was killed on the Aiguille de Roc in 1945 with his son Gilbert. Two other guides were killed in the mountains that same summer: Léon Balmat was killed while climbing on the Nonne and René Ravanel died on the Verte.

Le Lavancher guide Alfred Couttet and André Sauvage were the men behind the first mountain film. Couttet was killed on the Drus in 1925.

By the time he retired, Henri Garny had made 270 ascents of Mont Blanc.

d'Argentière. Where others just stepped across, Camille, because he was too short, stretched out his hands and caught hold of the rock opposite at the last minute. He is also remembered for the gusto with which he recounted the tale of the first ascent of the Nant Blanc face on the Aiguille Sans Nom. Forty years later he would show, to anyone who wished to see, the marks of Armand Charlet's crampons from the time Charlet had had to climb onto his head which was barely covered by his beret, to reach a decent hold. The effect was always the same, the listening tourist always came away with the impression that he had been talking to a man who was as hard as steel.

1. Camille Claret-Tournier
2. Joseph Couttet
3. Armand Couttet
4. Roger Pot
5. Paul Bellin
6. Auguste Cachat
7. Alfred Couttet
8. Benoît Couttet
9. Martial Payot
10. Madame Coty (guest of honour)
11. Joseph Demarchi
12. André Claret-Tournier
13. Edouard Pot
14. Fernand Bellin
15. Roland Simond
16. Marcel Borgel
17. Jacques Burnet
18. Paul Demarchi
19. Jules Bellin
20. Clément Comte
21. Georges Charlet from Les Barats
22. Ulysse Borgeat
23. Michel Claret-Tournier

The Compagnie was a rough assembly of characters and personalities. What they all had in common, however, was the ardent desire to take part in the guides' festival. Alfred Balmat, known as à la Maître, had restarted the festival after it had not taken place for some time. Even the emergency fund was woefully underfinanced and the gui- des' wages were no longer able to keep it afloat. In 1924, Balmat gave the group back a bit of cohesion and revived a tradition that continues to this day. From that point on, the 15 August would be a special day and all the guides would be honoured in the same way.

1934. In memory of the Belgian king, Albert 1ˢᵗ,
who had just been killed in a climbing accident in Marche-les-Dames (Belgium),
Roger Frison-Roche, Arthur Ravanel (son of Ravanel Le Rouge) and Georges Tairraz
were charged with planting the Belgian and French flags on the summit of the Pic Albert,
a buttress of the Aiguille de l'M.

In front of the guides' office in the late 1920s. From l. to r.: Roger Frison-Roche has his hands on the shoulders of Ulysse Simond, Paul Bellin hides Henri Perrot, in the centre is Roger Pot, Gustave Farini is the figure with the rope over his shoulder and Alfred Couttet is standing in front of Clément Comte who is leaning against the wall.

THE CITADEL IS BREACHED

A young guide, with a fresh outlook on things, would little by little find his place among the disparate groups that made up the Compagnie.

Roger Frison-Roche would become the chronicler of the changing times, when old guides crossed paths with the new generation.

Born in Paris to Savoyard parents, Frison-Roche arrived in Chamonix aged 17, to become the secretary of Chamonix's three tourism bodies: the tourist office, the hoteliers' association and the winter sports committee. His office was next to the Compagnie des Guides, just below the Mairie or town hall. He quickly became friends with Armand Charlet, Ravanel Le Rouge, Georges Tairraz, Alfred Couttet, and Camille Devouassoux who christened him the grand sifflet or 'big whistle' on account of his skinny frame. And when he had the time he would go climbing. He quickly came to the attention of his neighbours, the guides.

And he made his first ascent of Mont Blanc as a porter with Gédéon Semblanet. It didn't go too badly and seeing as his family was from the Beaufortain, a mountainous area in

the neighbouring department of Savoie to the south, the Compagnie decided to make an exception for him.

Frison-Roche recounts the story in his book Le Versant du Soleil. He writes, "*I had been presented to the Committee by sponsors: Alfred Couttet and Armand Charlet; my list of routes was sufficient. There were, on the one hand, those that I had done as an amateur and as a member of the Groupe de Haute Montagne, and others done as porter and assistant to certified guides. I came out top of my class for 1930. Without knowing it, I had just broken a centuries-old tradition. Up to that point only men born in Chamonix or Argentière could aspire to join the Compagnie. The bridge in Taconnaz to the south of the valley and the Col des Montets in the north were insurmountable barriers. [...] It would seem that seven years spent in Chamonix, that the extremely effective pressure placed on it by my sponsors had shaken the Compagnie to its foundations.*

As the President Joseph Démarchi, he of the handsome long side-whiskers declared: 'You are the first FOREIGNER that we have admitted to the Compagnie. Make sure we don't regret doing it.'"

R. FRISON-ROCHE

PREMIER

DE

CORDÉE

Roman

ARTHAUD

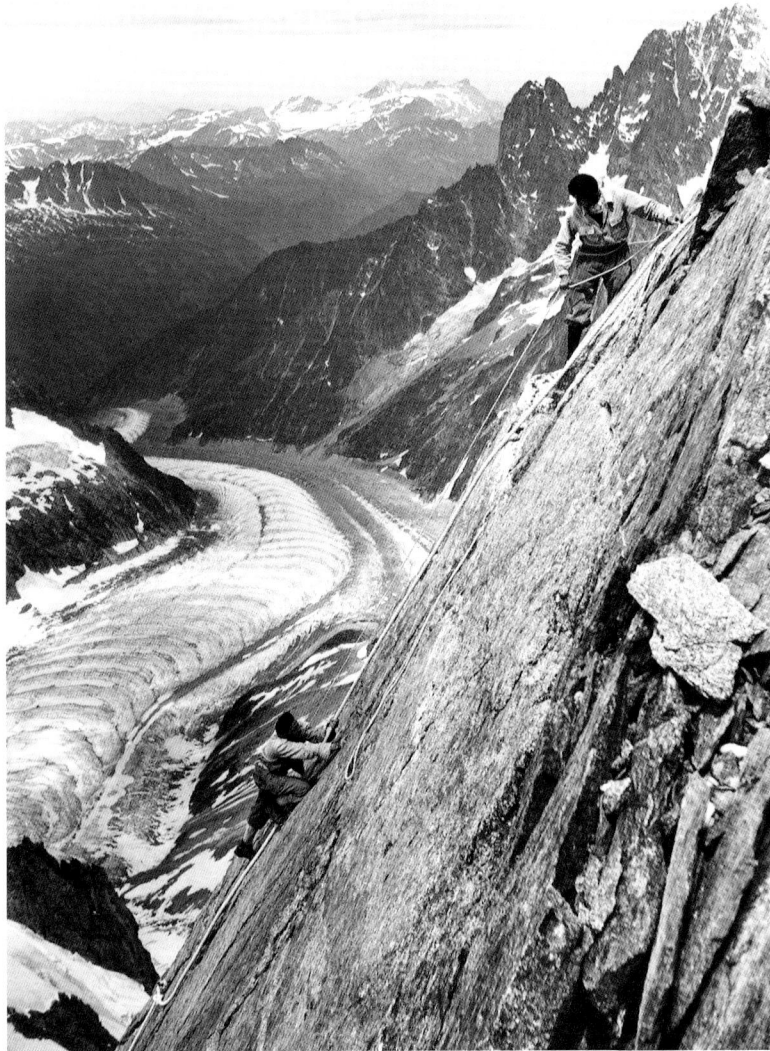

Rock climbing on the Dent du Géant. This photo, by Georges Tairraz, would be used on the first editions of Premier de Cordée.

The guides would not regret it, for Frison-Roche would assert his personality on the Compagnie and climbing during his years of tremendous activity and work. He was a ski instructor, the creator of the first school of mountaineering, the first specialist mountaineering journalist, all in the valley that never ceased to inspire him.

Like Armand Charlet, he too brought the image of the mountain guide up to date, but in a different way. Gone was the subordinate role, the shadowy figure who scarcely featured in mountaineering accounts. He would give the profession a sense of romance. Highly skilled and with a romantic aura, the Chamonix mountain guide was set for the future.

Little by the little the Compagnie started to change. In 1936, at the instigation of Armand Charlet and Frison-Roche, the first week-long training course for aspirant guides was set in place. While it was the Club Alpin that was responsible for trai-

ning guides in the care of tourists in all the other alpine and Pyrenean ranges, the Compagnie in Chamonix recruited its own future professionals itself. By 1911, the CAF already had 159 accredited working guides and porters. By 1890 the Société des Touristes du Dauphiné to the south already had over 100 guides.

This state within a state lasted until 1945 and the creation of ENA – Ecole Nationale d'Alpinisme – the national mountaineering school in Chamonix, the skiing section came shortly afterwards. This was proof of the power of the Compagnie.

Until then each spring, as described earlier, the future guides passed before a committee and an entirely oral examination, and the majority of candidates were accepted. As was also usual, they then gave a dinner for the committee, certain members of which did not weather the feasts well and it was customary to accompany them home with motherly concern...

Armand and Léon Couttet.
As with many guiding families,
it was the father
who introduced his son
to the mountains.

It stood him in good stead,
as Léon graduated
top of his class at ENSA
and later became a teacher
at the same school.

Training was empirical and the porters learnt on the job. Often the young novice would start out with his father or the guide that had trained his father. This being the case, it was understandable that many of the guides considered the place their own domain. Especially when it was his own father who had opened the doors to its magical realm to him. This was the case for Armand Couttet, a contemporary of Alfred Couttet and the Compagnie's President in the 1940s. His son, Léon, inherited his father's passion in life.

You didn't become a guide by accident in the Chamonix valley, nor for the money. It was certainly easier being a hotelier than doing the back-breaking work of guiding in the mountains. The magic was something different, and perhaps it came from the privileged relationships the guides have with their clients. Armand's daughters remembered how *"the clients would come into the big room where there sat the bed with a sofa on either side. They would sit there like great friends discussing plans for routes and trips for hours. Although they came from different backgrounds and very different lives, they shared the same dreams. And Léon, barely ten years old at the time, would hang on their every word for hours and hours."*

Not surprising then that this same kid would climb the Aiguille de la République with his father at the age of seventeen and would become both a guide (top of his class, 1946) and a teacher at ENSA. He could not help but smile when his father told for the umpteenth time the story of the bottle of champagne. It had been carried around for the whole summer and the client, who was a bit miserly, hesitated to drink it on their last outing. Léon's father solved the problem by throwing the still intact bottle from the summit, making one less thing to carry... This way of life belonged to nobody else but the Chamonix guides. Handed down from generation to generation, it had become almost hereditary. In fact, for a long time the Chamoniards were convinced this was true.

To have a real sense of the landscape of this place, as it moved and sometimes rebelled, you had to be born with your feet in the snow, or so the reasoning went....

SYNDICAT DES GUIDES
de
CHAMONIX - MONT - BLANC

TARIF

des Courses et Ascensions
1939

For a long time, the Grépon was one of the Chamonix guides' favourite routes.
In this photo Raymond Claret-Tournier belays his second on the famous C.P. terrace.

Left and below:
These photos show
the transporting
and blessing of the statue
of the Virgin Mary
on the summit of the Grépon
in 1927.
The statue is still there.

TO THE MONTENVERS WITH MADONNAS AND PIRATES

The mountain range in which these small and momentous events took place had very little to do with the massif as it is today. Even the popular routes have changed enormously.

At the beginning of the 1920s, the real hub of the range was the Hôtel du Montenvers. The greatest mountaineers of the day – the English, Italians, French and a few Americans and their guides - all stayed there.

The monchus would drink tea and discuss the stock markets and the revolution in China in front of the fire where larch logs crackled. The guides would come by from time to time, drinking endless bottles of wine in the guides' room. And it wasn't unheard of for some of them to have a bit of trouble getting up in the mornings. With the moonlight shining down on them from behind the Drus, the first parties would set off for the Dent du Requin or the Mer de Glace face on the Grépon.

And when there was not enough starlight, the first groups left the hotel with storm lamps, just after midnight. Two hours later more groups would set off for the other great classic routes such as the normal route on the Grépon, the Aiguille de Blaitière or the Grands Charmoz.

In the 1920s the Grépon would almost unseat Mont Blanc as the

most popular route in the massif.

It was a real benchmark and the guides knew all the tricks; the length of rope needed to move quickly, how to get over the difficult sections and the spikes and rock to use for belaying. Even the Knubel Crack on the Grépon, the first grade 5+ in the massif, was described in minute detail. The route description was incredibly detailed, describing the holds on the 25-metre pitch and the moves needed to get over the legendary crack.

Climbing with the equipment of the day was no small feat either. Certain products started to become available in Chamonix (Mr Sanglard opened the first sports shop in Chamonix in 1924) but the boots remained rudimentary. Roger Frison-Roche remembered them as being *"heavy, in thick and solid leather and studded. It was easier to climb on the Chamonix granite with soft iron ailes de mouches [bars on the edge of the soles]. They wore out quickly and had to be regularly 're-nailed' and resoled. On softer rock we preferred using tricounis [studded soles] made from very hard steel, we also used them for ice and compact snow. But it was a real feat to get up a grade 5 with that kind of gear!"*

The Chamoniards would become the jamming kings. And from the beginning of the twentieth century onwards, they were obsessed

Alfred 'Couttet Champion' poses for a photograph with his client. On the soles of the shoes in the foreground can be seen the famous 'ailes de mouches' (metal bars on the edge of the soles) and 'tricounis' (central studs) that were often used instead of crampons on snow slopes. However, these metal studs and bars proved less useful on the rock.

by the Grépon. The story is still told of the day in 1911 when Joseph Ravanel and his four brothers (Alfred, Jean, Camille and Paul), each with a client, met on the celebrated slab of rock. It was pure luck as none of them knew where the other was going.

Tough and wild, magnificent and legendary, the Grépon in any case had everything to make it the favourite route for guides and clients. And not a single guide failed to bring back a truly symbolic image from the top, a photo with the Madonna.

The men who installed the statutes of the Madonna that survey the valley from the bright summits of the Drus and the Grépon were gruff and tough.

The placing of the Virgin Mary on the Drus was the work of men from Argentière: the three Ravanel brothers – Camille, Joseph and Alfred – together with their cousin, Jules, Ravanel Le Rouge's son, Arthur, and the Abbé Couttin. Although colourful characters, these men were certainly men of faith!

Ravanel Le Rouge was at it again on 22 June 1922, when together with six other guides he installed another Madonna, this time on the summit of the Grépon. They are still there, silent witnesses to the passage of time and the folly of man's reckless obsessions.

But the Montenvers was not only a stronghold for those setting off on long routes, it was also a favourite venue for the Pirates.

The Pirates were guides who were coming to the end of their careers and it had been their favourite

Firmin Mollier, like most of the Chamonix guides, would become a 'jamming' specialist.

Rope espadrilles started to appear in the 1930s.
They weren't very sturdy and never lasted very long on the Chamonix rock.
In this photo we see Raymond Claret-Tournier sporting a rather fetching bandanna,
proving that some fashions are surprisingly timeless after all...

Alfred est galant envers gros trognon

Two of many images that exist charting the activities of the 'pirates'.

The typical image of the 'pirates' was of the men who cut steps and equipped their clients with socks for the crossing of the Mer de Glace. This in turn contributed to the image of the guides in the popular imagination.

Below: a head guide's cap worn by its owner at the Montenvers and the Bossons glacier. It allowed its wearer to attempt to impose order on his colleagues, not always an easy task given the strong characters of the guides.

spot for more than a century. With their moustaches smoothed down, faces tanned by the sun and eyes sparkling, it wasn't difficult to spot the old montagnards who offered to take those tourists desperate for excitement across the Mer de Glace.

In fact, this activity, often done in conjunction with work as a mule driver, formed an integral part of guiding as a whole. The Pirates also figured quite highly in the 'cahier des punitions', or punishments book.

These had always been colourful characters who didn't trouble themselves with what was considered good or bad manners and found it easier to sip absinthe than fruit syrup as they waited for their clients in the bar-café. Thus, onlookers often witnessed the comical spectacle of slender ladies guiding their would-be guides who appeared a little worse for wear.

In 1865, the Compagnie had already stipulated in its rules that they should *"not hold foreigners to ransom, [and should] not live up to the name 'pirates'"*. They got their name that would stick for almost a century, from their habit of descending like a group of buccaneers on clients at the station and 'pirating' or hijacking them as they stepped off the train.

At the start of the 1920s, there were still plenty of pirates

around. They worked mainly at the Montenvers but also at the Bossons glacier, where they would wait for their clients at the bistrot and were obliged to maintain a passage across the glacier with steps cut into the ice with axes. They are the figures we see on the postcards of the time, holding the hands of elegant ladies or hiring out old socks to people wishing to cross the ice. (Socks worn over shoes gave better grip on icy sections.) They also guided the crossing of the Mer de Glace up to Le Chapeau via the Mauvais Pas and the Torrent des Chaussettes, which gets it name from the socks the climbers wore, two routes that are no longer used.

In 1909 the Compagnie, in an attempt to avoid possible lawsuits and reign in these grandpa guides that were becoming a bit of a handful named two head-guides at the two glaciers. Decked out in an official cap (one of which survives in the Compagnie's office), their job was to ensure that the Compagnie's price structure and rules were respected, which was not always as easy as it sounds.

The Second World War put an end to the position. Demand understandably declined during those difficult years, but it was the receding glaciers that sounded the death knell for the work of the pirates.

It became difficult and even

impossible to cross from one side of the glaciers to the other and the old guides hung up their alpenstocks for the last time...

Crossing the Bossons glacier.
Crossing the Bossons and Mer de Glace glaciers
was very popular with tourists new to the mountains.
Yet the retreat of the glaciers after the Second World War
put an end to the activity.

Below:
the publication of this book
by Armand Charlet,
who was both a gude
and a member of the GHM,
would lead to a better
understanding of guide-
client relationships.

The Leschaux hut
in the 1930s.
Most of the climbers
who made their names
on the legendary climbs
of the Grandes Jorasses
started from here.

GUIDED AND UNGUIDED PARTIES, THE FIRST MISUNDERSTANDINGS

It is true to say that not all the Chamonix guides were exceptional sportsmen.

Armand Charlet recounts, in his book Vocation Alpine, the story of an Argentière guide who took for a three-day route: *"Three litres of red wine in his leather water pouch, plus two litres of white wine from Lognan [chalets above Argentière] and that is not including all that he consumed in the chalets and huts where there was a guardian…"*.

Accustomed to back-breaking work, some found it easier to drink absinthe and wine than mineral water. Old habits die hard and this was a closed generation.

Guides such as the one mentioned above would have enormous difficulty in adjusting to the new style of mountaineering.

The creation of the Groupe de Haute Montagne led to some serious mix-ups.

Most of the guides could not understand what drove these youngsters, often from good families, to set off with the most hare-brained ideas for routes in their heads.

Moreover, the Chamonix of the 1930s was still a village that was home to a close circle of friends and relations. They would follow, in spirit at least, one of their colleagues who had set out on a mysterious new route and weigh up his chances of success. All these mountaineers, amateurs or no, would meet up for the celebrated cakes served in the comfort of the Patisserie des Alpes or the PDA, as it was known. Climbers bivouacking on routes would dream about the famous PDA.

It goes without saying that this small community of climbers all knew each other and this group of young whippersnappers would soon come to irritate the guides for having dispensed with their services. Relatively soothing noises were made on the point.

Henri Bordeaux, a member of the Académie Française, wrote in the first issue of the revue Alpinisme: *"Mountaineering without a guide? Yes, but with an experienced leader who is allowed to give the order to turn back even when pride is involved and who feels responsible. Mountaineering without a guide? Yes, but among friends who know each other and who understand that a climbing group without a guide is only as good as its weakest member; whilst a mediocre mountaineer can be supported*

The traverse of the Arête du Jardin on the Verte in 1926.
For a long time cutting steps was deemed the best technique for moving up
snow and ice slopes in 10-point crampons.

by a guide and a porter and, in this way, be successful on difficult ascents." A few issues later, J. Legrand responded with: *"Alpinism without a guide is the highest form of alpinism and constitutes the mastery of it. An alpinist who, for no good reason, infirmity for example, always goes out with a guide leaves on with the same impression as a swimmer who never sets foot in the water without a life belt."*

These high-spirited youngsters would soon reject the guides, turning their backs on these father figures. The guides did not sense the rise of this new trend and while in France the unguided parties where in the minority, in Germany and Italy, thanks to clubs, a whole generation of climbers was being created; climbers who would never know what it was like to climb with a guide. During the interwar period, there was total incomprehension between the two sides; they were like chalk and cheese. On the one side were the hardline purists, on the other the temple merchants peddling promises of adventure. In huts they would often avoid each other. Few guides expected or accepted the confrontation. Most important for them was creating a clientele, the rest didn't really matter.

Near the Aiguille du Caïman in 1928.
The Caïman lies in the heart of the Chamonix Aiguilles and was first traversed (south-north)
by Mademoiselle E. de Ferré Perroux with Arthur Ravanel, Jean Ravanel and Alfred Payot.

*An attempt on the central spur on the north face of Grandes Jorasses in 1935
by Frendo, Chaix, Gréloz and Roch. Despite having an impressive list of climbs to his name,
Frendo still had to sit the guides' exams to join the Compagnie.
It goes without saying that he passed them all with flying colours...*

Edouard Frendo in the 1930s. He was born in Sfax in Tunisia and was the first city-born guide to make his way into the ranks of the Compagnie.

Below: René Rionda, Frendo's brother-in-law. The pair made the first ascent of one of the most well known routes in the massif, what is now the Frendo Spur on the north face of the Aiguille du Midi.

FRENDO, THE FIRST GUIDE FROM A CITY

Armand Charlet was one of the rare guides to build bridges between the two groups. A few years later, Edouard Frendo took the same step.

Frendo was not a typical guide. For a start he wasn't a Chamoniard and he was born in Sfax, Tunisia, where his father was a ship-owner. He discovered the mountains at the age of 14 and never left them. He really came into his own in the 1930s and he qualified as a guide in 1932 with the Société des Touristes du Dauphiné.

He was 22 years old and immediately set about trying his hand at the great challenges in the Oisans range. Together with some of the best climbers of the day, including Fourastier and Madier, he climbed some truly great routes: the Tour Carrée on the Roche Méane, the south face of the Rouies, the traverse of the Aiguilles de Sialouze, the second ascent of the Z route and the south face of the Meije, and the list goes on.

He then joined the EHM (École de Haute Montagne, Mountain School) as a sergeant. Frendo split his time between these two worlds, one giving him a certain moral rigidity and the other a desire to be in the mountains.

Gaston Rébuffat, with whom he did the second ascent of the Walker Spur, wrote of him that *"in his military guise he looks incapable of dreaming or laughing; he is of medium build, already a little plump and I had trouble understanding how he could climb so well; yet his agility surprised me and I noticed that he would laugh with his eyes in the mountains."*

He had only just` arrived in Chamonix and was already setting off on first ascents: a new route on a spur on the north face of the Courtes, the traverse from the Aiguille de Roc to the Grépon, and several attempts on the Grandes Jorasses. He really did climb for the fun of it.

He soon held sway in the organisation of all the new professional guiding courses. Gilbert Robino (a teacher at ENSA who put up a new direct route on the north face of the Meije in 1946) remembered him as: *"A serious chap who impressed us all. He had a prestigious background and was interested in anything that might improve techniques and equipment".*

It was obvious that Frendo aspired to joining the Compagnie. But here was the problem: he was neither a Chamoniard nor was he even married

Frendo started his career as a guide in the Oisans.
The Aigle hut in 1934, shown here in a photo taken by Frendo,
has barely changed since that time.

to a local girl. He applied to the Compagnie in 1939 and went straight to the point. A tough character, sure of the influence he could exert over others, he offered the Compagnie an ultimatum: *"Either you let me join or I'll start up my own guides company"*. The Chamoniards were impressed by his list of routes, perhaps even more so by his strong-mindedness, and by the fact that he was so at ease in an arena in which they themselves excelled. Nevertheless, they put a spanner the works. They refused to recognize his Société des Touristes du Dauphiné guide's diploma even though it had been certified by the CAF (Club Alpin).

For the Chamoniards there was only one kind of guide, and that was a guide from the valley.

Frendo gave in. With one of the best lists of routes of its time, he found himself on the guides' training course with the other aspirants whose only experience was an ascent of Mont Blanc or Le Buet. He naturally finished top of his class and became, with no great fanfare, only the second monchu, nine years after Frison-Roche, to be admitted to the Compagnie.

Perhaps more than Frison-Roche, who had close connections to the Chamoniards, Frendo represented a new era in the Compagnie. From now on, the best climbers in France had a chance of joining the hallowed club, provided they were patient of course...

The Aiguille des Grands Montets with,
behind it, the Aiguille d'Argentière and the Glacier du Milieu.

*Some of the guides were able to perfect their skiing technique
at the 1924 Chamonix and 1928 St Moritz Olympic Games.
Still dominated by the Scandinavians, they would not forget the lesson.
Gilbert Ravanel, with moustache, is in the centre of the second photo.*

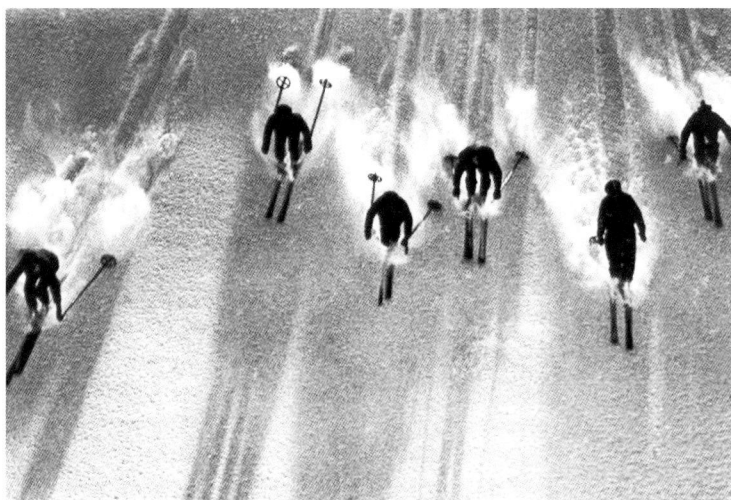

GUIDES AND SKIING

Given the setting, it was inevitable that the Chamoniards would take up skiing. Doctor Payot and Ravanel Le Rouge had discovered ski touring and Alfred Couttet had won one of the first French championships; others were bound to follow in their wake.

First there was Jean Ravanel who won the 1907 competition held in Montgenèvre (on the Franco-Italian border, just 100km from Turin). That same year Chamonix hosted its own competition. Fifty minutes after the first skiers set off, one competitor hurtled over the line. The champion was the guide Edouard Ravanel, who *"seemed to have left his house after having slowly savoured his cup of coffee"*, ran the title in the local paper.

In 1911 there were 21 skier-guides in the Compagnie and numbers were growing. Not surprising given the fact that in 1924 Chamonix hosted what was subsequently recognised as the first Winter Olympics. The world capital of mountaineering, the town threw itself into this new venture with enthusiasm. The whole town worked tirelessly for several months in preparation for the great event. Benoît Couttet, a future president of the Compagnie, was put in charge of the ice competition and every night he would carefully water the rink. So well honed was his technique, that the ice was as smooth and hard as the best rinks in Switzerland and Scandinavia.

And the contribution of the guides didn't stop there and a number of them competed in several Olympic games. Some, such as James Couttet and Charles Bozon (about whom more later), would win Olympic and World Championship titles. Six sports were included in the Olympic programme that year: ice hockey, speed skating, figure skating, curling, bobsleigh and Nordic skiing, which included the extended cross-country race (50km), the cross-country race (18km), ski jumping, the combined event (ski jumping and cross-country) and the 30km military race run by teams of four (a forerunner of the modern biathlon).

Alfred Couttet was the captain of the French team for this first international meet, and Kléber Balmat and Gilbert Ravanel represented the Compagnie. Of course, the games were overwhelmingly dominated by the Scandinavians.

Yet for the pioneers of the Olympic movement it was the taking part that counted. The Games were a fantastic showcase for a sport that was still in its embryonic stages and could only count around 3000 to 4000 regular skiers. Neither visionaries nor opportunists cashing in on the new craze, the Chamonix guides were genuinely passionate about the new sport and, having the infrastructure to practice it (the Brévent lifts were built in 1928 and the Glaciers lifts on the Aiguille du Midi in the 1930s), would be swept along by it. André Fournier, for example, became one of the founders of the French ski school as well as ENSA. There was more to come from the guides in the great skiing saga...

On the Combe de la Vierge.
The Requin hut
in the interwar period
was a perfect base for climbs
up the Mer de Glace,
which became a hugely popular
venue for spring skiing.

The Glacier du Mont Mallet
in spring 1934.

Cornice on the Col Supérieur du Plan on the Midi-Plan traverse with the Grandes Jorasses in the background.
This is considered one of the best photos in the Tairraz collection and was taken by Georges Tairraz in 1932.
Many photographers have tried to emulate him over the years but few have succeeded.

*Georges Tairraz
was the third in a line
of great mountain photographers.
He was a photographer and film-
maker and friend of Frison-Roche.
He came to symbolise,
in the years 1330 to 1950,
the complete mountain image-maker.*

AN ARTIST AMONG THE GUIDES

Finally, we could not bring this chapter to a close without mentioning Georges Tairraz. He never pulled off any great first ascents nor did he survive an epic drama, yet his images are no less fresh and relevant than they were when he first took them.

He presided over the caisse de secours (local benefit fund) for a long time, and did not have what one might call a traditional career guiding clients at the end of a rope. Yet he continued the family tradition, handed down to him by his father Georges senior and his grandfather Joseph, the founder of the dynasty, of journeying through the mountains, the poetry of their rocky faces never failing to charm him.

He was the mountain photographer of his day. His son Pierre remembered how *"he passed on his way of seeing things to me, teaching me how to take photographs, how to analyse landscapes, how to pick out the lines and shapes that provide balance in an image."* Georges, a poet of the mountains, accumulated dozens and dozens of fantastic shots in this period.

Then he turned his attention to the cinema. It was André Sauvage, with the help of Alfred Couttet from Le Lavancher, who made the first 'mountain film' on the Grépon in 1923. But it was Georges who had the real passion for the cinema. In 1924 he filmed L'ascension des aiguilles Ravanel et Mummery ('The Ascent of the Aiguilles Ravanel and Mummery') followed by Trois vies et une corde ('Three Lives and a Rope'), starring Frison-Roche.

After this time the films quickly followed on from one another and Georges was soon the technical advisor to every film whose action was set in the mountains. That is how he came to find himself suspended from a hoist at the top of the Eiffel Tower. A sheer vertical rise of 300m, the sense of nothingness below his feet was impressive even for a climber like Georges. He backed along a carefully balanced plank, holding his camera to him even tighter than usual. He carefully moved his way backwards to get the best angle for the shot, his stomach knotted with fear. He said afterwards that, *"as I moved backwards I kept telling himself that I was a Chamonix guide and I couldn't be afraid of heights"*. He too would never forget where he came from and even though his services were in demand with Walt Disney and the big Hollywood studios, he still felt most at ease with his friends from the valley.

With Frison-Roche and later with Gaston Rébuffat he beautifully illustrated man's voyages through the mountains. Here was another man who revolutionized the traditional image of the Chamonix guide.

Midi-Plan traverse in the 1930s. This really was quite an adventure when one remembers that the Aiguille du Midi cable car had not been built by this time and climbers had to walk up the length of the Mer de Glace and the Vallée Blanche to reach the start of the climb.

The Forbes Arête
on the Chardonnet.
Ulysse Simond is chatting
with his client and describing
the magnificent panoramic views
that stretch from the Swiss canton
of Valais to Mont Blanc itself
(July 1932).

THE END
OF AN ERA

THE 1950S BROUGHT GREAT CHANGES TO CHAMONIX.
THE CONSTRUCTION OF THE AIGUILLE DU MIDI CABLE CAR,
THE DIGGING OF THE MONT BLANC TUNNEL
AND THE CRAZE FOR SKIING SOUNDED THE DEATH KNELL
FOR THE TRADITION OF THE PEASANT-GUIDES.

The Second World War had temporarily brought life in the valley to a standstill but it survived the period more or less unscathed. Each guide got through the war years as best he could. Some were heroes, others were not.

Léon Balmat was one of those brave men, yet nobody at the time knew it and he hardly had to time to savour the new-found peace.

In August 1945 he was on the Nonne, just behind the Drus, with clients. His hemp rope was worn out but he couldn't afford to replace it. There was a rappel from the brèche or notch. It'll be alright this one last time, thought Balmat. His clients were down, as was a group of amateurs to whom Léon had offered the use of his rope. Now it was his turn to rappel and, with the rope passed around his body in an S-shape, he set off. All of a sudden the rope snapped and Léon fell, landing 100 metres below, and he died shortly afterwards.

One of his friends, a priest with a neatly trimmed beard, was inconsolable. The priest's name was Father Henri-Antoine Groues, better known as Abbé Pierre. He had been with the maquis, or resistance fighters, in the Vercors during the war and went on to found Emmaus, a charity for the homeless in 1949. He remembered his first meeting with Balmat in the guides' office in 1942. He was looking for a guide to take a group of disadvantaged youngsters up Mont Blanc. The head-guide called Léon in saying, *"listen, you're a good churchgoing lad,*

you couldn't look after the Father here, could you?" They climbed via the Grand Plateau, the Arête des Bosses and the Rochers de la Tournette and made it to the summit with no problems. Léon looked after his budding alpinists as they made their way back down. They finally got to the Glaciers cable car station, the precursor of the Aiguille du Midi cable car, and the young priest asked his guide how much he owed him. Léon refused any payment, saying *"listen, Father, this one's on me; it's my way of helping these kids."*

He was a generous man despite his uncouth manners and awkward air. It was then that Abbé Pierre, a priest at Grenoble cathedral who was getting ready to join the Resistance, put his audacious plan to Léon. He wanted him to set up a secret network of people in Chamonix who could help smuggle people wanted by the Gestapo over the border. Léon accepted and his barn became a meeting point for all those looking to cross the high-altitude mountain passes. No-one knew anything about it, not even the Austrians who during the occupation would from time to time sit on the stones outside Léon's farm in Les Pélerins. He would get nothing for his troubles as was evidenced by the sorry state of his rope, worn down to its core it would cause his death a few years later. Abbé Pierre still remembered this gesture more than fifty years later and would regularly visit Léon's family. His name had gently faded from the history books and Abbé Pierre thought it deserved recognition.

Alfred Ravanel at the Col de Balme above the village of Le Tour.
Every family owned four or five cows.

Clément Claret-Tournier with his cows outside his farm in Orthaz, near Les Bois.
Guide or farmer, most Chamoniards didn't see a difference and in years gone by the occupations
were indisociable from each other.

Previous page:
Marcel Charlet on the summit of the Aiguille du Moine.
Vibram soles began to make an appearance in the 1950s and this prompted an evolution in climbing techniques.

At the start of the 1950s flocks of sheeps were still taken across the Mer de Glace to graze in the 'alpages', high-mountain pastures, below the Drus.

CHAMONIX, A MOUNTAIN VILLAGE

Léon was buried in August 1945, just as Chamonix was starting to look like its former self.

A special report in Elite magazine about the Chamonix guides paints a few interesting portraits: *"some like the Balmats are big and straight men with a little of the peasant in their manner; others are more heavily built, such as Devouassoud whose delicate and sentimental soul contrasts with his giant's face and the simplicity of his manners."*

They were all farmers. Each farm had four or five cows, rarely more as the guides were not fanatical stockmen. Four or five cows provided them with just enough milk, and possibly meat if the summer season did not go well.

The summer season was the main time for tourists to visit the town. It was even said that a single day's takings from the cable cars in the summer was the same as the whole of the month of January.

Chamonix had striven to be a great tourist site and the explosion in the popularity of skiing had not yet happened, while plans for the second generation of ski stations, in the Courcheval mould, were still in their infancy. Instead, in the immediate post-war period, the locals went back to the land. There were the animals to look after, the Valais and Abondance cows to be fed and mucked out, ploughing to be done, seeds to be sown,

crops to be harvested, the barn or mazot (traditional outbuilding) to be repaired. Then there was the garden, full of beetroot, runner beans and kohlrabi, to tend. The valley looked like a kind of giant jigsaw puzzle with thousands of parcels of land, plots of oats, potatoes and buckwheat. A form of fodder called la choué was made on the narrow plots of land. For, as everyone had a plot of land, there wasn't much to go round and the Chamoniards had lots of children! Pork products were smoked around the boërne, an enormous traditional chimney usually found in the middle of the house, and milk was brought down from the Blaitière and Flégère pastures in enormous pails. That's not to say Chamonix was closed to the outside world. At the start of the summer, when it was time for the hay harvest, guides would come over from the Val d'Aoste in Italy to give a hand, and Swiss shepherds and fruit dealers would cross the neighbouring mountain passes. The old road that was still the only access route to the Chamonix, nonchalantly followed the bends in the river to the centre of what was still only a large but sleepy town.

In the 1950s there were still only 7000 beds in the valley. Not a great deal had changed for the Chamoniards.

'LA BELLE CLIENTELE'

Nevertheless, new places were becoming fashionable and the next generation of mountaineers chose to meet in Chamonix. They could be found in La Potinière, at the Brasserie des Alpes, at the Outa with its mini-golf course, at the Bar du Soleil where the world was put to rights nightly, or again at Chamonix's own beach where the sports centre now stands. The grand hotels were empty for the time being and the Majestic and the Hotel Mont Blanc were difficult to heat dinosaurs of a bygone age where it was impossible to make a profit.

The great and the good seemed to be a little more disparate now. The rich northern industrialists, the captains of industry and bankers – such as the Peugeot or Farman families – who would stay in the grand hotels or their private villas and make only the most minimal or concessions to everyday life, were becoming rare. More and more visitors were what were known as 'paid leavers'. Up until this point a guide could establish a good customer base in five years. Indeed it was not unusual for a guide to work with the same monchu for the whole of his working life.

Michel Payot, for instance, spent 40 years with the British climber James Eccles, who even mentioned Payot in his will. Frédéric Folliguet spent his career with a Geneva publisher. In the 1950s, Luc Couttet worked with four or five families, industrialists such as the Peugeots, Tiermens, Tiberghiens and Mazurels, mill owners from the north of France. Pierre Cretton guided the entire Michelin family and Alfred Ravanel looked after the Carmichaels, Reyniers and Manourys. One could list four or five families associated with each guide from the Compagnie. And the shared ambitions of client and guide mellowed in age until their excursions were no more than simple walks together. It wasn't unusual for client and guide to pass on their working relationship to their respective offspring, a kind of spiritual inheritance.

Time seemed not to affect this collective passion for climbing and continuity seemed assured. Yet if on the surface Chamonix appeared to have barely changed at all, its visitors were slowly but surely changing in character. The great and the good were becoming less and less faithful to their little valley; seduced by great journeys abroad, by exotic destinations and quieter valleys. And little by little they would desert Chamonix.

In response, word started to go around of hare-brained schemes that would shake up the sleepy valley. Some spoke of a tunnel under the mountains that would join France with Italy, others talked of the highest cable car in the world.

(L. to r.)
Clément Simond,
René Charlet and
Raymond Claret-Tournier
are awarded medals
in a ceremony
in the guides' office
for their part in a rescue.

MEANWHILE BACK IN THE GUIDES' OFFICE...

For the time being at least, the guides were more concerned with the coming season. They met daily under the same arcades that are still next to the town hall.

Armand Couttet, who was nearing his sixtieth birthday, always turned up on his bike. And like all the other guides, he would put his bike in the corridor next to the office. The famous office was a modest little room with a striped tapestry hanging on the wall, which had hardly changed since it was first opened.

Roger Frison-Roche compared it to a notary's waiting room. It was rectangular and deep, and a wide table with a waxed black cloth covering it stood in the centre. The head-guide often had to wipe off the rings from glasses left on the table before clients came in to see him. A stove that had seen better days made up the rest of the furniture.

Nevertheless, the place still had a certain atmosphere. A number of portraits, gifts to the company from clients, gave the apparently anonymous décor a bit of colour. There was Michel Croz, at the height of his powers, with a dedication by Whymper, and a yellowing photo of a visit by the French statesman Armand Fallières hung next to a portrait of the King of the Belgians on his return from the Drus. Further along were the maps, sketches and lithographs that would have been the pride and joy of any collector. In another corner sat crystals of smoked quartz and lumps of grey granite, sometimes used as bookends for the Compagnie's library. And then there was the famous corridor, which separated the guides' office from the Syndicat d'Initiative or tourist information bureau. Finally, there was the back room where the myriad tools of the guides' trade were stored plied high, one on top of each other. Hemp ropes were hung up all around the room and along one wall ice axes were stacked against each other, ready to go.

And above all this there lay a thick grey canvas stretcher and a huge rescue kit, a reminder that the guides could be called out at any moment of the day or night, even in a storm.

In the 1950s the mainspring of the whole operation was Joseph Burnet, an accomplished guide with 152 ascents of the Grépon to his name. He was a teacher by training and kept the Compagnie's accounts, edited the President of the Compagnie's speeches and organised the rescue operations. As many of the guides still didn't have telephones, he would get on his bike and go round recruiting volunteers for rescues. He would often start by asking around his neighbours in Les Coverays, opposite the Bois du Bouchet. That was why his brother Marcel, Edmond Maresca and René Tournier were often the first to set off. In fact, Marcel Burnet holds the absolute record for rescues, having more than 70 to his name.

Camille Claret-Tournier,
more often known as simply Camille Tournier (like all the Claret Tourniers),
was part of the old generation of guides who divided their time between
working in the mountains and on the farm. This would change in the early 1960s.

The famous Z pitch on the traverse of the Drus. This used to be one of the guides' favourite routes.

CAMILLE TOURNIER, MARCEL BOZON, CHARLES BALMAT, THREE VERY TRADITIONAL GUIDES

In 1946 ENSA, the ski and mountaineering school, was now training the guides and new faces started to appear. Among them was Léon Bellin – who at the age of 27 would become the guides' youngest President – Félix Martinetti, René Charlet and Edmond Cachat. There were also five newcomers who hadn't been born in the commune. Edgar Couttaz and Gilbert Chappaz were from Haute-Savoie and therefore had no trouble in joining; Louis Dunand, from Vallorcine, was the first guide to be admitted to the Compagnie from beyond the Col des Montets; and then there was Gaston Rébuffat from Marseilles and the Grenoble climber Lionel Terray.

After the arrival of Frison-Roche, Frendo and Livasic (who joined in 1944), these great mountaineers would confirm that it was possible to gain entry into Chamonix's mountain academy without being born there. Provided that you had the necessary technical and personal skills, obviously. Nevertheless, Louis Lachenal, Terray's alter ego, was curiously refused entry to the guides several years running. He was finally admitted in 1949 after three years of trying. Perhaps Lachenal's quasi-revolutionary climbing methods and happy-go-lucky habit of almost literally running up routes frightened the Chamnonix guides.

In fact the Compagnie was split. On the one hand

it wanted to open up its membership to those not born in the valley, while others considered this path a dangerous one to go down. In the end, it reacted on a case-by-case basis without setting rules or quotas.

The season would always start with the same ritual:
Guide: "But you know I can't start climbing until we've got the hay in."
Head-guide: "How long?"
Guide: "At least a week. And you're lucky. They won't be finished before mid-July in Le Tour."
The Camille Tourniers, Marcel Bozons and Charles Balmats of the Compagnie represented the traditional peasant-guides of the past who were as happy wielding scythes as they were ice axes.

Camille (Claret-)Tournier was one of the period's most charismatic guides. Born in 1900, he had a giant's build and a shock of white hair, and was the living incarnation of the old traditions. He truly loved the Compagnie, indeed he was its President for almost 15 years. The route on the Tournier Spur on the north face of the Aiguille du Midi is in part his work. And like many guides of his generation, he had a soft spot for the Drus and the traverse. The Flammes de Pierre, the Z pitch, the Pendulum, he could climb all of the route's famous pitches practically with his eyes closed. Then again having done it 58 times, he must have known virtually every crack.

Marcel Bozon at the Gaillands.

A delegation of guides in ceremonial dress visits Paris in 1952. From l. to r.: René Payot, Louis Dunand, Marcel Bozon and Charles Balmat.

At the age of 62 he was still climbing, this time on the traverse of the Aiguilles du Diable, with two other larger-than-life figures, Marcel Burnet and Gérard Devouassoux. Léopold, the son of Albert 1st, who would for a time also be King of the Belgians, was one of his clients.

Camille did visit Paris from time to time but loved his valley too much to be away from it for very long. It was neither glory nor money that interested him. The only things that really mattered were his sheep, the flock that he himself took up to graze on the Blaitière pastures. He had taken part in the Olympic Games in Saint Moritz, was Spencer Tracy's body double in the film The Mountain, was awarded the Légion d'Honneur (France's highest decoration) for the numerous rescues he took part in, yet what he loved the most was the peace and tranquillity of looking after his flock. It's unsurprising, therefore, that his nickname was le Berardi (the shepherd). He wasn't even forced to make a choice in life as the peaks and pastures formed part of the same environment.

Marcel Bozon, a colossus of a man, was another traditional guide straight of the mould. His best climbing days were in the 1920s and included, among other exploits, being a porter for Armand Charlet on his first ascent of the Arête Sans Nom on the Aiguille Verte. He was also awarded the Légion d'Honneur but he preferred not to talk about it at home on his farm in Les Pélerins. Work done and work done well, whether in the mountains or in the fields, that's what mattered to Marcel. Mr and Mrs Mazars, who he guided over several seasons, remembered him and his rough demeanour decades later: *"He wasn't very outgoing. He was a pure montagnard. He was an integral part of the landscape and he gave off such a sense of calm that, whatever the conditions, we felt as if nothing could happen to us. I remember when we were on the Brenva in a storm. His expression was impassive and didn't betray a single emotion. As if everything was just fine."*

The mountains, however, were not always gentle with his loved ones. His brother Anatole was killed in an avalanche beneath the Col de l'Iseran near Bourg Saint Maurice in 1939 and his nephew, Charles Bozon the ski champion, died in the early 1960s in an accident on the Aiguille Verte.

Like all the locals, that learned to live in the mountains' shadow, he by turns hated and also loved them. His seamed face and athlete's build gave him the look of a hard man. In fact, he was a softie who loved children. On top of looking after his own seven children, he also found time to pass on his passion for skiing to countless Chamonix youngsters. His hugely significant role was that of President of the French guiding union, the Syndicat National des Guides de Montagne.

Charles Balmat (extreme right) poses with members of the film crew for 'La Neige en Deuil' (released in the States as 'The Mountain'). The film's stars, Spencer Tracy and Robert Wagner, can also be seen in the photo.

A GUIDE IN HOLLYWOOD

Like the others, Charles Balmat, known as Barlette, had done his guide's training before the war.

As a porter, he had even accompanied Ravanel the Rouge in 1930 when he made the first winter ascent of the Grands Charmoz. The mountaineering community was a big family with various key figures. Paradoxically, Charles Balmat was descended from Doctor Paccard and not Jacques Balmat. He was thickset and often wore a beret and came from a line of guides, like most of the guides in the valley. His father Edouard and his uncle Adolphe had both spent their days in the mountains, yet Charles's future lay in quite an unusual path.

It was a path that started at the foot of the peaks that stand above the valley's floor and led him to the other side of the world, more specifically to Hollywood and Paramount Studios.

It was 1954 and the Americans were interested in Henri Troyat's novel La Neige en Deuil, which had been inspired by the 1950 Malabar Princess tragedy, when an Air India plane crashed on Mont Blanc. The studio wanted to make a film of the novel and so they went to Chamonix. Charles, whose grandmother had goaded him into taking English lessons, was made the assistant director. He immediately set about hiring 40 guides, to work as porters and body doubles for the stars. Camille

Tournier would be Spencer Tracy's double and Balmat's son Georges would stand in for Richard Wagner. With his practical experience, Balmat quickly proved to be indispensable. He explained how to hold an ice axe, organised the team's movements on the glaciers, monitored the weather conditions and scouted out the best crevasses and peaks for the film crew. The film crew called him Charlie and he made such a good impression that he was invited to go over to Hollywood to supervise the scenes filmed in the studio.

He wasn't sure, who would look after the livestock and harvest the potatoes? His four sons – Michel, Jean-Paul, Georges and Lucien (also guides) – convinced him to go, *"Go! We'll look after all that!"*

So, the Chamoniard who had never been abroad before, set off on his long journey. It took him 40 hours by plane to get to Los Angeles, which even included a stop-over in Iceland. He spent two incredible months rubbing shoulders with, and being dazzled by, the major stars of the day. He told Philippe Gaussot that he was *"literally blown away by the means the American cinema had at its disposal. It's unbelievable! To shoot the rock scenes, with close-ups of Spencer Tracy, they recreated an enormous wall of rock in the studio, the same height as the Aiguillette d'Argentière and the length of the climbing area at the Gaillands."*

Did Charles Balmat, Camille Tournier, Marcel Bozon and their contemporaries know that theirs would be the last generation of guides to work on the land and in the mountains, to be both farmers and guides?

The following decade would mark the turning point. The development of skiing, the construction of the Aiguille du Midi cable car and the Mont Blanc Tunnel would open up the valley once and for all and shake up the attitudes of its inhabitants.

Within the space of 15 years all the farming families had given up their livestock and, with the exception of a few diehards like Roger Bozon, the valley would change radically. Agriculture was to disappear from the valley, taking with it the nicknames that distinguished one Chamoniard from another. Gone were François Devouassoud known as 'the silkworm', Adolphe Folliguet the 'Boursollet bear', Jean Claret Tournier known to all as 'Jean à Béradit', 'pickaxe' Camille, Alexandre 'lourgni' Choupin, Alfred 'à la Caulade', Armand 'à la Bolnère', Alfred 'à la Maitre', André 'à Daubert', Luc 'à Besson', Alfred 'à Fantié'…

Was this a perfect way to attract novelists? Frison-Roche endlessly mined this rich seam in his novels, but these nicknames were also an absolute necessity. How else would you know which Couttet you were talking about when there were 700 in the valley, five of them called Alfred, all working as guides!

North face of Annapurna. It was first climbed by a French team and was the first 8000m peak to be conquered. The expedition's success owed a great deal to Louis Lachenal, one of the two Frenchmen to stand on the summit.

Marcel Schatz,
Maurice Herzog,
Gaston Rébuffat,
Jacques Oudot (doctor)
and Louis Lachenal
in a tent
at base camp.

Below:
Louis Lachenal
as a young guide
standing on the summit
of the Aiguille de Leschaux.

FROM THE EIGER TO ANNAPURNA, THE MAKING OF A LEGENDARY TRIO: TERRAY, LACHENAL AND REBUFFAT

For the time being at least, Chamonix was unaware of the revolution that would change it beyond recognition.

Instead, conversation centred on the two Chamoniards (by adoption) who had just made the second ascent of the north face of the Eiger. Lionel Terray and Louis Lachenal had just made their entrée into the pages of mountaineering history. And they certainly didn't sink back into obscurity afterwards.

Terray over the following two decades would make a huge impact on mountaineering, his name turning up time and again in books and journals. Lachenal was more of a shooting star, a rebellious spirit, a romantic who loved the mountains where he could be himself. Together they were the ideal climbing partnership.

They masterfully weathered a storm on the Eiger, shattered the record for climbing the Piz Badile and attacked the hard climbing on the Grandes Jorasses with gusto. Lachenal was a brilliant, modern climber who dreamed of linking up climbs on summit after summit, and Terray provided the ideas and the inspiration.

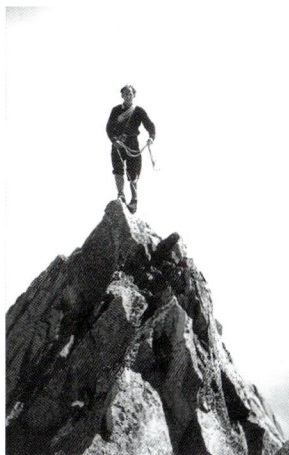

Lachenal carried the scars from his encounters with the mountains, including those from 18 operations on the stumps of the toes he had amputated after the Annapurna expedition. Annapurna was the first 8000m peak to be climbed and it was by Chamoniards: three guides, three leading lights of the world of mountaineering.

All three of them were exactly 29 years old when they boarded the boat that would take them, part of the way at least, to Kathmandu. They were all at the height of their powers. It was chance, the system of taking turns, that brought the shooting star of the climbing scene to camp 5 on Annapurna with Maurice Herzog. They set off together on Friday 2 June 1950 on what would be their own personal Via Dolorosa.

The two men were driven by different motives and Lachenal, even at high altitude, was still a guide. He knew that the line between success and tragedy was a fine one. On the summit of Annapurna, the cold, wind and fatigue biting into them, he knew they were very close to stepping over the line. He had even contemplated turning back less than 100 metres from the summit. But Lachenal was a man of his word and carried on for

Returning from Annapurna.
An exhausted Lionel Terray, suffering from snow blindness, is helped back to base camp by his Sherpas.

James Couttet
(World Downhill
Skiing Champion
1938),
Gaston Rébuffat
and Maurice Baquet
on the summit
of the Aiguille Noire
de Peuterey.

Herzog's sake. Lachenal really didn't care at all for any notions of triumph and glory.

He would write later, in his book Carnets de Vertige that *"[Herzog] told me that he was going on. It wasn't for me to question his motives; mountaineering is far too personal. But it seemed to me that if he had carried on alone, he would never have come back. It was for him and for him alone that I didn't turn around. That walk to the summit had nothing to do with national prestige. We were a team."* This self-sacrifice would cost him dearly. It would rob the master craftsman of the tools that were essential for his works of art, reducing him to the level of a clumsy amateur. He would have in front of him a mere five years of lectures, operations, writing, love and pain, before he was greedily swallowed up by a crevasse on the Vallée Blanche. The guides couldn't believe that Biscante, as they called him, had really gone.

Terray concluded the chapter on Annapurna in his autobiography, Les Conquérants de l'Inutile (Conquistadors of the Useless), that *"as the dream faded, we returned to earth in a fearful mix of pain and joy, heroism and cowardice, sun and mud, grandeur and meanness."*

Gaston Rébuffat also returned from the expedition deeply hurt, his idealism and opinion of men seriously shaken by the experience. He honoured his obligation not to say anything on the matter and avoided the controversy the expedition later provoked. He also refused all subsequent offers

to join expeditions and threw himself into his guiding work, his life's passion.

He soon found words to explain the enchantment and the beauty of an extraordinary profession. And the words he chose rang true. In 1960 he wrote in the French aviation journal Icare: *"The profession of guide is among the best in the world because man practices it on an Earth that remains untarnished. Few things survive unscathed in towns these days: there's no such thing as night-time any more, nor the wind, the cold or the stars. Everything is neutralized. Where is life's rhythm? Everything moves so quickly and makes so much noise! A busy man does not notice the grass on the paths, its colour, its smell, the light on it when the wind caresses it. The result of the curious encounter of the dough of humanity with the planet's terrain is men in a silence of forgetting! Coming across a snow slope as smooth as a pane of glass? Men destroy its weightlessness by working on it: cutting an artificial track through it. Confronted by a beautiful obelisk of rock? Men destroy its unwieldiness and demand their right to go everywhere. They are not having an adventure, they are living, simply doing their jobs."*

Rébuffat, the man from Marseilles, opened doors to the mountains, like a proud gardener opening the gates to his garden. He didn't stop with words and in the 1950s he became one of the greatest guides of his generation. Yet he was a guide and not a mountaineer. It was a difference of scale, and perhaps that is why he is remembered more

Rébuffat in action.
A graceful climber with an equally elegant style of writing, he painted vivid pictures of the guiding profession.

*Jean Farini
and Gaston Rébuffat (behind)
and James Couttet (in front)
on the summit
of the Aiguille de Pélerins
during their guides' course
in 1945.*

*The Walker Spur
on the Grandes Jorasses.
Gaston Rébuffat made
the second ascent
of the Walker and was
the first guide to dare
to guide a client on it.*

for his writing than for his climbing. Nevertheless, he was already proving his talent in 1945 when he did the second ascent of the Walker Spur with Frendo and put up some superb new routes including the north face of the Dent du Requin. He then climbed a number of challenging routes with a series of ambitions clients. He climbed the northeast spur on the Piz Badile with Bernard Pierre in 1948, the following year he was on the north face of the Matterhorn with Raymond Simond, and he guided Paul Habrand between 1952 and 1953 on the north face of the Grandes Jorasses, the Eiger and east face of the Grand Capucin. In so doing, he was the first man to guide three of the biggest routes in the Alps. Raymond Simond and Paul Habrand were certainly competent climbers, good enough to climb big routes without a guide. Yet back in 1950s they only had basic equipment, a rudimentary weather forecast and were very limited in their use of pegs and the routes they did with Rébuffat were quite exceptional. Indeed, at this time the Walker Spur had only seen eight ascents.

The indefatigable climber Georges 'the Greek' Livanos wrote about him in the annals of the GHM in 1985, the year Rébuffat died: *"I will not dwell on secondary considerations, it is Rébuffat the climber that interests me. I do not hesitate to restate here that he was the greatest guide of his day, and that is what counts. If a pantheon of mountaineers exists, it is with brotherly affection that he will be received into it by his peers, Michel Croz, Franz Lochmatter and Angelo Dibona."*

Over time Rébuffat has come to represent a kind of archetypal figure of the mountain guide. With his tall frame, his knee-length socks and his heavy knit sweater, silhouetted against a mountain ridge he had the air of an old engraving of a guide. His writing style became a reference against which others were compared, under his pen the mistral became 'generous', blackness was 'mineral', a first ascent was a 'signature in the rock', the Dibona route 'embodied climbing', the Dent du Géant was a 'miracle in granite' and the Aiguilles du Diable were a 'fantastical horseback ride'. Like Frison-Roche 20 years earlier, he knew how to give new life to the image of the Chamonix guides to whom he remained faithful to the end.

The great names and their exploits we have just evoked did not stop them blending in with their fellow guides when they all met up at the Compagnie. Paris Match, always a good barometer of how the rest of France views Chamonix, described them in its 5 August 1950 issue as follows: *"The kingdom of snow and ice that is Chamonix has its own nobility with their ropes and ice axes, and they are its guides. Their coat of arms is their guide's badge. Even if they were to become millionaires and never guide another monchu again, they would hold on to their medallions, their first badges of glory. If there is one guide held in greater respect than the others, it is Joseph Demarchi, the elder statesman. There is none more famous or better than the others and they form an ensemble cast with no stars."*

The Grands Mulets hut in the early 1950s.
The tracks in the background lead to the summit of Mont Blanc.

The rescue party photographed here in 1948 included Paul Demarchi, André Cachat and Georges Demarchi.

PAUL DEMARCHI, THE TWO-LEGGED SAINT BERNARD

The guides often made front-page news not just for their first ascents and climbing exploits, but for the rescues they carried out.

Until the establishment of the Ecole Militaire de Haute Montagne (the military mountain training school based in Chamonix and previously know as the EHM) and ENSA, when the system of rescues was reorganised, the guides had been more or less solely responsible for mountain rescues for the previous one hundred and thirty years. After this time from 15 July to 15 August, the height of the summer season, rescues were carried out by these two new bodies.

Yet at other times of the year the guides were in the front line. Over the previous one hundred years the Chamoniards had rescued hundreds of people, as a look in the rescue logbook still held in the offices of the Compagnie's will attest.

Irrespective of the risks involved, the vast majority of the guides were prepared to volunteer their services to help a fellow human being. Indeed in the 1950s it wasn't unusual to come across a guide with 30 to 40 rescues to his name.

Paul Demarchi was one of the finest examples of these 'conquistadors of the useless'. He was a member of the team that took part in a rescue on the Aiguilles du Diable in 1938. The Swiss alpinist Raymond Lambert and two friends were in trouble

high up on a flank of Mont Blanc. In the middle of February – it was -30°c with a metre of fresh snow – Demarchi took charge of the first rescue team. He walked all night and it took him 14 1/2 hours to get to the Swiss climbers, who were stuck in a storm at 4200m. They all came down alive but Demarchi, as well as three other guides involved in the rescue, had frostbitten feet. Demarchi was the worst affected and had to have several toes amputated.

But that didn't stop him and despite his handicap he continued to climb. His son, Jean-Paul, remembered how *"orthopaedic shoes didn't exist back then, so he filled in the gap in his boots with newspaper and climbed like that!"*

A true athlete who was passionate about his sport, he could never bring himself to completely turn his back on the mountains. He was put in charge of the Plan de l'Aiguille hut and carried the hut's stove, weighing over 100 kilos, from the Glaciers lift station all the way to the hut without putting it down a single time.

He had completely recovered from the amputations by the beginning of the 1950s. As proof of this, he and his brothers – Gérard and Roger, also known for their great strength – together with three guides from the Val d'Aoste were recruited to take the 1850m-long cable for the new cable

Bad weather on the Col du Midi.
Today just as in the past, this huge plateau can be dangerous
if the weather comes in and there are no tracks to follow.

Paul Demarchi on the summit of the Verte with clients.

Despite his amputated toes, he was still passionate about being in the mountains.

Below: before the widespread use of helicopters, rescues were carried out on foot.

car (a tonne of steel) down the north face of the Aiguille du Midi.

He will be remembered, however, for his time at the Plan de l'Aiguille. From the hut, a kind of advanced base camp, he took part in over 40 rescues, often setting off alone (before the other teams left Chamonix) and rescuing the victims from crevasses or routes and carrying them back to safety on his back. He didn't do it for money (the guides didn't even have their expenses paid at this time) nor for a sense of glory, he did it because he thought it was what he should do.

The weather at the beginning of April 1956 was unpredictable and seemed to change from one moment to the next and was particularly unstable in the mountains. Nevertheless, at his friend the ski instructor Henri Muckenbrunn's request he agreed to take both him and his Parisian client over the Col du Géant, on the Franco-Italian border. What Demarchi didn't know was that Muckenbrunn's client, Monsieur Ebel, was in fact wanted for gold trafficking in every European country except Italy...

On Thursday 5 April the three men had a coffee with Luc Couttet at the Le Chapeau buvette, the chalet offering refreshments to climbers and walkers above the village of Le Lavancher. They then set off for the Mer de Glace. No one would ever see them alive again. That afternoon they were caught in a terrible storm. A journalist sent to cover the story for Détective magazine described the scene: *"All hell broke loose at around 2pm. Suddenly, as if this wild mountain range were rebelling against the first caress of spring, what was chaos became a fury. The mountain enveloped itself in an ominous grey cloak and behind a swirling curtain of cloud, it howled with rage. The wind rushed and devoured its way through the valleys, whirling up the faults in the rock creating clouds of snow. And beneath the frenzied gusts, the granite creaked and groaned."* Demarchi battled against the elements for two days, just as he had done during the rescue on the Aiguilles du Diable. Then, one after another, the men feel into an eternal sleep on the edge of a crevasse in the middle of a snow slope. Demarchi's final act, as he sat at the foot of the Aiguille du Midi, was to plant his skis in the snow in the shape of a cross to show where they lay. It was his brother Gérard who found him frozen in the snow, his fingers still clasping his water bottle. The mountain had taken its revenge on one who had dared defy it.

Chamonix's Rue Vallot in the early 1950s.
Cars had yet to make an impact on the life of this large mountain village and its 2700 inhabitants.

Gilbert Chappaz (far right) on the summit of the Droites on a rescue mission with a happy ending. The rescue party reached the summit at the same time as the climbers Cornuau and Davaille (centre of photo) who had just made the first ascent of the north face of the Droites. They had spent five days on the face putting up one of the most committing routes in the Alps.

Below:
René Payot's accident had a great deal to do with the ambivalent feelings the Chamonix guides had about setting out to rescue Jean Vincendon and François Henry.

A WOUND THAT WOULD NEVER HEAL: VINCENDON AND HENRY INCIDENT

The Chamoniards have learnt not to trust the mountains and even in summer they remain wary. Experience has proved them right. The winter is still the most dangerous season and René Payot's accident only served to confirm their distrust.

On 3 November 1950 a Lockheed Constellation belonging to Air India crashed on Mont Blanc with 48 people on board. René Payot, leading the rescue team, set out for the Grands Mulets. René was extremely popular and came from one of the valley's most distinguished guiding families. In the mountains you could rely on him to break trail through deep snow and lead the most difficult sections, and when there were people to rescue he would always volunteer to help.

This time he was roped up to Pierre Leroux on the last rise before the hut. The snow was powdery making the snow bridges extremely fragile. They had just crossed a delicate crevasse when all of a sudden there was a dull crack and the entire slope on which they were standing slid away underneath them. Leroux threw himself to one side and was protected by the hole into which the snow was sliding but René was dragged into the

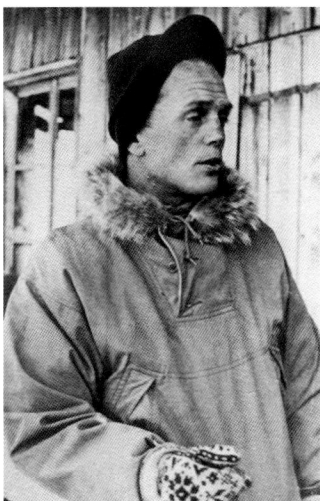

crevasse and buried under six metres of snow. He was a victim of the mountain's mort blanche (white death), in virtually the same spot where his brother Léon had been killed twelve years earlier. Except René's death was in vain, as all the occupants of the plane had been killed on impact. The sports journalist Olivier Merlin wrote his own tribute to Payot, another of the 'conquistadors of the useless', which was published in Le Monde on 7 November 1950. *"One often puts these alpine adventures down to a 'taste for the absurd'. It is this 'taste for the absurd' that confers upon our guides their greatness and nobility. Today this 'taste for the absurd' prompts the Chamoniards to race off and climb the lost peaks of Europe's highest arena. We should not be miserly in our praise and admiration for those men: they do more than just exemplify great sporting achievement, they do honour to the human condition."*

The guides owed their exalted reputation in large part to the rescues that they had been carrying out since the birth of alpinism itself. Yet in the 1950s, while the EMHM and ENSA took over during the summer season, rescues were changing.

The growing numbers of amateur climbers visiting the massif together

*Sledges, stretchers and poles made up the rudimentary rescue equipment of the day
and the rescues required huge human and logistical resources.
In this photo we see Léon Couttet (front) and Raymond Couttet carrying an injured climber down from the Plan de l'Aiguille.*

with the increasingly technical climbs being done made the rescues more difficult. The guides volunteering for rescues were starting to be overwhelmed by events. The following statement prepared by the guides' committee appeared in the press on 1 July 1956. *"The management committee of the Chamonix Guides requests that we widely circulate this warning addressed to those alpinists who, in a spirit of competition, pay no regard to conditions in the mountains as they are on their approach walk or while returning from a route, and to those who, out of conceit, undertake to climb routes beyond their capabilities, for they all underestimate the risks to which they expose the rescuers whom they expect to intervene."* This message seems strangely prophetic, as it appeared only a few months before the Vincendon and Henry affair.

It started on 25 December 1956 when an aspirant guide Jean Vincendon and his climbing partner François Henry set off to climb the Brenva Spur. The first winter ascent of the route had only been done a few months earlier, by Jean Couzy and

André Vialatte. While on the route, Vincendon and Henry were overtaken by Walter Bonatti and Silvano Gheser.

One hundred metres below the col both teams were caught in a storm and they were forced to bivouac. Far from improving the following day, the weather worsened. Bonatti knew that he had to reach the summit, find the ridges swept clean of snow and follow them down to the Vallot hut. He and his client pushed on and survived.

Exhausted by their efforts, Vincendon and Henry abandoned their bid for the summit and decided to take their chances on the north face of Mont Blanc. It was to be their undoing. And they found themselves trapped above a serac fall at one end of the Grand Plateau.

The alarm was quickly raised in Chamonix. Yet the rescuers had mixed feelings and were concerned that an accident like the one that claimed René Payot should not happen again. The slopes were loaded with snow and they would have to

follow the same route on which Payot had been killed. The guides also couldn't understand why the climbers would go and put themselves in such a situation in the middle of winter. The Compagnie refused to put the lives of fathers with children at risk to save two mountaineers who had to take responsibility for their own actions.

Can one blame volunteers for not wanting take part in a rescue operation they judged too dangerous?

Can one criticise them for their decision given that for decades they had carried out rescues, often at risk to their own lives, in all kinds of conditions? This time they were beaten by events and conditions. The attack launched on them in the press didn't change anything. Once again, the mountain had had the last word.

Lionel Terray tried to help but had to admit that his colleagues were right. Given the amount of snow that had fallen, any attempt to walk up to them would be suicide. There only remained the

option of an air rescue, which failed miserably when the helicopter crashed.

The two men died above Chamonix, while no one could come to their rescue.

The tragedy showed the limitations of the rescue system as it stood and it was the end of a legend: the guides would slowly hand over the job of rescuing climbers to a professional rescue service. Sadly, it was a painful transfer of power.

As climbing techniques and practices evolved,
rescues became increasingly difficult to stage.
Rescues involved teams from the EMHM, ENSA
and the Compagnie, yet events were running away with them.
With the increasing numbers of winter ascents
being made by teams throwing themselves at the big routes
such as the Grandes Jorasses and Drus,
rescues had to become more and more high-tech.

Léon Balmat
was a friend
of the Abbé Pierre.

Georges Bellin
was one of the best climbers
in the Compagnie.
Here is seen here on the Grépon
in the 1950s.

Joseph Burnet
was the Compagnie's secretary
in the 1950s.

Below, from l. to r.:
Aimé Desailloud,
Alfred Payot,
Jean Balmat,
Gilbert Ducroz.

Marcel Charlet
was a classmate of Georges Charlet.

A 20-man team at the Aiguille du Midi in 1958 after a huge rescue operation.
This was one of the first times gendarmes joined the guides in a rescue party.

Back row, from, l. to r.: Aimé Désailloud, Gilbert Ducroz, Marcel Burnet, Joseph Maffioli, André Braconnay,
Gendarme Peline, Clément Hugon, René Claret-Tournier, unknown soldier, unknown gendarme.

Front row, l. to r.: Fernand Bellin, René Charlet, Gendarme Roux, Fernand Claret-Tournier, Gérard Demarchi,
Doctor Dartigue, unknown gendarme, Camille Claret-Tournier, Edmond Maresca, Gendarme Véron.

Twenty-five guides have been awarded gold medals for 30 mountain rescues.

The 1960s saw a series of great winter ascents that made a huge mark on mountaineering.

THE BITTERSWEET YEARS

THE YEARS 1960-1970 WOULD GALVANISE THE COMPAGNIE
BUT THEY WOULD ALSO PROVE TO BE BITTERSWEET:
A TIME OF GREAT SUCCESSES AND ACHIEVEMENTS YET BITTER HEARTACHE
AND GRIEF. A WHOLE NEW GENERATION OF CLIMBERS DREAMED OF
THE MOUNTAINS. FULL OF HOPE AND ENTHUSIASM, THIS GENERATION
WOULD PAY A HIGH PRICE FOR ITS AMBITIONS.

The winter was like a permanently open bottle of champagne. Whether it was December or February and with the snows lasting the whole season, the valley was filled with the euphoria of a place that had woken from a deep sleep.

By the start of the 1960s, the Chamoniards began to explore and master the mysterious winter season. They had been wandering along their Haute Routes for decades but they had yet to tame the mountains in the heart of winter when they were blanketed in deep powdery snow.

It didn't take long, barely 10 years in fact, for the ski season to start earlier and earlier until 'spring skiing' became simply skiing.

In 1953 and 1954 there were still more than 40 Chamoniards leaving the valley for the new ski resorts of Courchevel and Méribel.

Yet by 1960 the ski instructor-guides, especially the younger ones, didn't have to leave the valley to find work. The opening of the Aiguille du Midi cable car offered new possibilities and the Vallée Blanche quickly became a classic ski descent. Then the Flégère and Grands Montets ski lifts joined the valley's blossoming winter décor. The short-lived tradition of skiing at the Brévent in the morning and the Midi's Glaciers piste was already out-dated. The guides had to meet new demands: off-piste skiing, day ski-tours and above all the Vallée Blanche.

The cramped yet quaint guides' office relocated and opened during the winter. In 1964 it moved next door to the Tourist Office and shared premises with the ESF (French Ski School). It didn't find its own separate and permanent home until the winter of 1972-3 when it moved into the presbytery, now known as the Maison de la Montagne.

The winter now had its own leisure activities, of which skiing accounted for a large part, and it would also produce some truly great mountaineering moments.

The main peaks had already seen winter ascents, mostly via the normal routes (the Grépon and Drus had been climbed in winter in as early as the 1920s), yet the big and technical routes up vertical faces had, until then, always repelled attempts by would-be conquerors.

By the end of the 1950s the great harvest of winter ascents could commence and René Desmaison, for a time a

*Four figures from the era
of the great winter ascents.*

*Fernand Audibert
on the summit of the Blaitière.*

*Christian Mollier in front of
the north face of the Drus.*

*Georges Payot
returning from the Olan.*

*Claude Jaccoux
on the first winter ascent
of the Arête des Grands Montets
on the Aiguille Verte.*

*Previous page:
Marc Martinetti on the first winter ascent of the west face of the Blaitière.*

A meeting in the guides' office in 1964 to celebrate the achievements of the group of climbers that had set out to do great winter ascents. From left to right: Georges Payot, René Desmaison, Fernand Audibert, Christian Mollier, Camille Tournier (President of the Compagnie at the time), Gérard Devouassoux, Marc Martinetti, Jean Fanton and Yvon Masino.

member of the Compagnie, would become their champion. He opened up proceedings in 1957 with Jean Couzy on the west face of the Drus.

These winter ascents were a little like modern-day crusades. The climbers embarked on their assaults of the mountains, enduring storms and glacial cold, combating rock coated in black ice like stoic sinners submitting to a kind of gruelling alpine penance. It became standard practice to spend four or five days clinging to a wall of rock. Clearing away 10 centimetres of snow to get to holds on climbs inspired a new technique. Advances had been made in equipment design and materials, but harnesses remained rudimentary and clothing manufacturers had yet to make the most of the relatively new nylon fabrics. Moreover, as the routes were done at the coldest times of the year, they looked something like alpine re-enactments of the Stations of the Cross.

Nevertheless, an entire generation of Chamoniards would throw themselves into this new discipline. As the numbers of peasant-guides dwindled the young had their minds set on first ascents. They were almost lupine in their appearance: lean with hungry expressions and tousled hair, they looked ready to pounce at any moment

and with such power that they bore very little relation to the climbing teams of days gone by.

They wanted to fight it out like the amateur climbers, training on the Leschaux rock routes, in the Vercors and the Calanques for the fun of climbing.

The older guides didn't understand. Climbing for the fun of it? At least with a client it made sense, but with your friends! The youngsters were different from their elders. Firstly because their training was done at ENSA, secondly their studies opened up their minds to new possibilities, and finally they were challenging the Compagnie's traditions. The group turned to itself for encouragement and support.

There were enough of them and they were sufficiently talented not to need the moral and technical guidance of the older guides. The most active among them – Gérard Devouassoux, Christian Mollier, Georges Payot, Yvon Masino, Marc Martinetti – were in a kind of race to pull off the best first ascents and their enthusiasm was so infectious that it even rubbed off on Fernand Audibert, a guide slightly their senior.

Just after the first ascent of the Aspirant-guides Route on the Rochers du Parquet in the Vercors. Gérard Devouassoux, with a slight cut to his face, is sitting next to Jean-Marie Germain (centre) and Jean-Paul Fréchin (right).

Gérard Devouassoux
on the first winter ascent of the north face of the Drus (8 & 9 January 1964)
with Yvon Masino and Georges Payot.

Fernand Audibert on the Fissure Brown
during the first winter ascent of the west face of the Blaitière (19-21 January 1964).

The famous 'PDM' trio.
As well as long time climbing partners, Georges Payot, Gérard Devouassoux and Yvon Masino were also great friends.

In March 1960 four men set off from the Désert en Valjouffrey. They turned their backs on the remaining chimneys just poking out of snow and headed into the small Fond Turbat valley. The long line of moraine leading to the hut was deserted and the Oisans in winter can be as austere as parts of the Arctic. The four men lugging their mammoth packs to the hut had a single objective in mind: the Devies-Gervasutti route on the north face of the Olan, one of the hardest routes in the range.

As was often the case later on, the group was made up of amateurs and professionals. Having said that, on the most challenging routes the distinction meant very little. Clients, on the other hand, did not have the physique or training for this kind of climb.

Jean Puiseux was the amateur in a team that also included René Desmaison, Georges Payot (son of René) and Fernand Audibert. Taciturn and measured in his gestures, Georges had a real thirst to prove himself. In future years he would take part in some of the greatest climbs of the day, including the north face of Huascaran and Makalu's west pillar. For the time being at least, he honed his skills scaling the fortress of the Olan's north face.

Fernand had taken up mountaineering relatively late in life. Perhaps that is why, at 28 years old and barely qualified as an aspirant guide, he felt he

had some catching-up to do.

The four men made their way through a metre of fresh snow. The technique hasn't changed much: take down suits, dig bivouac sites with shovels, set up tents on the face and take as long is necessary to climb the icy cathedrals of rock.

On the Olan it would take four days and was a kind of odyssey in reverse. They went from the shade into the light, climbed up through the cold for an instant of warmth. Desmaison described it in the CAF's magazine La Montagne. *"We climbed the final metre and emerged into the clear air of the west summit. We were bathed in sunlight. The dark wall of rock was beneath our feet. We were filled with an immense feeling of elation. We put down our packs and ropes on the huge summit. Far below and in the distance, at the foot of the mountains to the west, snaked the slowly darkening valleys of Valgaudemar and Valjouffrey. Lights were already starting to twinkle down there while we were still in sunlight. We were in mid-air, far from the rest of the world."*

Done in the beginning of 1960, the Olan was the first of the great winter ascents. Of course, the Chamonix guides were not alone in the Alps. While the first winter and direct ascents of the Eiger, Matterhorn and Grandes Jorasses were pitting the likes of Bonatti, Hiebeler and Haston against each other, the guides joined the fray in an

Roland Ravanel would make the Cirque d'Argentière his own secret garden.

almost completely disinterested manner, above all obsessed by a kind of sporting ideal.

More and more guides were climbing just for the fun of it. The snow was conspicuous by its absence in winter 1964 and the visitor could walk through Chamonix without coming across a single square inch of the stuff. For the band of climbers – Payot, Devouassoux, Masino, Audibert – the conditions were fantastic and they were joined by another guide, Christian Mollier. A great friend of Devouassoux, an excellent climber and a quiet man, the future sports teacher Mollier admirably complemented the team. With the addition of Marc Martinetti there were now six of them. With the snow stubbornly refusing to fall, they scrambled to launch themselves at their winter objectives.

Together or separately they pulled off the first winter ascents of the north face of the Drus, the Nant Blanc face of the Verte, and the west face of the Blaitière and the north face of the Grands Charmoz in the Chamonix Aiguilles. They even made a winter ascent of the Grands Montets ridge on the Verte. For this they were joined by the Chirve (Servoz-born) Claude Jaccoux, who was studying in Paris and usually climbed with Bleausards, as Fontainebleau climbers are known.

They also made attempts on the Frêney Pillar and numerous other sites in the Mont Blanc range, and for these seven young mountaineers, January

and February 1964 would remain an exceptional couple of months.

Another group – Roland Ravanel, Gilles Ravanel, Roger Fournier and Roger Ravanel – was scouring the Argentière basin and the Perrons chain and they too put up some great routes in the Gardes du Plateau and the Pain de Sucre des Perrons.

The famous crystal-hunter
Roger Fournier
was one of the most active guides in Argentière.

The 1960s were also a time of great travel for the guides.
Here Fernand Audibert, part of the team that went to climb the north face of Huascaran,
contemplates another great Andean challenge, the south face of Huandoy.

Whether they be Chamoniards, Zermattois or Sherpas, one montagnard recognises a fellow mountaineer. Here Everest climber Tensing Norgay presents Pierre Leroux, who had just made the first ascent of Makalu, with a silk scarf, a symbol of friendship and respect.

PIERRE LEROUX AND THE GREAT EXPEDITIONS

If at the start of the 1960s the trend for winter ascents revived the guides' fortunes, there were great changes afoot on the expedition front. After the limited rounds of 8000ers, there are only 14 of them after all, the French turned their attentions to more 'pointy' objectives.

Robert Paragot, Edmond Denis, Lucien Bérardini and Guido Magnone had already found their places in the history books with ascents of the south face of Aconcagua and Patagonia's Fitz Roy.

The Himalaya was still a vast untouched field of opportunities and the French had already eagerly set about making the first ascent of another 8000er, Makalu.

Led by Jean Franco, the entire French team, summited the 8463m high pyramid in eastern Nepal and the world's fifth highest mountain in 1955 with no fuss or fanfare.

As in the Alps the teams were made up of a few enlightened amateurs – Jean Couzy and Guido Magnone – and experienced guides such as Lionel Terray, Jean Bouvier, Serge Coupé, Maurice Lenoir and the hugely talented guide Pierre Leroux.

Originally from Paris, Leroux gravitated towards Chamonix working with private clients and, on occasion, the military. He was one of the greatest mountaineers of his day and had climbed the north face of the Eiger at the same time as Gaston Rébuffat, so naturally he applied to join the Compagnie. Since accepting Terray and Lachenal, the Compagnie had quietly admitted six other 'foreign' applicants. The 'foreigners' who added their names to the Charlets, Couttets and Bossonneys were Marius Nikolli, Fernand Pareau, André Braconnay, Marius Mora, Gaston Cathiard and Victor Schmit.

As the Chamoniards could not flatly refuse admittance to these highly competent men, they decided to test their powers of perseverance instead. Leroux described the ritual: *"It was a kind of rule that it usually took three applications before being admitted, one just had to take it on the chin..."* So it was that in 1955, with the Earth curving away beneath his feet as he gazed across at Everest and Lhotse, Leroux learnt that his application was held over for another year. Tales of glory from the ascents of 8000ers did not appear to have reached or very much

*The summit ridge of Jannu (7710m) has a magical air to it
and its first ascent was one of the great success stories of Himalayan climbing in the 1960s.*

bothered the Chamoniards. Yet it was only put back for a couple of years, as he was finally admitted to the Compagnie in 1957.

The same year the French Mountaineering Federation (FFM) decided to change tack, as all the 8000ers had been climbed. The FFM wanted to take Himalayan climbing in a different direction, seeking more technical objectives below the magic 8000m mark.

It turned its attention to Jannu, a peak next to Kangchenjunga (the world's third highest peak). In eastern Nepal near the border with India, Jannu is a Himalayan Drus to Kangchenjunga's Verte. Leroux was sent on a reconnaissance trip to the mountain together with Jean Bouvier and Guido Magnone and they spent a month and a half exploring the little-known surrounding area. *"It was a marvellous and carefree journey on foot, made with friends. Covering 30 or 40 kilometres a day for a month and a half, we walked up valleys, climbed small, 5000 to 6000-metre peaks, took photos and made sketches before crossing the pass leading to the neighbouring valley."* They explored the area, scouting out valleys and mountain passes, and recording a part of the Himalayas previously unknown in the West.

Eighteen months later, in spring 1959, they were

in India to make a first attempt. The team now had a few new members including René Desmaison. That spring they had to turn round just 300 metres from the summit, the climbing proving too hard for a team reduced to just two members, Terray and Leroux, strong enough to meet the challenge. The expedition leader Jean Franco had to console his friend. Leroux described the scene in his book, Guide. *"I came out of the tent and went and sat down a few metres away. It was hopeless and I started to cry. For it to come to this after months of focussing all our energies on a single objective was brutally disappointing... We were so close, it felt like we could still do it! I wept softly and little by little the initial stab of pain subsided. I went back to the tent and Jean Franco took my hand, saying 'Let it go Pierrot. We'll come back and next time we'll get Jannu!'"*

The expedition set off again in spring 1962 and reached the summit without a hitch. Terray, Leroux, Desmaison, Robert Paragot, André Bertrand, Paul Keller, Jean Ravier, Jean Bouvier and Yves Pollet-Villard all climbed the fabulous summit ridge on what some consider the perfect mountain.

André Devouassoux (right) in front of the Albert 1er hut
with Leopold, former king of the Belgians, and Camille Claret-Tournier.

*Never seen without a cap on his head,
a scarf about his neck, and smile playing
on his lips, André à Daubert,
as he was known to the people of Argentière,
symbolised a great guiding tradition.*

A GUIDE'S FATE: ANDRÉ DEVOUASSOUX

Even if attitudes were changing and climbers were making ever more audacious ascents, the Chamonix guides continued to perpetuate the old image of happy days in the mountains. At the start of the 1960s the figure of André Devouassoux symbolized the union of tradition and technical ability.

Rarely without his beret (later to be replaced by a cap), Devouassoux was considered one of the most active guides in the Compagnie, a Verte and Chardonnet specialist. The mere mention of his name was enough to create an aura of respect among one's peers in the mountain huts.

By the 1960s André à Daubert, as he was known in the valley, was no longer a young man. And at 54 years old he was hugely experienced. Yet the man who had accompanied Georges Charlet on the Verte's Couturier Couloir and had made the first guided ascent of the famous north face of the Aiguille d'Argentière, decided to slow down a bit. Watching his grandson, Raymond, playing in the fields in La Joux without his father, who had been killed during a rescue attempt, he realized it was time to stop doing long routes. And it wasn't for want of clients. They would visit him at the home his family had owned for generations opposite the church in Argentière. *"André, you wouldn't have a bit of time to go to the Forbes Arête, would you?"*

would come the question. Always smiling and with a deadpan sense of humour, he would pack his canvas bag, wrap his scarf around his neck and head out to join his clients. Like the majority of the guides he had work to do in the fields before setting off into the mountains. He would bring the hay in, sometimes not finishing before dusk, and it was often night-time before he reached the Albert 1er hut. He would then start out with his clients under starlight. He set a moderate pace; instead of rushing his clients, he wanted to share his high-altitude playground with them and had an unshakeable sense of joie de vivre. He was already known for his sense of fun in the 1930s, when he was spotted nailing the berets left on coat hooks in huts to the wall. A good number of guides were late setting off the following morning thanks to Devouassoux's prank...

His good humour remained undimmed by age or the harshness of the work and from time to time he would invent new games for himself and his clients. Such as the time, with Mademoiselle Barat, he did the traverse of the Perrons backwards. These stunts were perhaps a little unorthodox but they did show how much he enjoyed his job.

This despite the fact his family had been sorely tested by its relationship with the mountains. His

*The Tour Ronde: 'a cow mountain' ('une montagne à vaches')
as André Devouassoux called it. Nevertheless, it was here that he made his final ascent.*

uncle Jean Ducroz died on the Verte in 1919 and his first cousin Roger Devouassoux was lost on the same mountain 12 years later. His brother-in-law Jean Ravanel and nephew Gilbert were killed in a fall on the Aiguille de Roc in 1945, while in 1947 another of his first cousins, Auguste Devouassoux, was killed by rock fall on the Aiguille du Tour. Then in 1957 his son-in-law, also called Jean Ducroz, was killed during a rescue mission. One might have thought the family cursed. André decided to make the most of life and only do routes he wanted to climb. For that reason it was pointless asking him to take you up the normal route on Mont Blanc as it bored him...

He cultivated the personality the world saw and wouldn't have changed his sturdy Bonneval trousers and checked shirt for anything in the world. Just like his contemporaries, Camille Tournier and Michel Bozon, he was a peasant-guide who loved his farm as much as he loved the mountains.

They were one and the same for Devouassoux, which perhaps explains why he never reproached the mountains for taking his loved ones from him. That was the mountain way of life. The land had always been that way: it gave and it took away. He never spoke of these things with his clients and he was irrepressibly cheerful with a sharp mind and something of a way with words. *"Right, I've got*

to make a phone call", he would laconically tell his clients before spending a penny.

One morning in July 1960 he packed his bag as he always did with his 10-point crampons strapped to the top of his pack. He picked up his trusty Simond axe with its wooden shaft and told his wife, as he always did, *"don't worry, it's a cow mountain [walk in the park]!"* He had a point. The normal route on the Tour Ronde can be very easy and he had done it numerous times before. He was also guiding an old client of his, Charles Trédé, who in turn wanted to introduce his son to the mountains and climbing.

They spent the night at the Torino hut and perhaps Devouassoux told them the story of Doctor Colaud, whom he had taken on the traverse of the Drus. While he was changing into his espadrilles on the famous 'Z' pitch, the Doctor's nailed boots, which he had not clipped to his bag properly, fell all the way down the north face. The unfortunate Doctor then had to descend the entire route in his gym shoes, which were in tatters by the time he got back to Chamonix. The story always made Devouassoux laugh as it had a happy ending.

They set off at four o'clock in the morning. They walked in silence across the Combe Maudite and started climbing just above the bergschrund. They quickly reached the summit and the wea-

The Arête Kuffner, or Frontier Ridge, remains one of the best routes in the massif.
The Kuffner is just opposite the Tour Ronde and André Devouassoux would have got a good view of it
and its instantly recognisable 'Passage de l'Androsace' (seen here) on his last day in the mountains.

ther was glorious. They stopped at the top to take in the marvellous panorama surrounding them with Devouassoux pointing out the Brenva Spur, Route Major and the Kuffner (Frontier) Ridge. It was eight o'clock and knowing that the sun comes onto the east face quickly, Devouassoux decided to start down. He sent his clients down first while he held the rope tight above them. Jean-Louis Trédé gave an account of what happened next to the Dauphiné newspaper. *"I tried to my best to hold our guide and my father as they fell. I was in front when the stone hit André Devouassoux and didn't hear the shouts from the climbers on the ridge, warning us about the rock."* Spinning as it fell, the stone hit André Devouassoux on the head, killing him outright.

His name was thus added to the list of guides from the family killed in the mountains. And more family members were to die in the mountains in the years that followed: first a cousin, Joseph Ducroz, in 1961 and then a nephew, Roger Fournier, in 1976. They too were guides.

The fate of guides? A man's fate? Perhaps some families are cursed after all...

An eternal fraternity:
the guides' grave in Argentière.
All the Argentière guides killed in the mountains
are buried here.

A LA MÉMOIRE
DES GUIDES MORTS EN MONTAGNE

MICHEL CROZ _ CERVIN _ 1865
JOSEPH DEVOUASSOUX _ LES COURTES _ 1885
CLÉMENT DEVOUASSOUX _ LES COURTES _ 1885
MARC DEVOUASSOUX _ MONT BLANC _ 1905
JEAN DUCROZ _ AIGUILLE VERTE _ 1919
JEAN CHARLET _ DENT DU GÉANT _ 1923
CAMILLE SIMOND _ DENT DU GÉANT _ 1923
ROGER DEVOUASSOUX _ AIGUILLE VERTE _ 1932
ALPHONSE SIMOND _ COL DU MIDI _ 1940
JEAN A. RAVANEL _ AIGUILLE DU ROC _ 1945
RENÉ RAVANEL _ AIGUILLE VERTE _ 1945
JEAN H. RAVANEL _ COL DE BALME _ 1946
AUGUSTE DEVOUASSOUX _ AIGUILLE DU TOUR _ 1947
RAYMOND RAVANEL _ L'INDEX _ 1956
JEAN DUCROZ _ ENVERS DES AIGUILLES _ 1957
ANDRÉ DEVOUASSOUX _ TOUR RONDE _ 1960
JOSEPH DUCROZ _ GLACIER D'ARGENTIÈRE _ 1961
XAVIER CRETTON _ AIGUILLE VERTE _ 1964
VITAL RAVANEL _ AIGUILLE LA FLORIA _ 1965
ROGER FOURNIER _ ROCHERS DE LESCHAUX _ 1976
GUY DEVOUASSOUX _ GRANDS-MONTETS _ 1977
GEORGES BETTEMBOURG _ AIGUILLE VERTE _ 1983

*A challenging objective for a talented team.
Lionel Terray and Guido Magnone approach Fitz Roy
on the Argentina-Chile border.*

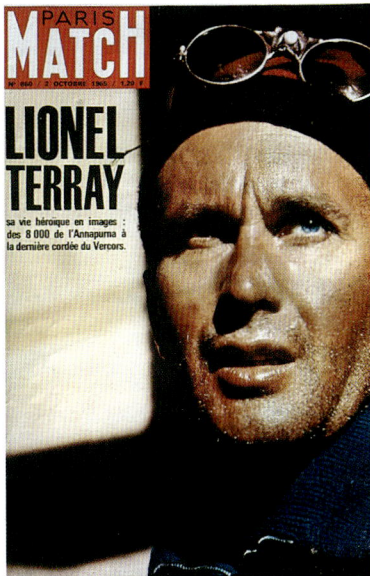

With his ascents of Annapurna, Fitz Roy and Jannu, Lionel Terray was undoubtedly the most well known French climber of his day and was often front page news, as these two issues of Paris Match can attest.

Below: Marc Marinetti was Lionel Terray's climbing partner on his fateful last climb. Their bodies were found wrapped around each other at the bottom of the Arêtes du Gerbier in the Vercors.

LIONEL TERRAY'S LAST ROUTE

Lionel Terray had been based in Chamonix for 20 years. In the eyes of the general public he was emblematic of the post-war generation of climbers, he set the example and was a modern-day hero with his strengths and his faults, just like anyone else.

A climbing heavyweight, he had revealed his sentimental side on his return from the Annupurna expedition. However, the days when he raced his way up the north faces of the Eiger and the Grandes Jorasses with Lachenal were long gone. Lachenal had been swallowed up by a crevasse on the Vallée Blanche in 1955 and on hearing the news Terray couldn't stop himself from exclaiming *"the rotten swine, he could have been successful at everything, even his death!"*

With his climbing partner dead, Terray felt a little lonely in the confines of the Alps and in the 1950s his thoughts turned to foreign destinations. He made first ascents Fitz Roy, mountains in Peru, Makalu, and the north face of Chacraraju, again in Peru. During this time he did not forget the Compagnie. He didn't always agree with some of its members but curiously he still felt the need to go back to it and take

groups into the mountain. So it was in 1958 when Terray the great Himalayan climber took a film crew up to the Couvercle hut.

Nothing seemed to dent his enthusiasm for mountaineering and here he was taking part in Marcel Ichac's Les Etoiles de Midi ("Stars at Noon"), one of the most successful climbing films ever made. There were no stars on the vast natural set, just a few friends – with Terray were Desmaison, Rébuffat as well as the Swiss climber Michel Vaucher – playing themselves. It was an international success.

Then he would go off travelling again, often with the help of his wife Marianne. He was on Jannu (twice) with Pierre Leroux. Yet despite succeeding on it in 1962, he was off travelling again. This time he went to Peru and then back to Nepal where he made a successful attempt on Nilgiri. That came to eight months away from Chamonix, he was becoming quite a globetrotter...

In 1964 he was off again, this time for Alaska and the splendid, unclimbed Mount Huntington. Terray was an enthusiastic forty-year old and, as is

Mount Huntington in Alaska, a journey into the realm of extreme cold.
On this expedition Terray found himself surrounded by a team of young climbers
that included Marc Martinetti and Maurice Gicquel.

often the case, he climbed with mountaineers that were sometimes as much as 20 years his junior. He was on the summit with Marc Martinetti, a talented young 23 year-old guide who had just joined the Compagnie.

His experience with these climbers from a younger generation helped him realize that he was no longer the climber he had been twenty years earlier, climbing the Eiger and the Jorasses with his mate Louis.

Nevertheless, he had reached forty and had matured since his adventures with Lachenal... At least on the outside. At heart, this great explorer of mountains had retained his youthful enthusiasm and vitality, which he described in his book Les Conquérants de l'Inutile ("Conquistadors of the Useless"): *"To be quite honest I had often felt it was time to stop before my luck turned – but these were times when I could not sleep for nervous fatigue, or when I got back to the valley exhausted after over-prolonged exertions. At such times I would typically*

dream of a quiet life, divided between the soft warmth of my own fireside and the love of nature. No sooner had I pulled myself together, however, than I would start to ponder on the past. The circumstances of daily life would start to seem petty, ugly and monotonous, until the memory of my more intense hours began to obsess me. I would find myself burning with desire to experience others as ardent, and once again I would hurl myself into the great game."

And the mountains were his playground. The great guide was still a great amateur at heart; as soon as the opportunity presented itself he would head off into the mountains once again. In any case, he didn't have anything left to prove, the Bonattis and Desmaisons of the world having taken over that role. He could have fun!

At the start of the autumn season Marc Martinetti suggested they climb the Arc en Cercle, a crack route on the Gerbier in the Vercors. The peaks of the Mont Blanc range were covered in a snowy pall bringing the climbing season to an end, so he

Armand Charlet and Lionel Terray in the 1950s.
The two men had a great deal of respect for each other.

accepted. The weather was unstable and Marianne was worried. Trying to reassure her, Terray called out as he climbed into the car *"the Vercors isn't the Himalaya you know!"*

Terray was perfectly at home on the twenty odd pitches of grade V and V+ crack climbing with a few sections of easy (A1) aid climbing through small roofs using etriers (small rope ladders). Wallcreepers flew over their heads, while below them the village of Prélenfrey looked tiny. They were pleased to reach the end of the final hard sections as now there were only grass-covered rock slopes to cross to get to the Gerbier ridges. They chose to keep the rope on as they crossed this final tricky section even though they couldn't belay each other. Suddenly one of them slipped. Now they were both sliding and there was no way of stopping their fatal fall.

Les Conquérants de l'Inutile
(The Conquistadors of the Useless)
a classic work of mountain literature.
This is the distinctive red cover of 1995 Editions Guérin reprint.

Terray had written in Bataille pour le Jannu ("The Battle for Jannu"), *"Under other skies, other peaks await us…"*

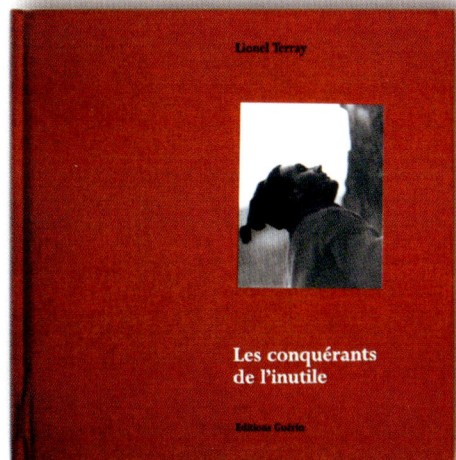

René Claret-Tournier poses with Otto Flich, an industrialist from the Ruhr, and Anderl Heckmair, one of the team that made the first ascent of the north face of the Eiger. The pair of them had the tricky task of guiding the German industrialist up Mont Blanc.

RENÉ CLARET-TOURNIER: MONT BLANC MAN

And what about Mont Blanc while all this was going on? One might have thought it had sunk from the limelight with all these other ascents being made.

Far from it. René Claret-Tournier was setting a record on it that is not likely to be beaten for quite a while. His climbing odyssey took him to the summit of the highest mountain in Western Europe five hundred and thirty times. In days, that is the equivalent of more than a year and a half spent at 4810 metres.

Things took off for Claret-Tournier after the Second World War. He had learnt German during his time as a prisoner of war and it proved to be very useful, as just after the war many of his climbing companions were Germans and Austrians. First was Otto Flich, an industrialist from the Ruhr, who employed Claret-Tournier and a certain Anderl Heckmair, one of the four climbers to make the first ascent of the north face of the Eiger. His distinguished clients also included Josef Klaus, the Austrian Chancellor.

René witnessed the evolution of climbing on Mont Blanc: *"At the start of my career I would often spend the whole season with two or three clients. They arri-* *ved in the valley with their chauffeurs and they would wait for their bosses at the hotel! While on Mont Blanc we would sleep in two small wooden huts. There weren't many unguided parties in the 1950s and there would quite often be 25 guides in one hut."*

The popularisation of the mountains led him to spend a great deal of time on Mont Blanc's snowy dome and some seasons he would climb it thirty times in a row. Whether it was battling his way along the Goûter ridge, crossing the Grand Couloir, climbing up towards the rocky outcrop of the Tournette and getting lost on the Dôme du Goûter, he had a wealth of good stories. The route from the Nid d'Aigle to the summit was packed full of memories.

He still had a penchant for mischief at the age of 80 and gleefully told the story of a young Swiss lady he guided. *"It was very cold that day and our gear wasn't as good as it is now. At around the Vallot hut my client suddenly had to answer a call of nature, but she couldn't undo her trousers as her hands were stiff with the cold. She embarrassedly turned to me asking for help. 'Don't be embarrassed, you're old enough to be my daughter', I quipped in an effort not to give her a complex given the*

Despite his attachment to Mont Blanc
and like all guides of his generation,
René would find time to pay his respects to the Virgin Mary
on the summit of the Grépon. The Chamoniards guides came to know
all of the mountain's slabs, cracks, ledges and pillars by heart...

circumstances. Once I'd pulled her drawers down, she could finally relieve herself and in return I got a hearty 'Thanks Dad'!"

Sometimes, however, he saw the mountain's dark side, such as the time he was there after a spell of bad weather. *"It was different every time; the people, the conditions, the weather. During a storm I'd often hear my clients saying 'luckily we've got a guide!' When in fact I was just as lost as they were and I just had to trust my instinct. In any case, I always refused to take clients out in bad weather. I once got stuck in the Vallot with Lionel Terray, and with us were four Spaniards who, despite the gusts of wind and our advice, wanted to climb. They left in*

the most atrocious conditions. We'd managed to get our clients under shelter and two days later the good weather returned and I set off for Mont Blanc again. I found the four frozen climbers sitting at the foot of the Rochers de la Tournette. They looked like they were sleeping peacefully but in fact they were dead, frozen stiff by the cold."

René did not have a single accident during his long career and even joked about the fact that the only time he had hurt himself was falling out of an apple tree. Which just goes to show what kind of a profession guiding can be, still one shouldn't forget Newton and his apple tree induced injury...

The west face of the Blaitière the day after a storm from the west.
In the early 1960s, the Brown route was still quite an extraordinary climb with its pitches of French 6a.

Charles Bozon
won the World Slalom Championships
held in Chamonix in 1962.
He was also a talented mountaineer.
In this photo he puts his '10 point' technique
to the extreme...

THE LAST BIG RESCUES
AND CHARLES BOZON'S GREATEST EXPLOIT

The turning point in mountain rescues came in the middle of the 1960s. This was a period of tremendous change, as exemplified by the use of helicopters, and the Chamoniards gave their all.

Let us start with the local boy Charles Bozon. Known to everyone as Charlot, he was at the height of his game in 1962 when he won the World Slalom Championships and was a kind of older brother figure to the French skiers Jean-Claude Killy and François Bonlieu. He was considered one of the best skiers in the world and had nothing left to prove, yet he continued `his wanderings. He had a genuine love of the mountains and mountaineering and never missed a chance to spend time on Mont Blanc's ridges and slopes.

In 1963 he was a teacher at ENSA and took part in an epic rescue mission on the Aiguille de Blaitière in the Chamonix Aiguilles. One morning that August a Scottish climber peeled off a route above the Brown crack and fell onto a rocky ledge. All Bozon and René Novel knew, as they climbed aboard the Alouette II helicopter that was to take them to the foot of the west face was that he was seriously injured. It looked like the weather was coming in and they had to move quickly. The helicopter dropped them, together with Gendarme Monet of the PGHM (Peloton de Gendarmerie de Haute Montagne, or mountain rescue police) and two

CRS men (from the Compagnies Républicaines de Sécurité, whose responsibilities include riot control and mountain rescue), off as close as it could get to the rock face. Not a word was said as they prepared their equipment and set off up the first pitch.

At 8pm a violent storm erupted, the deafening claps of thunder amplified by the walls of rock surrounding them. Gendarme Monet and the CRS men gave up somewhere below the Brown crack. They couldn't see further than two metres in front of them, the rain continued to fall and there was more hard climbing above them. Bozon was leading and climbed through the grade VI crack that looked more like a mountain torrent. They didn't have time to belay each other, as they had to get to the young Scotsman as quickly as possible. The rain fell even harder. They took half an hour to climb the remaining thirty metres up to the ledge. They finally reached the platform where the victim lay, he had slipped into a coma and his heart was barely beating at all. They had to get him off the mountain as soon as possible. Bozon hauled him onto his back and started down a long series of rappels. The CRS men below understood what was happening and shone a huge searchlight onto the rock face. The rescuers reached the bottom of the face at 4.30 in the morning and the injured climber was in hospital an hour later.

The arrival of helicopters caused a small revolution in how rescues were carried out in the massif. The guides still took part in a few rescues at this time but by the beginning of the 1970s they were entirely carried out by a specialist body made up of gendarmes and CRS men.

This was without doubt Bozon's greatest victory, in a human sense. But he would not have time to savour his succes. On 7 July 1964 he set off for the Arête des Grands Montets on the Aiguille Verte with a group of trainee guides from ENSA.

He no longer worked at ENSA and didn't have to go with them, as shortly before he had taken over the running of the Brévent cable car. Nevertheless, not having done the route before, Charlot thought this would be a great opportunity to pull his crampons on again and get his hands dirty. He arrived late and the cable car had already set off. It came back and he joined his former colleagues, including René Novel, in the car. They slept at the top station of the lift and set off at night to climb the long ridge overlooking the mountain's Nant Blanc and Argentière faces. At 8.30am they were nearing the Pointe de Ségogne. Soon they were on the final snow slopes with only a few metres to go to the summit. Suddenly the snow gave way under the weight of the climbers. They had loosened a slab of wind blown snow. The entire team fell into the Cordier Couloir and the lifeless bodies of fourteen mountain professionals were recovered from the bergschrund below.

The names of Charles Bozon, Maurice Simond and the aspirant guide Xavier Cretton had just been added to the list of guides from the Compagnie killed in the mountains. The accident on the Verte was a huge and terrible tragedy, yet it didn't stop the guides continuing to work in the mountains.

Can one stop a person with a real passion in life?

Although the PGHM was already starting to take shape, the guides would still rush to help as soon as they were needed for rescue missions and the two generations acted side by side. As on 26 August 1965, when Christian Mollier, Gérard Devouassoux, and Marcel Burnet set off for the Bonatti Pillar on the Drus, where two Yugoslav climbers had been stuck for eight days. They reached the green slabs in three hours and by midnight they had got the stranded Yugoslavs back down to a hut. Rescuers from the EHM had been trying to reach them for the preceding eight days...

Over the course of the years that followed, Gérard Devouassoux would become the leader of this new generation. Generous and brimming with ideas and plans, he would take part in numerous other rescues. These included the hugely controversial rescue, by several different teams including one led by Gary Hemming and René Desmaison, of two Germans who were trapped on the west face of the Drus. Then there was the first time a helicopter was able to set a team down on the Walker Spur on the Grandes Jorasses, and the rescue of Desmaison himself from the Jorasses.

The PGHM teams were getting stronger and better

Today all rescue operations in the Mont Blanc Massif are carried out by the PGHM,
yet members of the Compagnie des Guides might still take part in the event of a catastrophic accident.

organised and the guides were involved in fewer and fewer rescue missions. They had left their mark on rescues in the past, their faults as well as their humanity, as in 1945 when they recovered the body of one of their own, René Ravanel. They laid siege to the Verte, waiting 14 days for the weather to clear, to return the body to his widow, so as not to leave him in the mountains.

Climbing up to camp II with the Lho La (5800m),
a pass on the Nepal-Tibet border, and a small peak, the Khumbu Tse (6700m), in the background.

Everest and Nuptse (right) seen from Kala Pattar,
a classic view of the Roof of the World.

CHAMONIARDS ON EVEREST

Released from their role as rescuers by the start of the 1970s, one could argue that the Chamoniards had a little more time for themselves and were able to explore a little more of the world.

The Mont Blanc range naturally remained the cornerstone of the Chamonix guides' profession.

The 'PDM' team, of Payot, Devouassoux and Masino, dreamed of following in the footsteps of the great pioneering climbers who first went to Annapurna and Makalu. With Maurice Gicquel, a teacher at ENSA, the trio organised one of the first lightweight expeditions to climb a 7000-metre mountain. They chose Moditse Peak (7195m), a subsidiary summit of Annapurna South.

The experience would leave a great impression on them and a new era of Himalayan exploration was about to begin.

Once again guides and non-professionals, Chamoniards and 'foreigners' would join forces on some highly successful expeditions. These included a successful ascent of the west pillar of Makalu in 1971. Georges Payot was one of the group of mountaineers that was writing a new page in the history of Himalayan climbing and the following year he was on Nepal's Pumori.

A new project was quick to take shape in Chamonix:

the Compagnie's first Everest expedition. They chose Everest as at the time there had not yet been a French ascent of the world's highest mountain. Moreover, it had yet to be commercialized to the extent it is today and was still considered a kind of Cape Horn of mountaineering.

The provisional team was to be Gérard Devouassoux, Christian Mollier, Georges Payot and Fernand Audibert. They got a permit for autumn 1976 but were in competition with the Frenchman Pierre Mazeaud's team, which was planning to go in autumn 1974.

Fate would step in, when in October 1973 Mazeaud was named France's Secretary of State for Youth Affairs and Sports and he had to put his Everest plans on hold, his official responsibilities preventing him from going on expedition. He suggested to the Chamoniards that they exchange climbing permits.

The initial team grew to include Claude Ancey, Daniel Audibert, Jean-Paul Balmat, Denis Ducroz, the medic Eric Lasserre and the photographer and filmmaker Pierre Tairraz. The team was sponsored by the wine-maker Kriter, which had just financed a round the world sailing trip, the mountains perfectly complementing the sea.

Before leaving, Gérard Devouassoux had time to open the Office de Haute Montagne, an office in

*Gérard Devouassoux
in training a few days before leaving for Everest.*

Chamonix where climbers can get information about conditions and routes. The information is provided by mountaineers themselves and was the first of its kind to be set up in Europe.

After 19 days walking through the monsoon rain and under continuous attack from leeches, they arrived at the foot of Everest on 17 August 1974. Their objective was the mountain's long west ridge, a logical thread of ice and rock leading to the Roof of the World.

The nine-kilometre ridge starts at the Lho La and climbs 2800 metres to the summit of Everest, and at this time it was still unclimbed.

It was decided very early on that they would climb without bottled oxygen and camps sprung up along the route. They suffered from the cold as it tumbled over them from the Tibetan plateau and they were in the middle of nowhere, but they were in the heart of the world's greatest mountain range. They soldiered on and by carrying loads they were able to establish camp 1 at 5800m and camp 2 at 6400m.

On 7 September Gérard Devouassoux reported to his family that: *"Everything is working perfectly. We are making rapid progress and 15 days after starting out, we have almost reached the 7000m mark. I think we've done the most technically difficult parts of the climb and we've put caving ladders in the steepest rock sections. This is to avoid our ropes being swept away by avalanche or cut by rock fall. The monsoon isn't quite over yet and is sending us a great deal of snow. I think we'll have to wait until 10 September for the weather to get any better."*

As predicted, Jean-Paul Balmat and Claude Ancey were able to establish camp 3 at 7000m on 9 September. While they were doing this, Devouassoux, Pierre Tairraz and six Sherpas were carrying loads from camp 1 to camp 2.

It was then that a storm hit. They had time to take refuge in two tiny holes cut into a wall of snow. Tairraz, exhausted by the work they had just done, took half a sleeping pill. Devouassoux took the other half with a few gulps of soup. Tairraz immediately fell asleep, while the Sherpas continued to cut out a platform and Devouassoux heated up the soup for them.

Tairraz woke with a start and a terrifying feeling of being smothered. It was 7.20pm, what was going on? He was stuck, the fabric of the tent pressing against his mouth and his hands over his chest. He was still drowsy and at first he thought it was just the falling snow that had caused the tent to collapse. One of the Sherpas, Dordje, was also caught under the snowy blanket.

They had to face facts. An avalanche had swept over the camp. They struggled to free themselves

In the Khumbu on the walk in. First row, l. to r.: Christian Mollier and Gérard Devouassoux.

Sitting behind them, l. to r.: Sonam Galsen (sirdar), Pierre Tairraz (photographer and film-maker), Eric Lasserre (doctor), Fernand Audibert, Daniel Audibert and Jean-Paul Balmat. Standing: Claude Ancey, Georges Payot and Denis Ducroz.

for over an hour. By squirming and scrabbling they managed to tear the fabric of the tent and free themselves from the icy pall. Outside the darkness enveloped the mountains.

Nothing remained of the camp and the tent where the four other Sherpas were supposed to be sheltering had disappeared.

Pierre Tairraz set about organising the rescue and by chance he found his partner's shoes but not their owner. They dug away furiously at the snow. Suddenly there was a cry. Someone was still alive, just the other side of the snow-filled tent. It was where Gérard and his Sherpa, Yishi, should have been. They managed to recover Yishi alive but Gérard wasn't there. They dug and raked away at the snow with their hands, frantically probing, but they found nothing. It was as if he had vanished.

The three survivors' nightmare continued as they tried to recover the tattered remains of the tent. They found some overboots and a down jacket, just enough to survive at altitude, among a stash of gear they had made the day before. It was a long and icy night for the men as they ran events over and over in their minds.

With daylight they saw that a huge avalanche had literally blown through the camp. It had even reached as far as camp 1. Here the expedition doctor Eric Lasserre was witnessing another tragedy

unfold, as it became clear that another Sherpa had been swept away and killed by the blast of the avalanche.

Tairraz, Yishi and Dordje managed to get back to camp 1 where they were met by Georges Payot. Jean-Paul Balmat, Claude Ancey and another Sherpa were still stuck at camp 3 and it took them two more days to get back to base camp.

The Everest expedition that had started with such high hopes had ended in tragedy and pain, and it was out of the question that the guides continue.

Gérard Devouassoux and four Sherpas had seemingly disappeared off the face of the mountain. It wasn't until nearly 20 years later, and another expedition found their bodies, that the team was able to piece together what must have happened.

Devouassoux was found in the tent with the four Sherpas. He had probably been having difficulty sleeping and left his tent to have a friendly cup of tea with his Nepalese colleagues. The avalanche hit their tent and carried them all off the ridge and into the void. In death, all montagnards are equal...

Marcel Burnet on the Trident in 1971.
In the mountains and at the heart of the Compagnie he was a steady and hugely reliable figure.

Opposite the 4000m peaks of Saas Fee.
A former pisteur, he was hugely knowledgeable about snow and snow conditions.
Nevertheless, he was caught out by a wind slab avalanche.

THE GREAT GUIDE MARCEL BURNET

1974 was turning out to be a particularly black year for the Compagnie, as another of its great figures, Marcel Burnet, had been killed that spring.

If in the eyes of the general public the great guides were Gérard Devouassoux and Lionel Terray, for many Chamoniards Marcel Burnet was the embodiment of a true guide, the man who went in front.

Despite the 70 odd rescues he had to his name and the brilliance with which he accomplished his astonishing work rate, his reputation never really extended beyond the valley. It was as if this timeless play of light and shadow that had affected the guides since the very beginning of our story had only become more real.

Twenty years after his death, he was still fondly remembered, as Jean-Pierre Devouassoux explained: *"Marcel had conviction, technique and authority. He was, in a way, the Compagnie's de facto leader, morally speaking. In the mountains everything with him seemed easy. Beyond the sphere of the mountains, he symbolised the notion of going that extra mile and using one's skills to help others."*

Born in 1922, he finished third (together with Lionel Terray) in his class for his guide's exam but was never interested in making earth-shattering first ascents. He was a peasant-guide, happy to be

in the mountains with a real desire to share his passion for them and to take part in rescues.

In 1965, during the rescue of two Yugoslav climbers stranded on the Drus, the young men accompanying him where the greatest guides of their generation and even they had difficulty keeping up with him. He also had the respect of his peers and they would pronounce, *"you're going with Marcel? Then there's nothing to worry about."*

In March 1974, he was making his way along his thirty-sixth Chamonix-Zermatt winter Haute Route. He came to a short, doubtful-looking gully and started heading up it. The snow slid away beneath him and he managed to turn around only to be caught in a second snow slide that had started higher up. He was 54 years old.

He would be sorely missed, not least by his clients. One of them wrote a touching prose poem in his honour: *"He died in the mountains. He didn't have a choice. He had chosen to be what he was: a life spent on his feet, walking in front, breaking trail for others. Now words have little meaning; did they ever mean anything? We speak very little at altitude, our breath is too precious; but there's nothing to stop us smiling! A broad smile earned by reality matching our dreams. And the happiness he brought his family. A broad smile, simple and spontaneous, from which everyday*

gestures flow. 'Take the hold on the left!' 'Bring your foot up!' 'Smile!' Your body sways and the altitude increases... The rope runs through my fingers. There he is, he's done it! He turns to me smiling: 'Up you go! Your turn. It's easy, you'll see!' Everything's easy with him and a smile like his in front of you. We went anywhere, only to be with him. Once on the summit we would look for something meaningful to say, to thank him. We never thought of anything. So we just said 'It's beautiful! You haven't got a cigarette, have you?' He always had some (he always had everything) and handed over the packet. 'Help yourself. I've got my pipe.' Too much wind for the lighter? We'd light them from his pipe, his eyes glowing with pleasure.

If he hasn't come back, it's because he is sat up there, comfortable on his backpack, in his fiefdom of snow and granite, contemplating the heavens and the valley below.

Now when the wind comes in from the west and a wisp of cloud fades away above the Verte and the Drus, we, those Down Below, will say: 'Look, it's Marcel lighting his pipe!'"

That year the guides' course bore his name as a mark of honour and Marcel Burnet was still breaking trail.

1974 marked a real turning point. Whether by accident or an act of fate, the two guides who symbolised the Compagnie, inside and outside it, with their different temperaments, ideas, and techniques, died one after the other, less than six months apart. Two great changes were about to take place. The ideas espoused by the May 1968 protest movement would radically change the face of alpinism. The arrival of a new generation of city-born mountain guides and the creation of an independent guides' bureau (met with great resistance at first but accepted now) would contribute to the evolution of the guiding profession.

Marcel Burnet and Gérard Devouassoux were no longer there but the Compagnie had many more great pages of mountaineering history to write.

Marcel Burnet and his trusty pipe opposite the Grand Capucin.
He would let his clients savour the magic moment as they arrived on the summit,
saying simply "See, I told you we'd do the route."

The Compagnie 1971
1. Jean Charlet
2. Gilbert Ducroz
3. Roger Bozon
4. Jean Ravanel
5. André Ducroz
6. Georges Burnet
7. Michel Ravanel
8. Georges Payot
9. Camille Ravanel
10. Pierre Perret
11. Pierre Leroux
12. Pierre Couttet
13. Jean Payot
14. Alfred Payot
15. Bernard Devouassoud
16. Georges Deck
17. Clément Hugon
18. Roger Simond
19. André Braconnay
20. Jean-François Reymond
21. Raoul Simond
22. Paul Demarchi
23. Roger Simond
24. Victor Schmith
25. Marius Nikolli
26. Marcel Burnet
27. Gérard Burnet
28. Roger Ravanel
29. Claude Marin
30. Guy Devouassoux
31. Roland Ravanel
32. Norbert Bozon
33. Henri Thiolière
34. Bernard Burnet
35. François Charlet
36. Louis Ravanel
37. Gilles Ravanel
38. Roger Charlet
39. Humbert Ravanel
40. Joseph Bellin
41. Régis Devouassoux
42. Francis Bozon
43. Francis Carrier
44. Edmond Cachat
45. Léon Charlet
46. Gilbert Chappaz
47. Jean Balmat
38. René Maresca
49. Jean Claret-Tourner
50. Fernand Chatelet
51. Yvon Masino
52. Aimé Desailloud
53. Louis Folliguet
54. René Claret-Tournier
55. Georges Balmat
56. Gérard Bellin
57. Bernard Prud'homme
58. Lucien Balmat
59. Jean-Paul Fréchin
60. René Frosio
61. Daniel Audibert
62. Jacques Mechoud
63. Denis Ducroz
64. Roland Bozon
65. Edmond Maresca
66. Joseph Burnet
67. Roger Fournier
68. Fernand Audibert
69. René Charlet
70. René Peyrot
71. Alfred Ravanel
72. Claude Ancey
73. Yvan Charlet
74. Armand Comte
75. Maurice Cretton
76. Christian Mollier
77. Jean-Paul Demarchi
78. Jean-Marie Germain
79. Roland Couttet
80. Jean-Marie Claret
81. Michel Balmat
82. Claude Jaccoux
83. Gérard Devouassoud
84. Jean-Paul Chatelet
85. Roger Frison-Roche
86. Fernand Pareau
87. Norbert Fontaine
88. Louis Dunand
89. Raoul Bossonney
90. Michel Thivierge
91. Jaurès Charlet
92. Henri Dufour

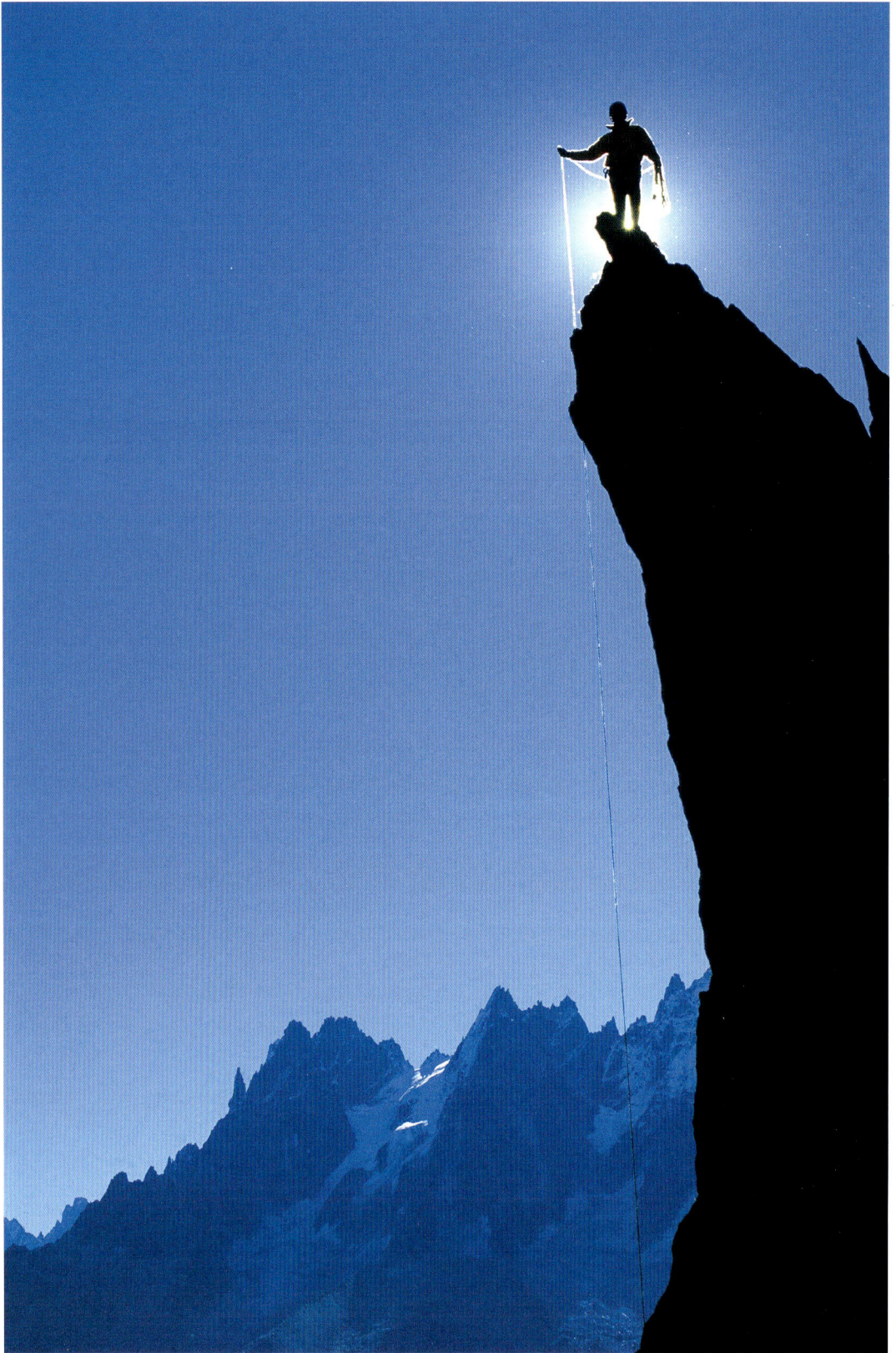

Hommage to Rébuffat: a guide stands on top of the Lames du Brévent.

A PERIOD OF GREAT CHANGE

WITHIN THE SPACE OF THREE DECADES, BETWEEN 1970 AND 2000, THE COMPAGNIE UNDERWENT A RADICAL TRANSFORMATION. THE PEASANT-GUIDES OF OLD GAVE WAY TO A NEW BAND OF MODERN MOUNTAIN PROFESSIONALS, SOME OF WHOM WERE FROM THE CITIES. IN FACT BY THE 1980S, THEY MADE UP THE MAJORITY IN AN ORGANISATION THAT OVER THE YEARS WOULD BECOME A MAJOR BUSINESS.

The 1970s saw several fundamental changes to the daily life of the Compagnie. Based in two rooms measuring 40 square metres under the arcades next to the town hall, the guides' office was starting to get a little cramped. The head guide would often hold meetings in the 'annexe', the bar opposite, and allocate jobs without even having to cross the street. Yet in the high season the famous tour de rôle would end up spilling out on the road in front and while this was picturesque, it wasn't very practical. In 1964 it moved into the tourist office together with the ESF. Mountaineering was the guides' bread and butter in the summer and, with the opening of the Grands Montets ski area and the arrival of a new generation of ski-tourers, skiing was becoming an increasingly important guiding activity in the winter, providing regular work for more than 20 of its members. The main bulk of the work was skied descents of the Vallée Blanche and, provided the crevasses and serac bands were passable, the season could quickly fill up. In 1965 the Compagnie had 500 clients with around 60 of them being groups coming at the end of the season. In 1969 the committee gave the go-ahead for the offices to move to the presbytery and in 1972 the Compagnie moved into the building it still occupies today. Pierre Perret was the Compagnie's president for 18 years and it was he who oversaw the move. The Compagnie now star-

ted to really find its feet and its independence. In the winter of 1972-3 it finally split from the ESF and organised its own off-piste trips. The first secretary, Annick, was taken on in the same year.

The rest of Chamonix was also busy at this time and the progressive opening up of the Grands Montets sector together with the growing popularity of Le Brévent and La Flégère meant a more diverse range of possibilities for visiting skiers. As well as being an international centre for mountaineering, it was quickly establishing a reputation for itself as a capital of skiing. A village with a reputation for looking inwards was being opened up to a whole new generation of skiers and climbers who made no secret of their wish to live there. Slowly but surely more and more mountain enthusiasts were joining the 3000 or so Chamoniards, and in two decades the face of the valley had changed radically, with family names from across France joining the Balmats and Charlets. This was a general movement and affected further afield than just Chamonix. In Les Houches, a predominantly agricultural community, four Young Turks – Jean Raphoz, Jean Clémençon, Bernard Dufour and Guy Peters – approached the mayor, Mr Glacon. They wanted to set up a guides' office. They were all independent guides and didn't imagine for an instant that they would be admitted to the

Les Houches guides' office 1974.
Front row (l to r): Gaby Dufour, Jean Raphoz, Marie-Claude
(receptionist), Guy Peters, Christian Dufour, Bernard Dufour.
Back row: Henri Pollet, Gilbert Pareau, Jacky Pourré.

Elie Hanoteau
during his ascent of the north face of the Eiger.

Compagnie. Not wanting to create tension in the valley, they had decided to open an office on the outskirts, away from the Compagnie. The town authorities granted their request but Fernand Pareau, a member of the town council, suggested that the Compagnie accept the four independent guides. The extraordinary assembly was called for 16 August 1970 and the age-old tradition of Chamoniard exclusivity, which had already been shaken by the arrival of a few notable names from the climbing world, was finally shattered. After much impassioned debate and to their great surprise, the four were admitted to the Compagnie by 26 votes to 18, with an enthusiastic Armand Charlet almost pinning their guides' badges to them on the spot. There was one condition; they were to be based in Les Houches. The Les Houches branch, followed by the Servoz office, provided a way for several guides who had only recently moved to the valley to join the Compagnie. It quickly accepted the likes of Gérard Pétrignet, Jacky Pourret, Elie Hanoteau, Jean Louis Allera and even locals, such as Gilbert Pareau and Eric Favret (the current president).

Elie Hanoteau was quite a special case. He was born in Belgium but quickly became part of the small Chamonix community. Yet he had to obtain French nationality before he could apply to join the Compagnie. He quickly established a high-class reputation as a guide in the mid-1970s, climbing the north face of the Eiger and taking clients on the Droites. As with the others, he was only admitted after a series of fierce debates. The words famously spoken to Frison-Roche after his admission to the Compagnie – *"you are the first foreigner that we have admitted to the Compagnie, make sure we don't regret doing it"* – took on a new resonance. Once again, the old frontiers were being pushed back.

After this, barely a year went by without a new event shaking up the old order established two centuries previously. In 1974, while the Chamonix guides' expedition set out for Everest, several young and talented guides were called upon as reinforcements for a summer that looked like being busy. Their main faults were their long hair and bold nature. These guides – Jean Afanassieff, Patrice and Giles Bodin, and Patrick Cordier – found themselves doing the normal routes on Mont Blanc and the Petite Aiguille Verte.

They played along and the following year duly applied to join the Compagnie as full members. But it wasn't to be. Their applications were politely but firmly and definitively turned down. So, in 1978, they decided to set up their own independent guides' office in the Rue des Moulins. What's more, they decided to call it the 'Compagnie des Guides Indépendants du Mont Blanc'. For the

Roger Ravanel
in the 1970s.
He would be one
of the first guides to take
clients on the Walker Spur.

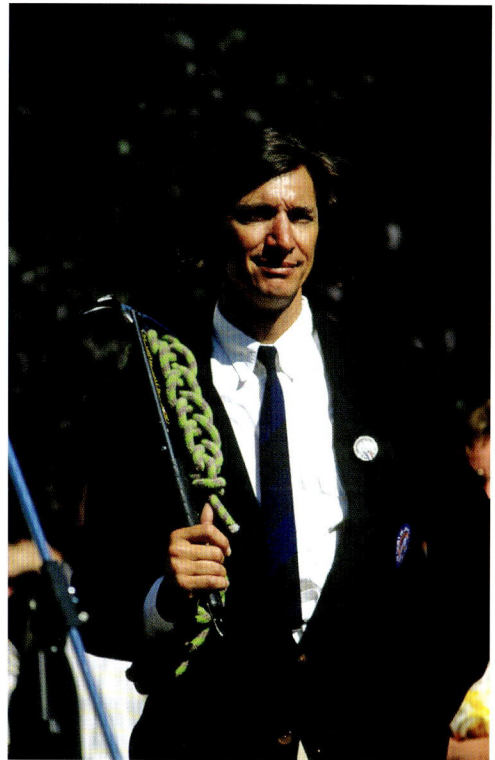

Jean Afanassieff
blazed a trail through
the climbing world
of the 1970s.
A founder member
of the independent
guides' office, he was
eventually admitted
to the Compagnie.

first time in its history, the Compagnie was facing direct competition. The general assembly of the French guides' syndicate held that autumn was the scene of some stormy exchanges. The meeting was dominated by the various guiding companies and the Chamonix delegation chose to attend in traditional dress. There were a few insults traded but eventually the new, independent association was admitted on condition it changed its name, as it might have caused confusion. The Chamoniards were 'reserved' in their opinions on the work of the slightly different newcomers at the beginning. Yet, as time went by, a degree of respect started to be established between the two organisations and the independent guides are now even invited to the fête des guides.

Things were changing in the mountains too. The exploits of, among others, Jean Afanassieff who made a solo ascent of the Walker Spur wearing jeans set other guides thinking. Even the hardest routes were now becoming more accessible and some guides were even considering taking a few handpicked clients on them. Roger Fournier, who died far too young, was probably the first man to guide the Walker Spur. Roger Ravanel was quick to follow in his footsteps. He didn't have the air of a high-level climber and looked more like a Cape Horn sailor, as hard as nails and ready for the very worst conditions. He also had two talented

clients, Marc Terraillon and Patrice Vandevelde, who were as good as some of the aspirant guides. Ravanel could climb pretty much any route with these clients, starting with one of the most highly-prized ones around, the Walker Spur. The route was tied up in the legend of the Compagnie thanks to ascents by the likes of Terray and Lachenal exiting the climb in a storm. But that had been 30 years earlier and, although the legend lived on, it was perhaps time to dust if off a bit. As far as Ravanel knew, and he was unaware of Fournier's ascent, no guide had had the nerve to take clients on the Walker Spur. In 1976 it was still considered a huge and potentially problematic undertaking.

A former manual worker, he was made of stern stuff and was prepared to meet the challenge. As a svelte young man he already had a number of fine climbs under his belt, including three ascents of the north face of the Triolet, the Tournier Spur on the Droites, the Route Major and Innominata on Mont Blanc and the west face of the Drus. Yet the Grandes Jorasses was a very different story. So, he decided to have a go at the route with another hugely talented climber of the time, Yannick Seigneur. They arranged to meet at the Montenvers but Seigneur failed to show up. This didn't stop Ravanel, who set off on his own. Just like everybody else who did the route at that time and as with modern-day guided ascents, he started

*Xavier Chappaz, Michel Arizzi and Jacques Fouque
on expedition in Peru.*

*Jean-Paul Balmat, Jean Fabre and Hervé Thivierge
bivouacking on Chacraraju.*

Serge Kœnig on Everest in 1988.

René Ghilini
is triumphantly
carried by
Peruvian villagers
after his historic flight
from the summit
of Huascaran in 1977.

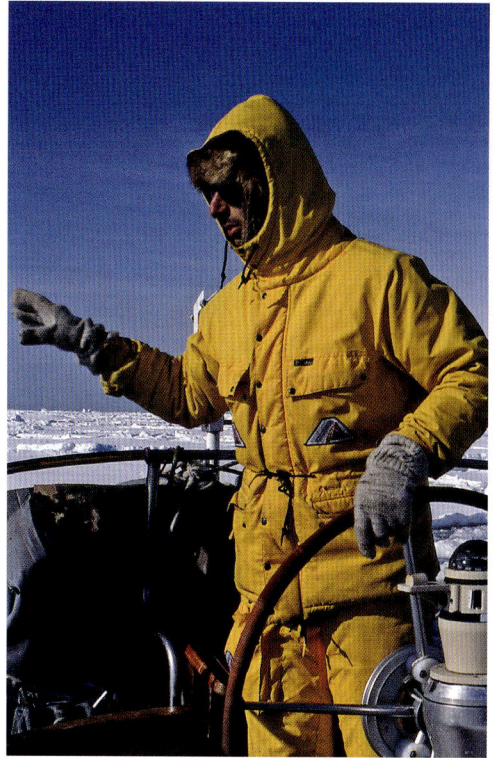

Philippe Cardis
on board his yacht,
Graham, in the Antarctic
in 1982.

in the morning, climbed as high as he could and bivouacked on the 'grey slabs'. This is an ideal bivouac spot above the Mallet glacier and opposite the barrier of rock formed by the Périades with a really remote feel. The following day the sky was overcast with the clouds, coming in from the west, already gathering around the Verte. The weather really started to deteriorate as he reached the 'red chimneys'. There was lightening and rain and then it started to hail. But this didn't stop our man who carried on, not as fast as today's top climbers but at a steady pace, a guide's pace. Water was collecting in his socks but he finally got to the summit. There was no time for self-congratulation, he had to drop in to the Italian Val Ferret. He had a second bivouac and spent the third night in a hut before reaching Planpincieux. Ravanel returned to climbing with other people and for a time was the Compagnie's president.

The end of the 1970s saw the emergence of a generation of globetrotters and expedition parties. It also saw the decline of national expeditions with the high point for French teams being the 1978 K2 trip, of which Daniel Monaci was a member. The trip nearly bankrupted the French mountaineering federation and now it was teams of friends that set about finding sponsors and exploring the Andes and Himalayas. The Compagnie also adopted this new approach.

In 1977, with Bernard Prud'homme as flight engineer and Denis Ducroz as cameraman, René Ghilini established an altitude record in a hang-glider above the Cordillera Blanca. Ghilini is another interesting character. Born in Domodossola, he spent his childhood in Chamonix climbing with the other local kids. He also managed to gain entry to the Compagnie without renouncing his Italian citizenship. He had no problems being admitted and with that became the first true 'foreigner' to join. This milestone in the Compagnie's development even passed unnoticed. Together with a group of friends, which included the American John Bouchard and Nicolas Jaeger, he scoured the Cordillera Blanca for climbs, putting up no less than 15 new routes (always Alpine style) over a period of five months. The most memorable images from the trip are those taken as he flew over Huascaran (where he set an altitude record). He flew over the villagers and landed in the middle of inhabited areas and local Indian carried him on their shoulders. The Peruvians even thought he was an incarnation of a legendary bird-man.

Perhaps the greatest display of his talents came from his climbs with Alex MacIntyre. Together they climbed the south face of Dhaulaghiri, once again in Alpine style, before acclimatising on the normal route on Annapurna as a prelude to an ascent of its south face. The trip ended in tra-

*Images
from fêtes des guides celebrations
in the early 1990s.*

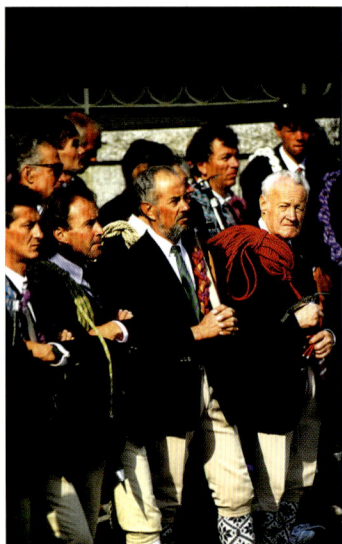

*The Compagnie's first accompagnateurs
at the 1981 fête des guides. Left to right: Thierry Ravanel,
Jean-Michel Humeau, Gilbert Mugnier and Eric Thiolière.*

*The fête des guides has even had visits from politicians.
Then president of the Compagnie Jean-Claude Charlet
stands with the prime minister of the time
Edouard Balladur (centre, front row).*

gedy, the death of Alex, who was hit by a falling rock while unroped. Ghilini descended alone and without a rope, the end of an incredible Himalayan odyssey.

Peru was very popular at this time, as there was no need for climbing permits and there were short approach walks. Hervé Thivierge at this time, when not putting up a new route on Chacraraju with Jean-Paul Balmat, could be found making the first ascent of a new route on Denali or climbing Yosemite's hardest routes with friends.

At the beginning of the 1980s, Xavier Chappaz, Michel Arizzi and Jacques Fouque were accompanying René Desmaison on his Andean expeditions. While, a few years later, Bernard Prud'homme and Serge Koenig were among the first westerners to be allowed back into Tibet (closed since the Chinese invasion) to try Everest from the north side. Although on that expedition the team had to turn back due to bad weather, in 1988 Koenig was the first Chamonix guide to stand on the Roof of the World. An exception to the rule was Philippe Cardis, who took to the seas and by the beginning of the 1980s was an Antarctica specialist.

Even affairs at more modest altitudes were changing. The creation of a new diploma, that of Accompagnateur en Moyenne Montagne (equivalent of the UK and US Mountain Leaders), would tempt other youngsters who didn't necessarily want to go into the high mountain environment.

Jean-Michel Humeau set up a desk in the tourist office while three local lads, Gilbert Mugnier, Eric Thiollière and Thierry Ravanel, attempted to have their training recognised by the great Chamonix guiding institution. All four of them were admitted to the Compagnie in 1981 and caused a stir at the 57th fête des guides by carrying umbrellas over their shoulders instead of ice axes.

Chamonix these days has around 10,000 inhabitants and has witnessed a population explosion. These days it is difficult to ignore the numerous young guides that come here from all over France and the world. Bernard Prud'homme, president of the Compagnie in the early 1980s, with the support of the committee decided to bring in new blood. The principle of quotas was abandoned. In 1986, 11 new guides were granted full membership (the average having been four a year before then), one of which was Christophe Profit whose application was accepted by unanimous vote. Of these 11, seven hadn't been born in the valley.

Today, over 50% of the guides are not from the valley or are not descended from one of the old Chamonix families. Although it hasn't flung its doors wide open, the Compagnie now accepts a whole range of candidates and one of the founding traditions has disappeared. You now no longer have to be born in the valley to join its Compagnie des Guides, a small step in keeping with the spirit of the new age and the dawning of the 21st century.

On a trip to Iceland,
with the air
of a round-the-world
yachtsmen.

FERNAND PAREAU, A LEGACY OF WISDOM

While it's true that mountains can shatter dreams and lives, their high-altitude embrace also allows others to live long and fulfilling lives. Fernand Pareau's career belongs in this second category and today he is the elder statesman of the active Chamonix guides. Although he rock climbs very little these days, he can often be found on the great Alpine 4000ers, always smiling and as dynamic as he ever was. Yet beyond his record for longevity and sporting exploits, he represents for many the ideal of a true guide. Humble and attentive, he radiates his enthusiasm and commitment. We can learn a great deal from Pareau, with the ever-present smile on his somewhat mischievous and young-looking face.

In his eighties, he is almost ageless having attained the age of contentment of men who are able to share and give of themselves. Yet nothing predisposed him to become a guide. He was born in 1925 in a small village in the Vosges (north eastern France) from where he was forced to join the 'Voluntary Work Service' by the German army in 1944. So he found himself working in the fields, to replace the German farm workers sent to the front. He returned after the war to find his village destroyed and joined his sister who had just moved to Argentière. She had met a guide, Léon Bellin, whom she married. In summer 1945, with his parents and two

brothers, Pareau got his first glimpse of the Mont Blanc range from the train in Sallanches. Its granite needles and glaciers crashing down into the valleys held him spellbound. This young man in search of a vocation had found his calling. His first climb was with Léon Bellin on the Brévent: *"... we exited pretty much where the cable car station is today having used three pitons on the whole route..."* In 1947 he met Hélène Ravanel, who would become his wife. He now joined another family of guides, that of Paul and Michel sons of Robert. Alfred Couttet, Hélène's godfather, gave them a twenty franc note, a huge amount for the time. He moved to La Chaufriaz, one of the most beautiful spots in the valley, to start as a farmer. He had three cows. He wasted no time exploring the mountains with his brothers-in-law. He worked as a carpenter and then ice salesman, collecting the blocks of ice from the Argentière glacier and selling them to hotels from Les Houches to Chamonix. He was back in the fields in the summer for the hay harvest, often working with the Ducroz brothers in la Joux. *"I waited for the hay to ripen. This was in July [...] often after a route in the mountains. When I had harvested my hay I would do others in Le Tour, Le Lavancher and Les Houches. We were given half of what we had cut."*

He worked as a porter for the Tré le Porte hut (since disappeared) and explored the massif while

On the south ridge
of the Moine
in the 1970s...

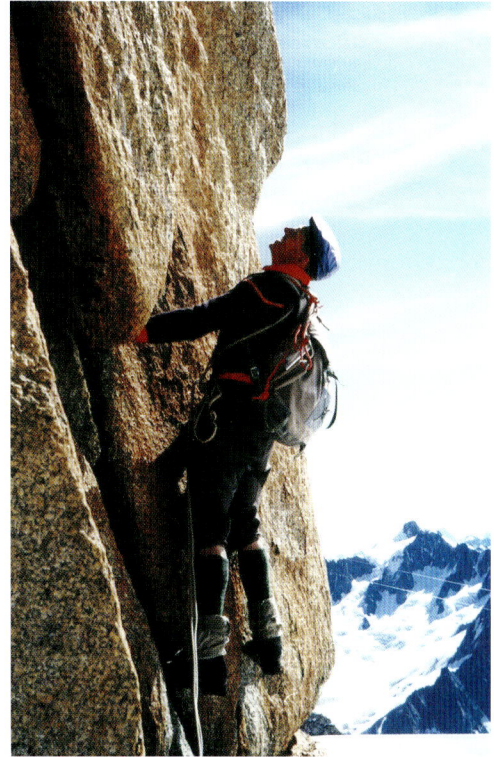

... or in the
Argentière basin.

carrying 58-kilo loads on his back. He completed the aspirant guides' course in 1953. There was no need for a long list of routes back in those days: *"We were trained on the job. Once you had your aspirant guide's certificate and knew a bit about technique, you learnt the real job by following a guide. At that time we weren't allowed to go out alone."* He joined the Compagnie that same year. With the support of the Ravanel and Ducroz families as well as Léon Bellin, he had no problem getting in. That summer he met his first client: *"It was 16th August 1953. At that time we were assigned our routes on the evening of the 14th. The 15th was the [guides'] festival, which finished with dancing. The guide whose turn it was must have had too much to drink, as he didn't wake up on time! So, the head guide asked me if I could take the Oudotte family to the Requin hut. Bernard was 15 at the time and is still my client now."*

At the same time as he was finishing his guide's training (the school was in Les Praz, skilfully managed by Armand Charlet), he joined the SNCF. It was 1956 and Pareau was responsible for maintaining the line. *"People didn't ski the Vallée Blanche or even go off piste in winter back then and I had a family to feed. My team shovelled the snow away from the line between Les Tines and Vallorcine. There was lots of snow then and one winter André Ducroz measured 24 accumulated metres of snow in*

Le Tour!" Hence it was only in the summer that Pareau got to put his crampons on, setting off on daily climbing marathons in the mountains. One such occasion was the day he set out to climb Mont Blanc with Roland Couttet, who was at the time an aspirant guide: *"We jumped a crevasse around the Grands Mulets area and one of our clients managed to stab himself in the ankle with his crampon. We decided to carry on. We stopped below the Glacier Rond to take off our crampons and have a quick drink. But his muscles had cooled down and he couldn't stand on his foot. So, we carried him. He weighed 83 kilos! We got back to the Plan de l'Aiguille at six thirty in the evening. And I had to meet someone at the Albert 1er [hut]! But I didn't have a car. I got to Le Tour and started up the moraine, and I reached the hut at midnight. I then set off at two thirty in the morning to do the three cols! There was no cable car at the time and we walked down. I was absolutely knackered, but we didn't have the choice back then."*

He continued to work like this for decades, going from working in the mountains as a guide to maintaining the valley's railway lines. He had moved to Le Lac, Servoz, in 1956 and in 1976, after having set up the guides' office in Les Houches (with Guy Peters, and Gaby and Bernard Dufour), he retired from the SNCF. He was 51 and made the most of his newfound free time, enthusiastically devoting

even more time to the mountains. He started to travel, trekking and climbing in several countries. Yet one of his great strengths, above his climbing exploits, was his ability to develop real and lasting relationships with entire families, taking parents, children and even grandchildren into the mountains. For Pareau, a guide really was like a proud gardener opening the gates to his garden, as described by Rébuffat. Pareau shared these transcendent moments of enjoyment in the mountains – their beauty and their difficulty – with his clients. And the tributes collected together by François Eric Cormier for Pareau's seventieth birthday can attest to this:

"It was through his long pauses that he spoke to me about the mountains. He would put his hand on my arm and say, 'You know… walking… climbing… going higher and higher… Ah!' I hire a guide. But he's not a guide, he's a friend, a dear friend." Henri Debrue.

"I'm still young but I hope that one day I'll be as wise as Fernand. Then I will have achieved something!" Arnaud Boudet (now a guide).

"To find oneself surrounded by nature with him is to feel the call of life deep inside oneself." Colette Boudet.

"In 1994 I climbed Mont Blanc with Fernard, having only been on the Weissmies with him before. On the summit I held out my hand to thank him. But Fernand grabbed me by shoulders and said 'on the roof of Europe, we embrace'. I will never forget his fraternal gesture." Gérald Jaton.

One of the France's best ice climbers, François Damilano, joined in the tributes:
"The recurring question was:
what are you going to do when you're older?
Invariably I would reply: I'm going to be an Eskimo or mountain guide.
I had two heroes when I was five or six. Although I didn't really realise it at the time, the first one was a fictional character. Apoutsiak was a little Inuit boy and I found his adventures, as recounted by Paul-Emile Victor in the famous Père Castor series, absolutely engrossing. My other hero was real and I saw him each summer. He would go off in the mountains, which already fascinated me even then. Sometimes he took my parents. He must have been indestructible, as he always came back with stories full of danger and ambushes.
I remember.
I remember that afternoon on the snows below the Index. Fernand picked up little Sylvie and me, one kid on each knee. The three of us slid down the entire

On his travels once again, this time in Nepal.

snow slope at what seemed to me to be breakneck speed. Fernand certainly was incredibly strong. A little later someone explained to me that Eskimo diplomas were pretty difficult to get hold of, so I opted for guiding instead. Thank you Fernand."

Fernand is unquestionably a humanist and he has passed on his passion first and foremost to his children, Yves and Gilbert, with the latter becoming a guide like his father. He might have been content to be an extremely good guide with a remarkable career. But the young man in him still remembered the astonishment of seeing the mountains for the first time. As a man of conviction, he has remained true to his ideals. And living next to the Route Blanche, the main road through the valley, and witnessing the environmental damage – melting glaciers, crumbling mountains and climate change – he could not witness it without making a stand. He feels we have a duty to protect the massif. He has taken part in all the campaigns and protests since the fire in the Mont Blanc tunnel in 1999. He is always the first person to arrive at the roundabout, leading to the tunnel, to set up the protest banners. And he has even tried to convert the law enforcement officers to the cause who showed their gratitude by breaking his nose. But you can't keep a good man down, and he is convin-

ced the mountains need to be protected, for both himself and for others: *"When we think of the trouble our ancestors had in preserving the mountains. They knew they had to be treated with respect. They didn't damage them. And if only we had thought a little bit about it beforehand, we certainly wouldn't have let them build this corridor for lorries through the valley. We would have known that we were ruining it! But the idea of this 'cash cow' right in the middle of Mont Blanc was too tempting for some and still holds sway over more than one person in the valley!"*

Fernand is certainly a committed combatant with a keen intuition. And former president of the Compagnie, Xavier Chappaz, praises his intelligence in an article that appeared in the Dauphiné Libéré (the local paper for the region): *"It is a real pleasure for guides to follow in Fernand's footsteps and take up his struggle for the environment. He is a wise man who has much to pass on to us. He does everything with a smile, tenderness and good humour. He has a positive outlook and takes an interest in the future of others and in the legacy we are leaving younger generations. He has an eye on the future."* Hence, one understands why he was chosen to be the first person to carry the Olympic flame through Chamonix on its ways to Turin in winter 2006. And the flame burns on inside him.

Daniel Monaci on the south face of Chacraraju in 1978.

Robert Chéré and Daniel Monaci were one of the leading climbing teams of the 1970s. On the first ascent of their route, Nativité, on the Aiguille du Midi (7-9 March 1974).

DANIEL MONACI, THE GREAT SOLO CLIMBER

A final slope, almost an end in itself, and a team was already preparing to cross the curling snowy lip. They were going slowly, as is always the case at altitude. Up here the route straddling its southeast and south faces, Mont Blanc has a Himalayan feel. That day the Arête de Peuterey was like a gateway to the north and the men were pummelled by the winds sweeping the face. Three teams from the GMHM were making their way up the hard icy slope. Commandant Marmier, at the front, had just crossed the cornice with his second not far behind. In a hushed silence, presaging the tragedy that would follow, the cornice collapsed releasing a tsunami-like mass of snow. The men braced themselves against their ice axes. They could do little else in the face of the wall of ice. The wave swept everything away before it and one team and then another was carried off down the slope. One of them, Jérôme Saadi and Jean-Jacques Vaudelle, was carried onto the Frêney face. By some kind of miracle the other team of Xavier Gargeas and Serge Koenig (who would later join the Compagnie) were spared, their rope catching on a small spike of rock.

Lower down a solitary figure knew this was the end, on a mountain that he had known for so long. A fraction of a second later and he too was swept away by the mass of snow and ice. Like so many other great mountaineers before him, he fell down Mont Blanc's Brenva face. He had chosen a path, easy ground for him, that many promised themselves they will do and which few actually ever manage.

By the early 1980s, Daniel Monaci was one of the great names of mountaineering. He had just returned from the French K2 expedition where he had led the way at almost every single stage of the climb. Under his long curly hair and thick beard that gave him the air of a druid, was one of the best mountaineers of his day. Yet there was nothing to predispose this son of Italian immigrants to take up climbing. Nothing in fact other than being born near Bergamo and as a child reading accounts written by Walter Bonatti, originally from the same city. Monaci grew up in the Maurienne valley and at the age of 12 he tended flocks of sheep and goats at the foot of the Aiguilles de Belledonne. By 17 his penchant for solo ascents was already starting to show itself. In June 1969 he made the first solo ascent of the Couloir de la Corniche on the Pic de Frêne in the Belledonne Massif. Although he was outgoing and fun-loving, he quickly set about solo climbing almost everything. At the age of 19 he attempted and succeeded in making the second solo ascent of the north face of the Drus and moved to Chamonix the same year. Chamonix at that time was still a small town that was quiet in the winter. Yet Monaci didn't arrive unnoticed and even the

Daniel Monaci at a stance in Yosemite.

On the first winter ascent of the Bonatti-Zapelli on the Pilier d'Angle.

old guides had to accept he had talent. He had a strong but unassuming personality, two qualities highly valued by the locals.

He was 20 when he did his military service with the EHM and the same year he became an aspirant guide, alongside Hervé Thivierge. He had no problem joining the Compagnie. Thivierge remembered *"even though he could be a bit secretive, he made the ideal climbing partner as he had an even temperament, no matter the circumstances. He was always incredibly kind and he lived for the mountains, his head full of projects and routes to climb. He was meticulous and prepared his climbs down to the last details."*

Despite his small frame – 60 kilos and 1.62m – he had huge energy and found the mountain wilderness he sought on his winter ascents. Interviewed in Le Point magazine in 1974, he explained that *"in the winter you known straight away where you are. The extremely low temperatures, violent winds, and the ice and verglas on the routes make them three times as hard as they are in summer. I go there to test myself."* And his ascents were pretty testing, as at the start of 1974 he made the first winter ascent of the Couloir Cordier on the Verte. A month later, together with an equally talented partner, the gendarme Robert Chéré, he was on the route on the Aiguille du Midi where Georges Nominé had died. They climbed straight through the seracs on sections of over 80° ice, a must for the time. After 60 hours they finally exited the 'Voie de la Nativité', exhausted but elated.

Monaci and Chéré formed one of the greatest climbing partnerships in Chamonix. They were both perfectionists and loved the mountains, which proved a winning combination. They climbed the Shroud on the Jorasses in seven hours. Seven hours as opposed to the 13 days it had taken Desmaison and Flematti on the first ascent just seven years earlier. They made more and more winter ascents. Perhaps the most remarkable was the first winter ascent of the Pilier d'Angle over three days (22-24 December 1975) via the Bonatti-Zapelli route which had only been done twice before, in summer. Monaci was friends with everyone and climbed with some of the most talented young guides around, such as Hervé Thivierge and Michel Arizzi. In 1976 he graduated from the guides' course top of his class, which was accompanied by much celebration...

The following year the three sidekicks, this time accompanied by Jacques Fouque who would also join the Compagnie, headed for Yosemite. They climbed the length and breadth of the valley. Of course they climbed The Nose and also made ascents of seven other routes, including Yosemite Point Buttress and climbs on Washington Column, the Royal Arches, Sentinel Rock and Middle Cathedral Rock. For the fun of it they also had a go on the great 50-metre Tyrolean traverse on Lost Arrow Spire, which sees you suspended over metres of nothingness and is a guaranteed adrenaline kick, even for a guide...

On the summit of Chacraraju
with Jean-Paul Balmat and Jean Fabre.

Daniel Monaci, Michel Arizzi and Philippe Bruere
receive their guides badges, 15 August 1976.

In 1978, Monaci and Thivierge, together with Jean-Paul Balmat and Jean Fabre (the only guide who is also a graduate of the French civil service academy, the ENA, and a Marseillais to boot), headed for Peru. Their only reference points were Lionel Terray's accounts and black and white photos, which were dated even then. They set out in Terray's footsteps with the firm intention of traversing Chacraraju, the same peak that Terray had climbed. Twenty-metre high cornices dampened their ardour and they wisely turned their attentions to other equally technically challenging objectives. They climbed five peaks, four of which via new routes: the west couloir of Yanapacha (5400m), a hard ice route up the south face of Pisco (5800m), the south face of Chacraraju (6000m) and the south face and east ridge of Taulliraju (5875m). Everything went like clockwork with the ever-present threat of avalanches triggered by earthquake in the back of their minds. After all, this was where the town of Yungay had been wiped off the face of the earth by a catastrophic landslide that started on Huascaran, a nearby peak.

He spent the summer season guiding in Chamonix, among others, the Bouche family, loyal clients he shared with Hervé Thivierge. The autumn and winter found him back soloing in his dream mountains. His impressive list of ascents included the Marteau, which had just been climbed, and the Lagarde-Ségogne Couloir on the Aiguille Caïman. After this he left for the French expedition to climb K2's south-south-east spur. Fifteen men for one mountain. This may have seemed a little excessive for an efficient climber who loved to move quickly

and alone. He was in the leading team and turned back a little before Thierry Leroy who continued to 8550m, less than 150 metres from the summit.
Perhaps that was why he turned back to his first passion and one of his greatest exploits, the first winter ascent of the Pilier d'Angle. Robert Chéré had died a few years earlier on the Verte and this time Monaci was alone. What was he thinking about as he set out? He was 28 years old and had just become a father. Usually so meticulous, this time he dropped his pitons while on his bivouac. He would have to turn around. It was the middle of the night when he climbed up towards the Col de Peuterey. He could see headtorches higher up. It was three teams of climbers, the men from the GMHM. Daniel was still on the slope. *"Ok, see you on the Peuterey ridge, we can follow each other,"* Monaci said. One of them took a last photo that day, 15 February 1980. Behind the figures in red you can make out a solitary figure, his rope trailing behind him in nothingness.

The first team was already on the summit ridge. One man stepped up, then another. All of a sudden everything was falling away as the cornice collapsed, dragging the team of two and Monaci down with it. He hadn't stood a chance and disappeared down the Brenva face. He had written the following passage about the Pilier d'Angle in his notebook. *"Why did we do that winter ascent? For the technical challenge, for the route's isolation, for the pleasure of climbing or simply for those extraordinary moments?"* A few extraordinary moments, the summary of a life and a passion.

Claude Jaccoux
on an approach walk,
1980s.

CLAUDE JACCOUX, THE INVETERATE TRAVELLER

Alpinist, Parisian dandy, teacher, mountain guide and pioneering expedition leader, Claude Jaccoux is the living embodiment of the multi-faceted
nature of Chamonix alpinism, of a universal brand
of alpinism nurtured in the mountains of one valley and exported to mountains the world over. Yet,
his career did not get off to a flying start. He was
born in Servox in 1937. Almost an asset these days,
back then it was a world away from Chamonix: the
valley ended in Les Bossons and that was that.
Thus the family was made up of teachers, customs
officials and postal workers. Claude had barely
had time to gaze up at the mountains before the
family moved to Paris.

These were carefree years in the French capital
and he was head boy for humanities at the prestigious lycée Henri IV. He spent his summers in
the family home in Servoz, avidly exploring the
mountains as an outlet for his boundless energy.
His friend, Jean Jonot, introduced him to a whole
new world, that of Fontainebleau. *"The forest was
made up of various gangs: we had our rocks, routines
and our own makeshift bivouacs. And just like Robert
Sonnelier, none of us was any kind of hotshot."* Nevertheless, he developed a passion for the mountains
on these rounded lumps of sandstone. A penniless
student, his summers in Vieux Servoz gave way to
mountain bivouacs. As an apprentice alpinist, his

life lessons were gained climbing and he learnt on
the job with a kind of innocence that led to more
than one extremely narrow squeak. Even so, he
made rapid progress and his mentors were the likes of Guido Magnone, Robert Paragot and Jean
Couzy, young Parisian climbers who were shaking
up the world of mountaineering. Like them, he
racked up some impressive climbs, and in 1958 he
made the fourth ascent of the Walker Spur. He also
put up a handsome new route on Tozal del Mallo
in the Pyrenees. This was born of a desire to travel
beyond Mont Blanc and its standard routes.

A young teacher in Paris and then Strasbourg, his
thoughts turned increasingly to guiding. The one
drawback was that he had long hair, dressed like
a hippie and walked the streets of Chamonix ba-
refoot. In short, this wasn't really in keeping with
the standards of the day and he was refused entry
to the aspirant guides' programme two years running. This was somewhat puzzling given that some
of the successful candidates only had the normal
route on Mont Blanc to their names. They did,
however, have the support of the various branches
of the Compagnie des Guides. It would take the in-
tervention of Lucien Devies, the president of what
was then known as the FFM (French mountaineering federation), for Jaccoux to be accepted as an
aspirant guide. On the guides' course he met Armand Charlet, who already had him in his sights.

The Compagnie's 1966 expedition to the north face of Huascaran, one of its first trips abroad. The south face of Huandoy is in the background.

Claude Jaccoux, Michèle Stamos and his famous client Jeremy Bernstein opposite Nupste. They were some of the first people to trek to Everest base camp.

The Young Turk and old hand were initially wary of each other but a profound sense of respect soon developed between them. His 28 months of service with the EHM (alpine troops) as aspirant guide gave him an opportunity to integrate into valley life and naturally it was Armand Charlet who supported his application to join the Compagnie des Guides. He was the first Chirve (Servoz man) to join the Compagnie, which prompted the following laconic observation from Charlet: *"We consider Servoz part of the Chamonix valley."* Geographical boundaries had relaxed a little and Jaccoux, the pioneer of new places and spaces, didn't mind this minor inaccuracy at all.

Jaccoux left his teaching job to devote himself to his new profession. He settled into a routine, guiding in the summer and working as a ski instructor in La Plagne in the winter. Whenever he had the chance, he would take up other challenges and in 1964 he made the first winter ascent of the Arête des Grands Montets. In 1966 he ventured out of the valley to join the successful expedition, which also included Georges Payot, to climb the north face of Huascaran. He had already explored Algeria's Ahaggar mountains and had been well and truly bitten by the travel bug. It would take a meeting with a particularly bad client to really launch him further. Jeremy Bernstein is a leading physicist, renowned author and contributor to the *New York Times* magazine (even appearing on its cover). Together they made a highly improbable climbing team. Claude entertainingly recounted their exploits in AlpiRando magazine: *"He arrived in Cha-*

monix with a head full of ambitious projects, yet he was so frightened in the mountains that he actually achieved very few of them. I met him on a tour de rôle. He was so funny that I always ended up forgiving him… We hardly ever managed to get anything done, no matter where we went, and I ended up doing the routes on my own. He was incorrigible and despite his fear of the mountains, he always came back for more. He couldn't sleep the night before doing a route. He looked drawn the next morning and would set out as if being led to the slaughter. The best days for him were the bad weather days. One morning at the Couvercle hut, after it had snowed all night, he was so happy that he fell to his knees on the terrace shouting: 'Jesus Christ, patron saint of mountaineers, be praised!'"

While Claude couldn't take his client further than the Col des Nantillons, thanks to Jeremy he got to explore new mountains. He had already set out to explore new faces but had he actually ever escaped the way he would with his companion? In 1967 he flew to Kathmandu, the DC3 landing on a grass runway, and found a room in the only working hotel. He set off on his trek to Everest base camp, starting 40 kilometres from the Nepalese capital. The trek took two and a half months, more than enough time to immerse oneself in the spirit of travel and adventure. He was now an inveterate explorer, always one step ahead of everyone else. The following year he was in Pakistan, exploring and climbing Naltar Peak. His success here prompted him to seek out even more exotic lands, such as Afghanistan. Following in the footsteps of the French adventurer and journalist, Joseph Kessel,

On Aconcagua's superb south face.

Relaxing with a Sherpa.

he took his travelling companions and clients on an extraordinary journey. The mountains merely served as an excuse to explore and like highland cavaliers, they galloped across these mysterious lands. Jaccoux was now convinced that more than just climbing, the real adventure lay in meeting other peoples and cultures. He pored over maps and set off to discover each new area that opened itself up to tourism.

After Kashmir, he was one of the first westerners to explore Ladakh. He always managed to attract a distinguished team of amateur explorers with the time and taste for adventure. For them joining Jaccoux meant heading for unexplored mountains and unknown peoples. There was no fixed programme to follow and each moment was just as much a discovery for the guide as it was for his clients. This was what made the trips so successful.

Jaccoux set off on his adventures into Terra Incognita with good humour and generosity. There were no trekking companies or detailed itineraries at this time. They were there to be invented. On his return, he still found time to get involved in his professional body and was the president of the French guiding syndicate. Other lands and places fascinated him. Over the years his trips gradually led him higher and higher. To 6500 metres, 6800 metres and then 7200 metres on Trisul with the Italian guide Allberto Rey. On the walk in they came across Sadhus on their way to Nanda Devi. When he could, he invited guides from the Compagnie, such as Bernard Prud'homme and JF Charlet on Annupurna IV and Roger Ravanel on Trisul. Together with Michel Vincent, he was the first guide to offer high-altitude trips, to mountains such as Kun in India, Annapurna IV and then Mustagh Ata.

But he didn't forget his first love, and together with Bernard Domenech and two clients he put up a new route on the southwest face of Mont Blanc. With the arrival of the first trekking companies in the 1980s the two men stepped up a gear, setting their sights on the 8000ers. They were the first to organise commercial expeditions to 8000-metre peaks: Gasherbrum II in 1985, Shishapangma in 1986, Cho Oyu in 1988 and Everest in 1989, which attracted no less than 18 clients. This team of 'clients' included a band of highly talented climbers such as Jean-Mi Asselin, Eric Escoffier and Chantal Maudite, to name only the most well-known of their number.

Their three-month siege of the mountain ended in failure at 8400m that year. Organising these expeditions was taking up more and more time and Jaccoux, a man with a passion for the freedom of the mountains, was starting to realise that it was more the job of an accountant and quartermaster than a mountain guide. Thus, he abandoned his high-altitude expeditions and returned to guiding. Yet he still sets aside a bit of time to explore some of the most beautiful areas of the world, mostly in autumn. He has been on over 60 treks in Nepal as well as numerous other destinations. But these facts and figures are not important, certainly not for a former literature teacher turned explorer. A calling that took him to some of the least well-known spots on the globe, where he could make sense of life, long before the word adventure had been tarnished by the notions of mass tourism and commercialisation.

On Nuptse's summit ridge with Everest in the background.

GEORGES BETTEMBOURG, ARCHANGEL OF THE MOUNTAINS

A shooting star in the firmament of guides, Bettembourg cemented his reputation in the Himalayas. Bettembourg was not a name from the Chamonix valley. Yet, he was from a long line of guides on his mother's side. His grandfather was Georges Charlet, the brother of Armand Charlet.

And as we have seen, he was an accomplished guide. Georges Bettembourg's father was also a guide but he disappeared back to his native Briançon, abandoning his wife and child. Georges grew up in the heart of the village of Argentière in a family that lived and breathed the mountains. He and his mother lived with his grandparents, with the man whose first name and passion for the mountains he shared. His guide and crystal-hunting uncle Jean-Paul and his cousin Jean-Franck were on the floor below. There was only two years age difference between the two boys who played together and no doubt shared their secrets and dreams with each other. The Charlet clan numbered 10 at this time and crystals played a particularly important role in the family life.

A few years earlier Georges's grandfather and uncle had claimed to have discovered a seam of gold up at the Col du Passon and at school, Georges junior was known as 'Jojo pépites' (nugget Jojo). An affectionate nickname, it turned out to be quite appropriate for a generous man who had a healthy appetite for life and all it offered. But the gold was no more than an anecdote. What really fascinated the family members were crystals: the lumps of smoky quartz and fluorite that sparkled out from the mountain ledges and cracks. The boys' grandfather took their education in hand. It wasn't to be gained from books or grand theories but from the ground. He taught them about the Chamonix granite and the rock's weaknesses. Their hands quickly bore the stigmata of their hunting sprees and they soon learned to spot the signs of a good vein.

They were now rock hunters. Spring 1968 provided them with an opportunity to start in earnest. While the country was crippled by strikes and unrest, the Cirque d'Argentière was a haven of calm and the brothers (they were as close as brothers) clambered over the broken terrain, sounding out walls of rock and dangling at the end of vertiginous abseils. All that for a few crystals?

They saw it differently. Jean-Franck recalls how *"our grandfather told us: 'you'll see when you're guides...' We didn't understand what he meant, it didn't make much sense. Even though we loved reading about Bonatti and Terray, we couldn't understand how all those thousands of mountaineers could leave the mountains without even having taken the time to look for all those crystal treasures. The climber's vocation came later and in the end all our climbing in the moun-*

Georges Bettembourg and Hervé Thivierge on Corsica's Teghie Lisce.

Jacques and Catherine Cuenot, Hervé Thivierge and Georges Bettembourg enjoy a bivouac in Corsica.

tains away from the classic crag routes, over a whole range of different terrain proved to be excellent training for the Alpine careers that lay in store for us."

They quickly started to build up quite a repertory. Bettembourg was beginning to know bits of the Cirque d'Argentière like the back of his hand. His favourite high-altitude spots were now the Aiguille d'Argentière, Pointe des Améthystes and the Col des Cristaux. And they were becoming hugely talented alpinists while they were at it. Georges passed his aspirant guide's exam at the age of 20 and graduated top of his class to become a full guide in 1974. He was in good company, as other new young guides for that year included Patrick Vallençant and Anselme Baud...

He joined the Compagnie in 1971. For his part, Jean-Franck spent several years studying away from the valley. Yet as soon as the opportunity presented itself, the two men would meet up and head into the mountains. Over the space of a few years, Georges, accompanied by his cousin and other like-minded climbers including Hervé Thivierge, put up around 30 new rock and ice routes. Each time they set out to do a new route, their primary concern was the crystals to be had there, and the climbing came second. And it's no coincidence that a great number of these new routes appeared at the Argentière end of the valley.

Yet it was at the other end of the valley, on the north face of the Pélerins with Daniel Audibert, that he found a pink fluorite octahedron, which

remains to this day one of the most exceptional specimens of fluorite found in the massif. This extremely rare piece still bears the name of its finder: Georges.

As a ski instructor, Georges would head to Stevens Pass in the United States each winter. Here he refined his crack-climbing technique and found another treasure, Norma. This was the same Norma who has such a presence in his sadly premonitory book La Mort Blanche (White Death). His life was split between summers in Chamonix and leading climbs as a guide and winters on the other side of the Atlantic. Then Bettembourg, whose other experience hardy extended beyond a few treks, met the expedition climber Yannick Seigneur. This was 1978. The two men were hugely ambitious. Seigneur already had Makalu's west pillar under his belt, while Bettembourg had the insouciance of youth (he was 28) and an incredible level of fitness on his side.

At a time when there were only a few national expeditions, which mainly involved jumaring up fixed ropes, they set out to climb Broad Peak Alpine style and without bottled oxygen! Images of the two of them running over moraine simply as training would mark an entire generation of climbers. They gave the Himalayan climbing of their father's generation with miles of fixed ropes and crowds of porters a bit of a beating. They finished the climb in three days. Georges wrote later that he had turned around half an hour from the

1979, on the slopes of Kangchenjunga. The wind can be your worst enemy.

*Georges,
his face haggard on his return from the mountain.*

summit. We will never know if Yannick Seigneur reached the top of a subsidiary summit or the true summit itself...

Georges was starting to be noticed and this is how Gilles Chappaz, the editor-in-chief of *Montagnes Magazines*, described him in September 1981: *"He has an odd kind of relaxed look with something of the crafty but amiable loafer. He looks you straight in the eye and has an expressive face that gives off a sense of mischief with just a whiff of insolence. The overall impression is of an enormous desire to communicate, to talk... And he can certainly talk. A great deal. A slightly troubled look comes over him when he's looking for the right word and his ideas aren't always expressed with total clarity. But this is not a person looking for conclusive black and white answers. Rather, he wants to develop a sense of the moment, of its truth. He's really not interested in ironing out the contradictions that spice things up. Thus discussions inevitably meander slightly towards confusion. Yet, he exudes such a sense of sincerity and spontaneity, irony and tolerance that he must have a pretty sensitive side too."*

A sensitivity that he put to use on the world's great mountains. On the way to Broad Peak, he had an encounter that would change his life. The meeting was with Doug Scott, who describes it in his book Himalayan Climber: *"In Skardu, on the way to K2 in 1978, a jeep screeched to a halt and a chap with a mop of black hair and a huge smile leapt out. He said 'I am Georges Bettembourg. I will climb with you one day, but now I am off to Broad Peak – goodbye!' [...] There were not at that time many who had climbed above 8000m alpine-style so Georges was enlisted."*
In the space of five years Georges Bettembourg, together with Doug Scott and crew, would become one of the best Himalayan climbers of his time. He was the one of a select band of Frenchman invited to join the British climbers and few have followed

in his footsteps. Thus, Doug Scott the mountain bear joined forces with a curious character from the Chamonix valley.

In 1979 they were on Kangchenjunga. At 8586m, it is the third highest mountain in the world and gives challenging and dangerous climbing. Frank Smythe wrote in 1930 that there *"isn't a single mountain face in the world that begets as many avalanches as this north west face."* Then there is the filthy weather. Situated at the end of the Himalayan chain, it lies in the path of the winds rushing between the hot and humid Bay of Bengal to the south and the cold and dry Tibetan plateaus to the north. Violent and unpredictable winds regularly batter its complex, chaotic summit. The face they wanted to climb was gigantic: all three thousand thoroughly uninviting metres of it, with serac falls for that added touch of danger. After much discussion, the team opted to make a detour via the west side of the north col. They found a 1000-metre high slope reminiscent of the north east spur of the Droites finishing at 6900m. Georges was keen to get to work and possibly overstretched himself doing carries and fixing ropes. Perhaps he was trying to make up for the fact that he was the only Frenchman!

They reached 7900m and that night the wind raged, whipping up one of the tents and Georges's sleeping bag in its frenzy. They went down, dazed and confused, eyes frozen and bodies exhausted. A little while later they were on the mountain again. Once again Georges threw himself into the climbing, over zealously perhaps. The howling wind showed no signs of abating and Georges, exhausted by his efforts, abandoned his attempt considering it too dangerous. The three others had the summit in their sights while he headed back down to base camp. The following day the wind, which had been storming for the past five

A truly great climb: the first ascent of Shivling's east pillar, a 13-day climb. Rick White, Greg Child and Bettembourg on the summit in Doug Scott's photo. Summer 1981.

With Patrick Vallençant and Jean-Louis Etienne during their attempt on Broad Peak.

weeks, finally died down and the Brits had made it to the summit. This was the third ascent of Kangchenjunga, made more noble by being done Alpine style. Official histories only have space for summiteers but it didn't bother Georges. His mind was already elsewhere, on other high altitude quests, he had found his Holy Grail. He sent the following message from their base camp: *"On the north col of Kanch, I felt torn between my mind as it communed with the Infinite pulling me up towards it above my head, and my physical shell, which was cold and wanted to go to the loo and was tying me back down to earth. At that moment, I had an intense sense of the joy and wretchedness that is to be a man. It was amazingly pleasant and extraordinarily painful all at once but most of all it was real!"* He hadn't planned anything and had no career plans or any thoughts for his relationship with Norma the American, who was never far from his thoughts but would soon move out of his life.

That autumn he was back in the Himalayas with Doug and Mike Covington. They had no less than three peaks on their hit list. First up was the north face of Kusum Kangguru, an ethereal taster for the climbs to come. Next came the north face of Nuptse. After having fixed ropes on it, they climbed the huge face that culminates at 7800m in just three days. On the way down, sapped by their efforts at altitude, they had to face the Ice Fall. Massive sections of it had collapsed and it extended a further 100 metres back. It took them over nine hours to cross the mountainous chaos of crumpled ice. The team of iconoclasts had broken with convention for a second time. Free-spirited and still young, they had once again shaken up old-style Himalayan climbing. They were some of the few climbers to follow in Messner's footsteps. And like Messner, Georges attempted a solo ascent of Everest. Unlike Messner, Georges turned

around at 7600m. He stopped to gaze philosophically at the beauty and poetry of the surroundings. The expeditions now came one after the other. In 1980 he made an attempt on Makalu (turning round at 8000m) and made the first skied descent of Makalu II before joining Patrick Vallençant on Broad Peak where they made a skied descent from 7600m. The following year, again with Doug Scott, he was one of the team to make the first ascent of the east pillar of Shivling in India.

It took them 13 days and 60 pitches of sublime climbing to reach the top. In 1982 he was in Bolivia trying out his latest invention – the 'ski-voile', a precursor to speed riding – that he had already tested on the north face of Mont Blanc. Summer 1983 he was back in Chamonix as usual. The mountains were bare that summer, stripped of their carapace of ice. Rocks could be heard tumbling down the huge slopes of the mountains in Chamonix at night. It was a good season for crystals. Georges explored the Aiguille Verte together with Jean-Franck and two clients and friends, no doubt following in their grandfather's footsteps. It was a glorious day in the mountain cirque that they knew so well. Their packs were full of crystals of smoked quartz and they only had one more abseil left to reach the bottom. All of a sudden there was a terrible noise 400 metres above them. The mountain was tearing itself apart. A pillar of rock on the Contamine Route had collapsed. A tide of rocks crashed over them. They were washed down with the abseil stance and ropes. Jean-Franck found himself dazed and alone with one client in the middle of a mountain face that now looked more like a landslide. It was too late for André Reynaud and Georges. Their bodies lay on a carpet of rocks with crystals glinting in the last rays of sun, just as Georges had among his contemporaries.

Georges Payot followed the family tradition and became a guide with the Compagnie.

*Georges Payot
on the summit
of the Aiguille Verte
having made the first ascent
of the Contamine route
with Jean Martin,
André Contamine
and Pierre Labrunie,
26 August 1962.*

GEORGES PAYOT, A PASSIONATE WITNESS

For a long time Georges Payot smoked a pipe, which made him look a little like French chansonnier Georges Brassens. And like Brassens, Payot has also cultivated some lasting friendships and has probably been heard to sing the odd off-colour song in his time. His white beard and thinning hair means he has something of the bard about him and you might momentarily take him for a wise old man.

From a long line of guides, he could have made a career simply as a mountaineer without having to guide clients, but that wasn't his style. He made several first ascents in the Alps and the Himalayas and as a teacher at ENSA he has trained generations of mountain professionals. Yet he has had an extremely low profile over the past seventy years. You might say he fell into the 'guiding cauldron' as a child, like a mountain Obelix. And, as he likes to remind people, there have always been guides in the family. The first, Pierre-Joseph Payot, was on his father's side, and became a guide in 1793 and was followed on his mother's side by Jean Payot (it's a common name in the valley...) in 1842. They were all farmers but had numerous other trades and Georges's father René had trained as an upholsterer. It was his father who gave him a taste for the mountains. He was a guide and head instructor at the EHM. He died on 6 November 1950 when he was swept into a crevasse by a snow slide

below the Grands Mulets hut. Georges was only 13 years old when he found himself in Paris Match, photographed carrying his father's crampons and ice axe at his funeral. Perhaps it was because of this traumatic personal experience that he kept the media at arm's length.

The years that followed in the inward-looking Chamonix valley were not easy and he earned a living as a porter in the local luxury hotels. At the age of eighteen, anticipating his call up for national service, he joined the air force as a cook. On his return to the valley in 1957, he was faced with finding a job. As most of his friends had become guides and he was no worse than any of the others, he thought he would give it a go. He could boast three routes in the Aiguilles Rouges, done under the supervision of guides from the Compagnie, and one as 'an amateur', on the northeast ridge of the Aiguille de l'M. But this didn't matter, as his tutor Armand Charlet was at the height of his game and gave Payot plenty of opportunity to perfect his art. He spent weeks at a time in huts, practising on ice and rock, and doing large numbers of traverses – the Charmoz-Grepon, Aiguilles du Diable and Courtes – learning ropework. He was an aspirant by the time he was 21 and applied to join the Compagnie, as was expected of him. He did his first routes as a professional with Marcel Burnet. He

Payot bivouacking on the Olan, winter 1958.

*Yannick Seigneur and Georges Payot
on an expedition to Makalu's west pillar.*

also started climbing with other young men from the valley, such as Christian Mollier, Marc Martinetti and Yvon Masino. He first teamed up with Gérard Devouassoux in 1960, on the Bonatti Route on the Grand Capucin. The famous Payot-Devouassoux-Masino climbing team, known affectionately by friends and colleagues as PDM, was starting to take shape. Two or three of them would regularly go down to climb in the Prealps and the Calanques, sometimes with Martinetti who had a motorbike. They were the first guides to climb for fun like this. The old guard didn't always think much of these exploits, as for them climbing was work. But this didn't bother Georges and friends and their thoughts turned increasingly to these escapades during their courses. They were forbidden from climbing at the weekends. Georges tells an anecdote of one of his guide's courses in 1961: *"One Sunday in June, René Desmaison, Yves Pollet-Villard, Fernand Audibert and I set off to climb the northeast pillar on Mont Aiguille [in the Vercors, south of Grenoble]. We were found out and got a serious dressing down. The following day was an ice training day on the Mer de Glace and we were just made to run up and down slopes. 'So, you want to do routes on Sundays, eh? A bit tired are we?' No, it was useful training. We felt good in the mountains, we got on well and that was a great help and gave us a real boost."*

Together with his brothers-in-arms from the valley and René Desmaison (Georges was one of his first

climbing partners), he would take part in some of the best climbs of the 1960s. He was in the team (with Fernand Audibert, René Desmaison and Jean Puiseux) that made the first winter ascent of the Devies-Gervasutti route on the Olan. This was one of the first modern winter ascents on a difficult route. Four years later the PDM team knocked off the north face of the Drus using three bivouacs and an epic involving nineteen bottles of champagne in the valley afterwards. He added the first traverse of the Chamonix Aiguilles in winter (with Christian Mollier) and a winter ascent of the Nant Blanc face of the Aiguille Verte (with Desmaison) to this record. That made a total of nine bivouacs in the heart of winter over less than three weeks...

He has a taste for fine climbs and the good things in life and sees no difference between so-called amateur and professional climbing. In 1962, together with André Contamine, he made the first winter ascent of the central spur on the north face of the Aiguille Verte.

He has produced his best performances on expedition, beyond the Alps. According to many, his ideal climbing partner was Robert Paragot, with whom he went to Huscaran and Makalu. Payot, according to Paragot, *"wasn't very talkative but when he did speak, it was words of encouragement. He's a quiet and optimistic person."* In 1966 he and Claude Jaccoux were members of an expedition to the north face of Huascaran. His suffered his first oedema

During the 1974 Everest expedition.

With Christophe Profit and Olivier Besson, returning from a route on the Envers du Mont Blanc.

on his first night at altitude and was evacuated down to the town of Yungay, spending his time on tourist visits to Cuzco. One might say he was now in some senses vaccinated against altitude and went on expedition after expedition with an incredibly laid-back attitude. In 1971 he was part of the team chosen by the French mountaineering federation to make an attempt on Makalu's west pillar. At a time when a lot of teams were happy to repeat the normal routes on the 8000ers, the French decided to up the stakes and try this poker-straight pillar. Payot reached the 8000-metre mark and the expedition was a success, with Yannick Seigneur and Bernard Mellet reaching the summit. But even before then, Payot had already become a Himalayan regular. In 1970 he had got a taste for high altitudes on the south summit of Annapurna with Devouassoux, Masino and Maurice Gicquel. He was really smitten and in 1972 he made the first ascent of the south face of Pumori (7145m). The entire team, mainly composed of teachers from ENSA, reached the summit. From the summit he no doubt gazed across at nearby Everest. This was his next objective together with a team made up entirely of guides from the Compagnie. Yet it was to end with the deaths of Gérard Devouassoux and two Sherpas, in an avalanche. Despite the death of one of his best friends, he set out again and in 1978 made an attempt on the southwest pillar of Dhaulaghiri. *"It was another expedition planned by ENSA teachers. Our goal turned out to be harder that we had thought.*

Complex mixed terrain and the strong Tibetan winds meant we missed out on the summit."

He was asked to join the French expedition to K2 the following year, but turned the offer down recognising that he had had enough. That did not stop him from returning for several years running to Nepal's Manang, to train Nepali mountain guides. He also went back in 1986 to try a new route on Annapurna, an expedition cut short by the death of Benoit Grison. And he was back again in 2000 for the fiftieth anniversary of the first ascent of Annapurna.

He has turned his attention since this time back to his first love. With no fuss or fanfare, he has spent his well-earned retirement almost apologising for climbing with the next generation who in turn are proud to have him with them. At the age of 62 he joined Yann Delvaux and Richard Perez on Half Dome's Regular Route in Yosemite. He has also sampled the delights of Wadi Rum's magnificent sandstone routes and climbs in Australia with his nephew Alain (joining the latter's 80-year old client Jacques Landry to make a particularly energetic mature climbing team!). And at 64 he was off to Denali. Even these days the likes of Christophe Profit and Benoit Robert enjoy climbing with this grandfatherly figure, who has never lost his love of the mountains. And some in the valley ask where it will all end, as his energy and enthusiasm seem boundless.

Christophe Profit soloing the American Direct on the Drus.

Jérôme Ruby,
Fred Vimal
and David Ravanel
in the early 1980s.

PUSHING THE LIMITS

Lionel Terray announced in the 1950s that he didn't think there was *"any challenge left in the Alps that would change the face of mountaineering."* Yet every generation of climbers has done its best to prove the contrary. For two decades it was winter ascents, often with the talented and inspired René Desmaison leading the way. They were carried out like some kind of well-oiled ritual and in keeping with the ethics of the day, with no previous ascents allowed, absolute autonomy and total commitment. But by the end of the 1970s, the greatest challenges had been met and once again the rules of the game came under scrutiny.

The following two decades would turn things upside down, and not just in the sporting context but also sociologically and even geographically. Chamonix wasn't spared these changes and it was no longer the cliché of a typical mountain village. Tourists arriving in the resort were now greeted by the brand new Chamonix Sud complex, which drew its inspiration from the modern architecture of the new housing projects in Sarcelles and Vaulx-en-Venin, before being confronted by a series of concrete towers next to the central square. There had been a radical shake up of ideas and withdrawal to a completely Chamoniard identity, was becoming increasingly difficult. A new generation of climbers arrived in Chamonix. They didn't just stay for the summer season, they wanted to explore the massif and live in the valley the whole year round. They did various odd jobs and had, for the most part, set their sights on becoming guides.

Looking back, those years were exciting, vibrant and dramatic yet brought surprises and contradictions. In the artistic world, music styles were blending and melding with boss nova, disco, rock and reggae all finding their audiences. The geopolitical context was also changing. Chernobyl and the collapse of the Soviet Union meant received notions were now being questioned. This was also the beginning of mass consumption and the sales of the first home computers. Young people were discovering that, unlike previous generations, their lives were less than idyllic as they were now having to contend with the effects of Aids, the hole in the ozone layer and a nascent realisation of the extent of the damage to the environment. The cinema was dominated by massive American studios, which were launching blockbusters such as ET with huge world-wide publicity campaigns and distribution deals. The planet seemed to be spiralling out of control while space-time was shrinking. The mountaineering world was caught up in this maelstrom and traditional alpinism adopted a range of different approaches, trends and styles.

The hugely talented and eclectic climber Thierry Renault is as strong on rock as he is on ice.
On the first ascent of Shiva Lingam above the Argentière glacier, one of the first grade VI ice routes.

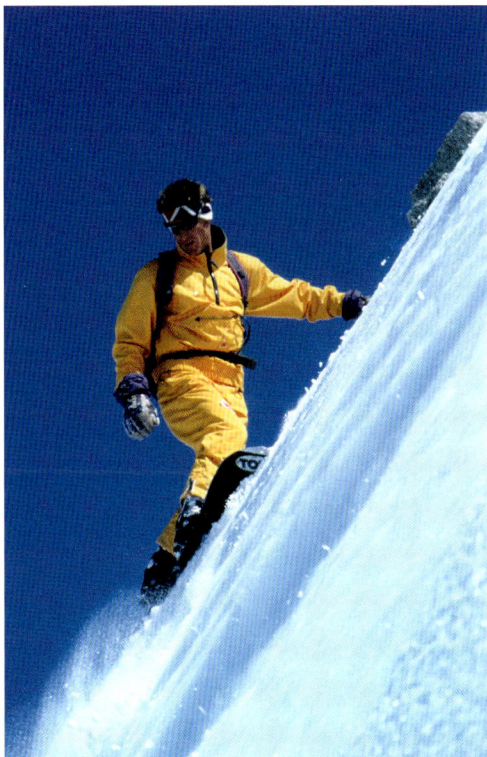

As good a snowboarder as a climber, Eric Bellin extreme snowboarding.

Thierry Renault free climbing a route called Ma Dalton (F7b).

Little by little free climbing started to step out from under the shadow of mountaineering to become a discipline in its own right. Michel Piola and the superb routes he put up across the massif were among some of the key elements spurring on the evolution of the discipline. Climbers could also now climb a route without having to reach a summit. Patrick Gabarrou, together with a number of different climbing companions, set about exploring the Alpine massifs, starting with the Mont Blanc range. And the arrival of hang gliders and then paragliders allowed a whole host of projects to link up climbs and routes to take off. Jean-Marc Boivin's solo ascent of the Matterhorn in 1980 and his linkup the following year of the south face of the Fou and the American Direct on the Drus with Patrick Berhault shattered previous records. This was the start of the years that saw climbers truly pushing their limits. These exploits were relayed onto our television screens and discussed in magazines.

Alpinism as a philosophy of life, taking priority over everything else for weekend escapades, had become a sport if not a profession in itself. Climbers were training as hard as top athletes, and adhering to diets and strict training regimes. Considerable improvements were made to equipment: curved picks for axes, new rubber soles for rock boots and Gore-Tex clothing, to name but a few. In just ten years, grades were given a pounding: French grade 7 then grade 8 rock climbs

were now the benchmark standard for climbers who thought they were any good. On ice, the grade VI threshold was broken and legendary grade VII routes started to appear.

At the start of the 1980s, Christophe Profit was only 22 years old but was already one of the best climbers of his generation. He understood the importance of the whole package, how attractive it was to the media, starting with the specialist magazines (which were already hiring helicopters and collaborating with the major national papers). His first great coup was on the American Direct on the Drus. He climbed it several times, refining his technique and performance, before soloing the 1100-metre route that includes several pitches of French 6b! At the time, he and his rivals – Eric Escoffier and Jean-Marc Boivin – battled for the title of the 'fastest man in the mountains' and he amazed the world of mountaineering with his exploits. He is particularly famous for his linked winter ascents of the three great north faces of the Alps – the Grandes Jorasses, the Eiger and the Cervin – in March 1987. His brand and style of climbing marked this 10-year period and culminated in a fabulous ascent of K2 in 1991 with Pierre Beghin.

Yet he was not the only climber in this frenetic race for top performances. Thierry Renault is not only known for his pioneering ice routes but is also a brilliant and eclectic mountaineer. Together

Dédé Rhem and Jérôme Ruby on the first snowboarded descent of the north face of the Triolet, June 1995.
A superb shot by Philippe Fragnol.

François Marsigny on the first ascent of Divine Providence, August 1984.

Alain Ghersen on the first free ascent of Divine Providence (with Thierry Renault).
One of the best climbers of his generation, Ghersen's impressive list of climbs includes, among many others,
the first winter solo ascent of the Bonatti Pillar, the first winter ascent of the Directissime Jori on the Frêney
and the first solo ascent of Divine Providence. He was also responsible for Au Sud Nulle Part,
the first grade F8a route in the Mont Blanc chain...

Extreme snowboarding and skiing, BASE jumping, mountaineering and climbing: multi-talented guides Sam Beaugey, Pierre-André (Dédé) Rhem and Jérôme Ruby.

They also joined Christophe Profit and Jean Blanchard for some back to basics climbing on Pumori and Kantega.

with Christophe Profit, he linked the north face of the Pilier d'Angle, the Piola-Steiner route on the central Frêney pillar and the classic route on the central pillar before finishing up the Innominata Ridge! On granite with Pascal Etienne, he completed a host of routes on the Aiguille du Midi: the Contamine plus Jules de Chez Smith plus Super Dupont and the Rébuffat. That's not forgetting his climbing further afield. In Yosemite, for instance, he once held the record for the fastest ascent of The Nose, climbing one of the biggest walls in the world in just 12 hours.

Linking up routes and rapid ascents quickly became the watchwords of an unrestrained form of climbing mainly done by French climbers, which some British observers teasingly called 'the French Touch'. Young climbers flocked to join them. With their colourful clothing, they were far from the image of Rébuffat. From Fred Vimal via Eric Bellin and Christophe Crettin to Dédé Rhem, Jérôme Ruby, Alain Ghersen and, a little later, Jean-Christophe Lafaille, their heroic exploits were accompanied by colourful stills and film footage. Rhem and Ruby are famous for their snowboarded descent of the north face of the Triolet that was captured on film. Yet the tragic deaths of some of the climbers of this time and the sheer number of their exploits brought this era of mountaineering to a close. Most of those involved turned their backs on the limelight, no doubt wanting a bit of downtime and freedom.

François Marsigny was one of the rare climbers of this time to pursue a career in a more classic form of mountaineering. While still studying architecture in Paris, he was influenced by a shooting star of the climbing world, Benoit Grison. He steered a course between hardcore amateur climbing and a natural desire to be professional in his work. Thus, he made the first winter ascent of the Cascade de Frêney in a 70-hour roundtrip from Paris. Together with Patrick Gabarrou, he put up one of the most notable and the hardest routes in the Mont Blanc range, Divine Providence on the Pilier d'Angle.

This is certainly not an exhaustive list. Yet it should be noted that the majority of these great figures from the 1980s, part of the climbing elite, have joined the Compagnie and have put their extraordinary talents to good use in helping others. Two generations of these exceptional climbers set their sights on goals that were far from the microcosm of the Chamonix valley. In 1998 and 2001, for example, Christophe joined forces with Sam Beaugey, Dédé Rhem and Jean Blanchard on new routes on Pumori's south pillar and the southeast pillar of Kantega. In exporting itself beyond the Mont Blanc Massif, Chamonix alpinism has returned to its original principles, those of magnificent routes and close friendships. It has come full circle and Chamonix alpinism has gone back to its roots.

Jean-Paul Charlet, with Roger Fournier, explains the finer points of crystal hunting to a client.

The heyday of the 'Daltons'.
Left to right:
Jean-Franck Charlet,
Daniel Lagarde,
René Ghilini
and Roland Cretton.

GUIDES AND CRYSTAL HUNTERS: A LONG TRADITION

Both crystal hunters and guides were for a long time an essential part of Chamonix life and the crystal trade was flourishing when de Saussure first visited the valley. Crystals were very fashionable at that time and decorated the chandeliers of palaces in Venice, Vienna and Rome, as well as jewellery, snuffboxes, the hilts of swords and even garters. De Saussure described the Chamionards thus: *"Searching for crystals and hunting are the only occupations that remain the exclusive preserve of men. Happily, far fewer men are occupied with the former of these occupations than before; I say happily, as many have perished [in doing it]. The hope of sudden enrichment, of finding a cavern full of beautiful crystals, exerted such a powerful attraction that they exposed themselves to the most dreadful of dangers and a year hardly went by without men perishing in the ice and over precipices."*

More than two centuries later the situation is very different. Mountaineering has become a sport and only the odd, rare collector is still fascinated by crystals while the vast majority of the guides have turned away from crystal hunting. Those that do collect, do so as a hobby. Thus, over the entire first half of the 20th century there was only a single large discovery recorded. In 1929, on the first ascent of their route up the north face of the Aiguille Verte, Georges Charlet, Alfred Couttet

and André Devouassoux came across a magnificent outcrop weighing several hundred kilos with some crystals jutting out by over 30 centimetres. But this was the exception, not the rule. Paul Payot wrote in 1950, almost nostalgically: *"In the windows of some souvenir shops you can still see a few sheets and blocks of rock crystal, the last vestiges of a flourishing trade that existed since the Middle Ages and which is now gone."*

The fate of Charlet Straton's mineral collection is a sign of the huge indifference to crystal hunting there was by 1954. When the Le Planet hotel, which he had had built, was sold to become a holiday centre, his collection was scattered among the rubble. A local boy, Roger Fournier, gathered up a few of the discarded specimens. He would go on to become both a great guide and a crystal hunter.

On the fringes of the guiding fraternity, there are still a few passionate collectors prepared to scour the most inauspicious terrain in their quest for minerals. A guide from the Oisans region, Roger Canac, compellingly describes the attraction these stones can exert:
"One is a crystal hunter just as one is someone from the mountains. It is a state of being. Most of all, it is a passion. [...] Minerals speak to the heart and to the intellect for they are at one with the stars; they are stones that sparkle, that are both fragile and robust

Daniel Lagarde and Roland Cretton
discover a smoky quartz 'four' or cavity lined with crystals.

Daniel Audibert and Georges Bettembourg
with specimens of fluorite.

and can be held in one's hand. Crystals cause a quiver to run through your soul and through those who come across them as they explore the granite needles. Sometimes they are as translucent as the ice that falls from the roofs on clear winter mornings. Sometimes they are embellished with beautiful lemon-yellow, topaz or smoky hues through to the deep ebony of black quartz. Rock crystal is born from the protogine that nourished it and the clouds it contains come from the sky. It was once believed that the high altitudes exposed them to cosmic rays from the stars. We now think that the natural radiation produced in the granite gives them their attractive, indelible smoky appearance. It's the Earth's alchemy."

The flame burned the longest in Argentière, and Georges Charlet passed on the tradition. No doubt dazzled by his first discovery, this excellent guide would regularly scour the south face of the Verte, the Aiguille de Leschaux, the Chardonnet and the Aiguille d'Argentière for treasure. He introduced his son Jean-Paul to his unusual quest. It was Jean-Paul who introduced Roger Fournier to crystal hunting. After a few exchanges Jean-Paul Charlet took Fournier mineral gathering and his passion for crystals was born.

A talented rock climber, he did some great routes including a guided ascent of the Walker Spur on the Grandes Jorasses and the northwest spur of the Droites. And he never lost his passion for crystals. His boldness and enthusiasm led him to

make some exceptional discoveries. His notable finds included a remarkable collector's piece he uncovered near the Pointe des Améthystes that is a smoky crystal topped by an amethyst 'cap'. He and Charlet were the first crystal hunters to visit and climb the range's great rock walls.

He was a collector at heart and he left behind after his death (in the Leschaux area) one of the best collections in the Alps. Other groups were formed during this time, as if at a stroke the local rocks were at their most sparklingly radiant. Armand Comte from Chamonix often joined forces with Jeannot Tournier and Michel Comte and his first find dates back to 1959. Freddy Couttet is well known for his knowledge of crystals as are the Cretton family of Argentière.

Do they collect for pleasure or for financial gain? It is difficult to say but thanks to their hunters, crystals have rejoined the collective imagination of the locals and the guides. They are fascinated by them, much like the Conquistadors were by Eldorado; a mix of financial gain and a heady quest for beauty, where adventure is wrapped up with the most extravagant dreams. For most of them it becomes an all-consuming passion and little by little the crystal hunters have found their place again in the valley. The 1968 mineral exchange even gave them a degree of legitimacy and exceptional pieces were brought out of storage.

Another team of guides/crystal hunters - Jeannot Claret-Tournier and Armand Comte - with their summer's haul.

Jeannot Claret-Tournier in action.

But don't be fooled into thinking this is easy money. The most stunning pieces are found on the most crumbling and exposed rocks faces where rock falls are regular occurrences or they require rummaging through unstable bergschrunds, and they always have huge backpacks to carry.

And then even once you think you have the crystals things can still go wrong, as happened to Armand Comte near the Aiguille Croulante. *"It was Palm Sunday 1960. We had walked up to the Couvercle hut on skis. We'd spotted a vein just above the bergschrund at the base of the Aiguille [Croulante]. We followed a couloir, traversed across a steep section and then it started it ease off a bit. On a ledge in the slope we could see a lump of granite lying upside down. Turning it over we found a wonderful selection of pure, unbroken crystals. The lump weighed a good 60 kilos and we wondered how we were going to get it down. We suggested to Michel Comte and Robert Coquoz, who were with us, that they go and bring up a sled from Chamonix. We belayed them through the trickiest sections, as the terrain was pretty unstable. It took us two hours and when we got back to our lump of granite, to our utter amazement it had disappeared! The wall faced south and we had stood it up on a little patch of ice. It hadn't occurred to us that the sun would be so hot and would soften the ground. We found it in pieces on the ground at the foot of the wall. We were pretty upset..."*

As the valley opened up to foreigners, the next generation of crystal hunters to explore the mountains came once again from Argentière. First there was Jean-Franck Charlet who with his cousin, Georges Bettembourg, followed in their grandfather's footsteps.

They continued the family tradition (crystal hunting in September and searching through veins that had already been explored) but quickly moved up a gear. Up until that point, crystal hunters had mostly stuck to the base of the rock walls and maybe 100 or 200 metres above the bergschrund at the most. The massive technical face climbs (such as those on the Droites, Courtes and Grandes Jorasses) had yet to be explored. Bettembourg was an innovator and rappelled down the most inaccessible faces. This was how he discovered one of the most beautiful pieces of fluorite to be found in the Chamonix Aiguilles. Others followed in their wake. René Ghilini, also a guide from the Compagnie, started crystal hunting in the 1980s and discovered a magnificent outcrop on the north face of the Requin. The following day Bettembourg was to uncover another one. Each asked Jean-Franck to join him and they ended up forming a team of three, two of them crystal hunting while the other acted as the guide. This lasted until 1983, the year that Georges was killed on the north face of the Aiguille Verte. The remaining two teamed up with another guide, Roland Cretton, and Daniel Lagarde and set about clim-

Kim Bodin
one of the young generation
of guides with a passion
for crystal hunting.

Jean-Franck Charlet
is just as active as ever.

bing the hardest routes around, as they were all accomplished mountaineers. They also climbed all year round. While their ancestors viewed it as an additional activity, the three guides and Lagarde would 'professionalize' the local tradition. They were faultless in their organisation. As soon as the conditions were good enough, one would act as the guide while the other three explored the rock faces. They no longer waited for the supposedly dryer late autumn period. They were soon nicknamed the 'Dalton brothers', after characters in the Lucky Luke cartoons, as they seem to come through some incredible scrapes. With their torn clothes, enormous backpacks and calloused hands, they looked more like stonemasons than mountaineers and top-level climbers. They would happily chat about mountaineering and routes but were less forthcoming about their finds although the twinkle in their eyes would often give them away. After all, did Stevenson ever give the precise location of Treasure Island? They would discretely scour the rock faces, which up to this point had never been explored by crystal hunters. On the north face of the Requin, on a vertical wall of rock over 400 metres above the ground, they made some incredible finds, one outcrop weighing over 100 kilos.

Nevertheless, they brought it down by hand. Following an incident with a group of Swiss crystal hunters on the north face of the Grandes Jorasses, a law had been brought into place in the Mont Blanc range stating that crystal collecting was still allowed but only using 'human means' (ie. no dynamite or helicopters...). They were always the first to leave and often returned only after the last climbing parties. Staggering under the weight of packs that would make Himalayan Sherpas proud, they spent 15 years combing the range for treasure. They loved the freedom of the mountains and climbed the steepest, most isolated walls in the massif on their quest for these precious stones, following their childhood dreams. The death of Daniel Lagarde in the Montroc avalanche and Roland Cretton's gradual retirement to become a sculptor brought an end to the foursome. Jean-Franck carried on, teaming up first with Dédé Rhem and then Kim Bodin. Yet numerous guides from the Compagnie have been tempted at one time or another to give it a try. Indeed, others have taken up the challenge. Whether they are discovered by guides or not, or members of the Compagnie or others, every year an extraordinary new find is made. Their holy grail is no longer an outcrop of smoky quartz; nowadays they are looking for pink fluorite.

Gaston Bachelard wrote: *"The crystal hunter is the one who, in some way, has his hands in a cluster of stars where he can caress their gems."* In three centuries of mountaineering, nothing has changed in the Mont Blanc region.

Visiting the Périades sector is a bit like a journey to the ends of the Earth for a non-climber but it's a veritable paradise for crystal hunters for whom there is even have a bivouac hut perched high on the ridge.

Jean-Franck Charlet discusses his passion for crystals

"There have always been crystals in the family. My grandfather, Georges Charlet, would climb the Verte in the 1930s only for the crystals. He had found a fantastic outcrop on its south side, just below the summit ice fields at over 4000m. He went back to the difficult north ridge on the [Aiguille de] Leschaux as well as the Courtes, Chardonnet and the Aiguille d'Argentière for the same reason. Later on, he introduced my father Jean-Paul to mountaineering and guiding for the crystals. And he became one of the most dedicated crystal hunters around. I only wanted to be one thing when I grew up: a crystal hunter. By the age of 25, after several years spent sat in lecture theatres, I was sure of one thing: I would be a guide and a crystal hunter. In 1981, René Ghilini discovered a superb outcrop on the north face of the Requin and the following day Georges Bettembourg found another one. They both asked me to join them and make a team of three, to act as guide while they looked for crystals. That's how it was until 1983. That year, 1983, was great for crystals. Georges and I took our best clients with us on the Contamine Spur on the north face of the Verte. And we found some outstanding pieces. We were setting up our final abseil in the last rays of sun when a huge section of rock came away 400

metres above. Georges and André were no longer with us. I don't know what it was that compelled me to throw myself back into the job and crystal hunting. My lifelong friend René joined me and he understood. The flame that we had lit with Georges couldn't be snuffed out that easily. Our team needed more members. I knew Daniel Lagarde was a great guy and was good in the mountains. I also knew his address and that he would like the hard work and the adventure. With him onboard, it looked like we had a chance of getting a good team together again. At that time there was another guide/crystal hunter, Roland Cretton, wandering the mountains on his own. And his natural understanding of the rock and quirky sense of humour meant that, naturally, he became our fourth member. Thus our four-man team was complete.

My earliest childhood memories date back to one autumn, when my father would come home in the evenings with his latest pickings. He would put his big pack down on the floor in the kitchen and delicately bring out the heavy stones wrapped up in old newspapers. The magic would happen over the sink, as in contact with water, the lumps of rock would be transformed into sparkling jewels. I only had one wish: to be a crystal hunter when I grew up."

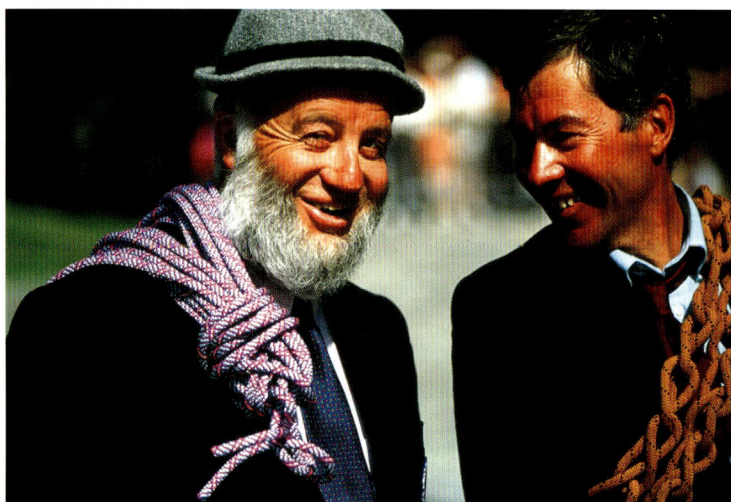

A weathered face and a mischievous expression. JP Devouassoux and Pierrot Ravanel at the 1992 fêtes des guides.

JP DEVOUASSOUX, THE GIFT OF SHARING

That day, 27 December 1998, the sky wavered between dark and light, suspended as if in anticipation. JP knew the Col de Balme area like the back of his hand. As a child he would take goats to pasture here and he had explored every gully, bowl and slope on skis, like a prospector panning for nuggets of gold. That day, however, he felt the thin, early season snow-pack presented a danger. As a precaution, he got his clients to wait in a safe spot and moved forward, exclaiming, *"Oh my goodness! Stay there and don't move. I'll have a look."* There was a dull thud, a cloud of snowy dust and a silence descended on the man and his trademark white beard. In an ironic twist, he appeared a few days later on French TV, skiing through perfect powder and talking about his friend Eric Tabarly, who had disappeared at sea that summer. Both snatched away by what they loved most.

With his solid square-cut shoulders, powerful hands, weather-beaten face, a mischievous glint to his eyes, a tenor voice with the occasional quaver and a Tyrolean hat permanently screwed onto his billiard-ball head, JP was one of the most striking figures in the valley. He was president of the Compagnie's relief fund (caisse de secours) for three years and was sensitive and humane with a curious and open nature, the noble embodiment of a guide who leads his clients. Not motivated by

incredible first ascents or prestigious climbs, he sought out serenity in the mountains with the rope serving as a symbolic link between two enthusiasts. He and one of his clients, Mademoiselle Barrat, made an incredible team. She was all delicate movement, while he stood for controlled strength. With neither partner directing their movements or acting as leader, a symbiosis emerged between the two climbers. His client's impossibly slow pace was matched by JP's endless patience and affectionate respect for his exceptional client, whom he took to some amazing routes.

A surprising detail is that she was originally his father André's client. André having died on the Tour Ronde as a young man, JP, as he was known throughout the valley, took over a few years later. His extremely hardy client was from a prominent Huguenot family and also happened to be a woman but she became the most senior of the active alpinists at that time. With a patient and steadfast manner he took this dedicated mountaineer, who was by this stage in her 70s, onto north faces more commonly the preserve of younger athletes. They started with the north face of the Col de la Verte and the big 4000ers in a partnership that would last for over 20 years.

He shared this spirit of fun with both his clients and his friends. This is how Alexandre Galperine

Many Argentière residents consider the Aiguille Verte as their mountain. It dominates this Alpine village and gives it meaning.

wrote about him in his book 'Traces pour JP' (Tracks for JP), published by the Compagnie. He didn't speak of him in the past and instead used the present tense, so in keeping with JP's personality: *"As with certain other guides, JP is at the same time an intellectual and a man of action. He is from the school of observation, not discussion: his way of looking at the mountains, seeing a world that can be transformed, resembles that of a painter. There is a serac band on the Argentière glacier. We study them every time we go past them with JP, as it's a continuous game of construction and de-construction. It's like a vast building site, a great white canvas, a canopy on a ceremonial elephant, or a temple for an ambivalent and unsteady religion [...] Take a good look, says JP, we don't need to go to Angkor Wat [...] This won't last long, there might be nothing left by the next run."*

He also had his own way of skiing: *"A tune sung by JP whose name we can't even remember is more evocative that the air we breathe. While stationary, JP has the air of a Romanesque statue. Once he has set off down a slope on skis, he grows in stature and relaxes into it, as if in some kind of waltz. His movements delicately hug the terrain, like a cloud clinging to a summit. When we turn around with him we see the cadence sketched out by his tracks. These curves and arabesques and their accompanying lines leave loops and curls in the snow, a figure drawn by a guide. A figure that can take on the shapes, colours and sounds of the mountains…"*

JP was not a solitary star. He needed partners, brothers with whom he could share, think up and construct his adventures. He had numerous friends and some of them, such as Louis Folliguet, were more than just acquaintances. He shared a passion for ideas and places with Folliguet and JP would often help him to bring his projects to fruition: *"The two friends would ski with, in turn, the Bonneville sous-préfet, the president of the ski lift authorities and a financier; the sous-préfet to authorise it, the president to make a decision and the financier to say yes."*

Together with Xavier Chappaz, he advanced the cause of the Compagnie: *"He was a mountain bandit. While others saw him set off with a simple backpack, he was actually carrying a bag of tricks. Following his own set of pistes and weather map, his peasant's instincts, the colour of the sky and the texture of the slopes, he would find snow as light as the fine sawdust made by skilled carpenters. He always skied where no one else went and he always found great skiing. He wasn't afraid to tell people about it and to remind those, who weren't already convinced, that sticking too closely to the weather forecast meant you often ended up in the bar."* He was like an older brother to Chappaz, helping him get to grips with his role as president of the Compagnie and giving him a few common sense tips. *"For your information,"* he would say, as a kind of memo for good

The 1997 fêtes des guides.
JP, president of the caisse de secours at the time,
walks with Roger Frison-Roche, the doyen of the Compagnie.

Mademoiselle Barat
is honoured at the Argentière fêtes des guides.
Like his father before him, JP was her regular guide.

sense and good ideas. He was totally selfless yet was always ready to defend the relief fund, the bedrock of the Compagnie. The fund was sacred and a vocation and he called upon a great many virtues to defend it, including authority, complicity, charm and humour. He would indulge in a certain amount of horse-trading and if necessary he could be pretty wily in negotiations. He even went so far as to soften up a tax official who had decided that this pillar of generosity should be taxed. He told him stories of avalanches and broken families and the taxman was greatly moved by this bear of a man with tears in his eyes.

His three-year tenure left a lasting legacy: the Euro campaign, an exhibition of paintings held in the Maison de la Montagne, the introduction of artwork to the posters for the guides' festival held on 15 August, kids from the valley designing the posters and drawing their idea of a perfect mountain, his membership of the guides' choir and a final guides' ball held in the salle des fêtes which burnt down just after he stepped down.

His life was filled with music, painting and poetry. This man who was born on a farm in the heart of the village of Argentière, among the sounds of cowbells, mollycoddled by his sisters and protected by a loving father, opened his mind to the world as one opens a window to let in the light. His outlook on life was guided by a quest for beauty,

which he would happily share with others.

One of his own guides was the Belgian businessman and patron of the arts Jean Pierre de Launiot who introduced him to the great works of classical music. He was just as passionate about opera as he was about the mountains and would visit the great opera houses with his wife Arlette. Over the years he became one of the great ambassadors for the valley and shared his dreams with a huge number of people. He clients included government ministers and world-class businessmen. He had a talent for initiating meetings and friendships and it was he who was the inspiration for this book. He introduced me to numerous Chamonix families, facilitating encounters and obtaining confidences that were only made because it was 'JP from Argentière'.

One day we were sitting outside a café in Argentière, opposite the Aiguille Verte, and he took me to the cemetery a short walk away. It isn't a sad place and it sits under the protective gaze of the Verte and the Chardonnet. Locals stroll through the small plot of land in the centre of the village on walks or to pay their respects to ancestors, and JP wanted me to grasp the spirit of the place. As we stood by the tomb for the guides and in just a few simple yet powerful words, he helped me understand and gain a greater appreciation of Argentière. *"Do you want to know what Argentière is about? You see the tomb for the guides: it holds my*

Mademoiselle Barat in her 90s on the Pyramide Vincent in the Monte Rosa Massif.

uncle, my brother-in-law, my father, my cousin and my best friend, they all died in the mountains." He didn't need to say another word; he had let me know that when he had to die, he would prefer it to be in the mountains. He wasn't being fatalistic and it wasn't sad, that was just the way it was. When it was his turn to make his exit, he wanted to his see friends again and be reunited with them. That day I understood his visceral bond to his village and to his job.

Wherever he went, he took a piece of the land that was so dear to him in his heart. One of his best clients invited him to the United States and he found himself having lunch with John Kerry and his wife, who had just got married, before being taken on a tour of the White House with a group of American senators. He was introduced to John Glenn, one of the first Americans in space, and gave him a geography lesson about Mont Blanc. For him every day presented the opportunity for joyful communication and he would often guffaw *"isn't my country beautiful!"* Two or three words spoken with what was almost modesty were enough to make him happy. The 'gift of sharing', he would have certainly approved of the epithet. On the eve of the winter that would be one of the most terrible in Chamonix's history, JP returned for a final time to the mountains he was so fond of and which he loved to share.

On his skis at the Grands Montets
he was a peerless creator of perfect turns.

The Pointe Chaubert on the traverse of the Aiguilles du Diable.

*Sylvain Frendo
belaying on the traverse
of the Aiguilles du Diable.*

'GRANDES COURSES': LONG CLIMBS IN BIG MOUNTAINS

Whether you are a competent climber or not, the idea of the 'grandes courses', classic long routes, is an invitation to go on a journey of exploration. For a guide it is the ultimate challenge. He is climbing at the very limit of his capabilities and not only has to confront the realities of the terrain but also the expectations of a climbing partner who expects everything from him: technical skill, safety and stamina. In short, the guide has to take all the pressure of the climb while appearing to remain rock-solid and unwavering, not unlike the surrounding slabs of granite...

Guides such as Roger Fournier, Roger Ravanel and, a little later, Elie Hanoteau had already shattered one taboo in the 1970s by taking clients on the Walker Spur and the Eiger. By the beginning of the 1980s, there was real power to be had in getting a big mountain route in the tour de rôle.

Three guides explain their routes, with each guide obviously having his own take on the situation. Vincent Couttet, for example, jumped at the chance as soon as he was given a big mountain route and he remembers being given the American Direct on the Drus that way. With a wave of a hand he had a new climbing partner, a Canadian client, a complete stranger. The ritual is always the same: the guide interrogates his prospective climbing partner on what he or she has already

done; making the client recite the route names as if in some kind of bizarre Latin exam. Yet this is not enough if you are faced with a huge climb, for although some clients can perform extremely well in the oral exam, they can sometimes bring out a few surprises on the practical. Vincent had fine-tuned his practical test: *"He had to be able to do the Lachenal in 2 1/2 hours and link it up with the Rébuffat in 2 hours. If he could go at that pace, could climb well and quickly, he was going to be able to second me on a long face route."*

Thus, in 1986, he climbed the north face of the Drus, the American Direct and made an attempt on the Bonatti Pillar. In 1987, the era of the great linked climbs, he did Williamine Dada on the Blaitière, traversed to the Fontaine ledge and bivouacked there before rappelling down and climbing back up the south face of the Fou the following day.

Jacques Fouque and Michel Arizzi had suggested this route two years earlier, having just come off the traverse of the Chamonix Aiguilles. *"I had heard from Michel Bellin that you could traverse the face and that was how he had climbed the south face of the Fou five days running. It was a new and logical idea. I made my calculations down to the last gram for this project. I climbed without a pack on the hard sections (moves of French 6c) and hauled the gear up,*

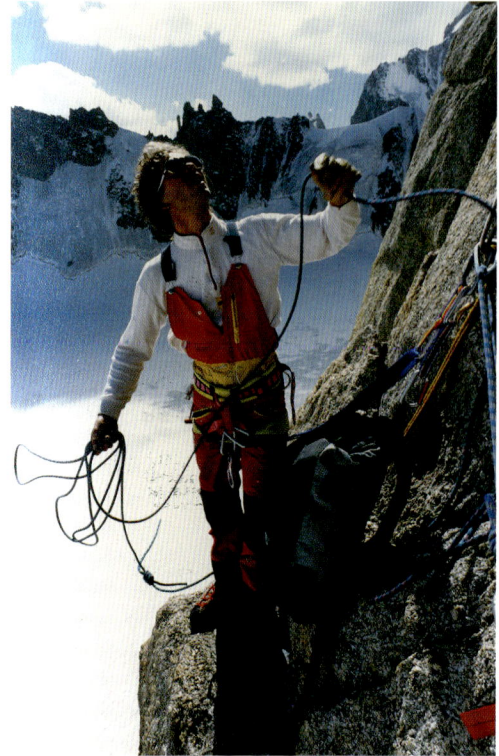

just like in Yosemite. At the bivouac, far from anyone, we found a watermelon that some mates had hauled up with them on the traverse of the Aiguilles. The following day we were completely alone and started rappelling. It's really impressive being on this kind of face. We were caught in a shower of fine hail as we were on the exit corner. The Chamonix Aiguilles had a phantasmagorical feel. We rappelled down the west face in torrential rain. We had no choice, as we were in rock shoes and there was no way we were going on to the Spencer [Couloir] without crampons."

He did some of the best climbs in the range, the kind that really make a career. And yet, ironically, he admits that this is not necessarily the most profitable strategy. The rate for a long route is obviously proportional to its difficulty and size, but at the same time it is a pretty random business. Vincent didn't have time for anything else and often passed clients on to other guides, as he was waiting for a window in the weather. The best example of this is the Walker Spur, the much-coveted pillar that has so many stories and so much symbolism attached to it. *"There is a spot in Les Tines from where you see it. I could tell by just looking at it without binoculars if it was in condition or not. The primary challenge was to find the right window to climb it in, ahead of the crowds. I wasn't working the first time I climbed it, with Eric Favret. I then did it two more times as a guide. I knew the*

29 pitches and belay stances by heart. I started up the corner 30 minutes before daybreak. As the sun rises, you suddenly realise the size of the task ahead of you and you ask yourself the fateful question: can I do this? You sense the responsibility for the entire climb resting on your shoulders and in a fraction of a second you have made your choice. You know you have to manage both the climbing and your client. You have to watch, protect and encourage him, take breaks and eat snacks at the right moment. It involves some very specific logistics to manage the strain as well as the climbing. The second time I was with Franco Obert, who had a 60-year old client, and we were on the summit by 1pm."

After 10 years of this pace, Vincent decided to slow down. *"I didn't want the big routes to become commonplace. I had tried to be innovative and I wanted to move on to something else. I never made any claims to be a top-level climber but on these kinds of routes it's will power and desire that make the difference. A desire to share, to explore and make advances, to innovate."* The search for something new is perhaps the key to success. And that was how Vincent Couttet found a way to climb the Aiguille Verte by a rather surprising manner: climbing the Arête Sans Nom and descending via the Arête des Grands Montets in time to catch the last lift down. After a trip to Yosemite, he decided to focus on other things, away from the big classic routes, and

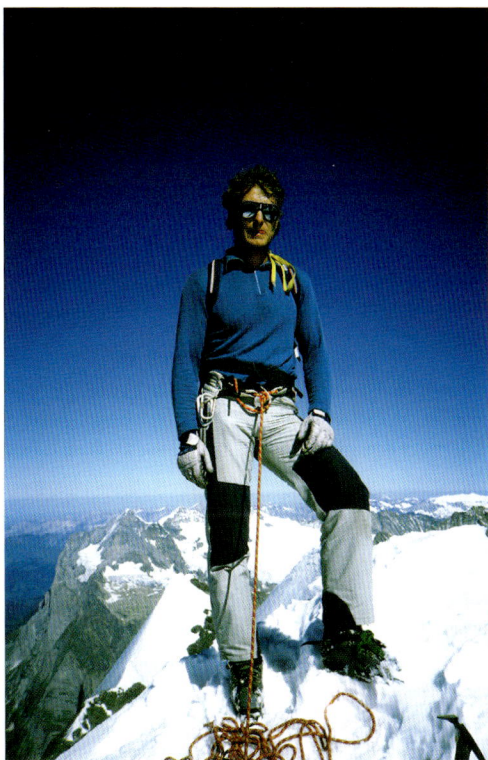

Michel Arizzi
at the top of the north face
of the Eiger.

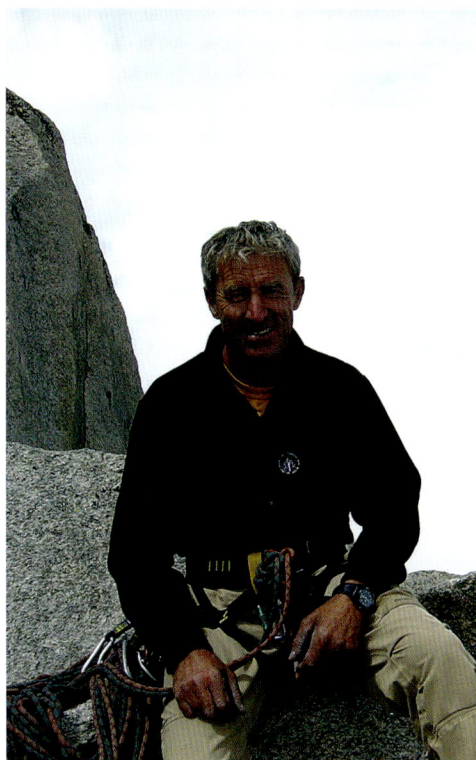

Jacques Fouque
on the traverse
of the Chamonix Aiguilles.

set up a company specialising in climbing equipment; a logical continuation and a way of adapting to the profession.

Michel Arizzi is a good example of staying power. He hasn't stopped since the aspirant guides course and his first routes, climbed with Daniel Monaci. He is an extremely strong climber and, before part of it collapsed, he climbed the Bonatti Pillar five times in a row. He also takes his strongest clients on the Grand Capucin, Walker Spur and the south face of the Fou. He recognises that 20 years ago he had more time to prepare his clients: *"Some would come to Chamonix for three weeks. I had time to train and prepare them for the main project. Nowadays, with the climbing walls and crags that are being developed all over the place, people are sharper when they arrive and, as long as I know them, we can think about setting off immediately."*

Over such a long career, he has collected a group of around five or six enthusiasts and he regularly suggests climbs to them. *"There are all kinds among them. Some barely know how to tie on and rely on me but I can go anywhere with them. Others are almost as good as guides themselves but just don't have the opportunity to find partners and we can swap leads."* He has noticed a change in guiding and mountaineering as a whole. *"These days the summit is less important than it used to be. We can quite easily do a route that doesn't go to the summit. The most impor-*

tant thing is the enjoyment. And I take more and more people on climbing trips to places like Morocco." He has often teamed up with Jacques Fouque, who he considers an extremely talented guide. For him there is an emotional difference as well: *"I have quite a relaxed temperament but in this kind of terrain you have to be totally vigilant. You have to expect just about anything and you have to be able to put your foot down even if you're with a team of top business leaders. It's a question of staying Zen, like the famous time on the Aiguille Noire de Peuterey. We were up with the sun and left the valley early in the morning. We were on the summit by midday and were caught in a terrible hailstorm. The air was electric and my [female] client squeezed my arm so tightly that I had bruises for a long while afterwards. Two hours later there was 20 centimetres of snow and it was fine again."* Over his 30-year career he has also noticed differences in the climbing calendar brought about by climate change. The time for doing some ice routes in the mountains is shorter now and they are often done in the spring or even the winter.

Marc Cereuil has witnessed a transition. He admits that he would not accept the job of guiding a client on these kinds of routes in the tour de rôle. The emotional bond is too strong for him, as is his attachment to the classic values of mountaineering, and he prefers to train up his clients

Marc Cereuil
exiting a route
on the north face
of the Aiguille du Midi.

Lionel Pernollet
on a long Yosemite
aid route.

and guide them on a journey that ends with one of these great climbs, a high point and final destination. He has been a guide since 1991 yet he doesn't see himself as an expert. He accepts that within the Compagnie there are some who are more technically competent than him, while he knows how to steer and direct his clients so that at a given time they will be ready and will give their best. *"Personally I am not ready to take a request like that in the tour de rôle. I wouldn't want to. I need to share their dreams with them, to help them progress and to be a simple facilitator when I think that all the elements are there. When the team is going well, when those emotional bonds have been established and the conditions in the mountains are perfect."*

He is also the only guide to talk about a personal equilibrium, which means when the guide is ready and in the right frame of mind, when his emotional and family life is in balance. A sense of equanimity is also a key factor. No matter how many times the guide has climbed with a particular client, the pressure rests squarely on his shoulders in this kind of terrain.

Although the client has renounced any responsibility, the guide must not even feel it. Cereuil remembers a time he was guiding the north face of the Eiger with Christophe Profit who had the second client. *"We decided to turn back on the*

Hinterstoisser Traverse because of stonefall. The face really wasn't in condition. I was with a client called Gaelle and although she was a strong climber, I could see that she was totally overwhelmed by the sheer size of the face. That shows the difficulty of the route, especially when nothing goes to plan."

He also found being with another guide on this route made it even safer. *"I have a great deal of admiration for the old guides who perfected climbing with porters. It provided youngsters with a real opportunity to learn and to second, in case the conditions were bad, the older climbers. It was a real safety net."* That day he and Gaelle got back down without any problems, reminded that climbing big routes is not just a simple mathematical equation. *"I have four or five clients like this, three of whom are women. I have to pay tribute to their fortitude and I know they have no unrealistic desires and I understand them well enough to know when they are on form. I would say that big routes are also being able to do a climb that's not as hard with a less capable client. We have to give our very best in those instances. I took some climbers on the traverse of the Aiguilles du Diable and the Arête des Grands Montets and for them it was the absolute high point of their climbing career and I had to call upon all my skills [as a guide]."* He also admits to doing around five big routes per season, when there are perfect conditions and he is on form (which doesn't happen every year). He

Croz Spur, north face of the Grandes Jorasses, 1980s.

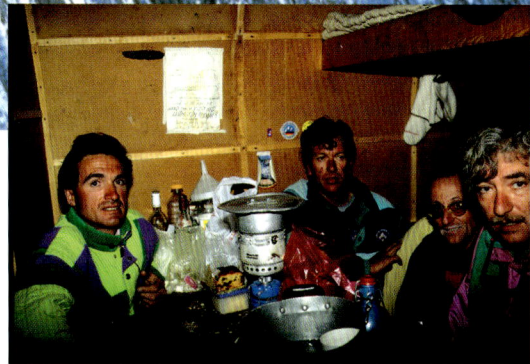

*Christophe Profit, often cited by fellow guides
for his professionalism, with Gilbert Pareau
who also enjoys the respect of his peers,
with their two clients at the Canzio bivouac.*

leaves a period of roughly ten days between each route, enough time to let mind and body recover. He estimates that since 1991 he has had around three seasons like that, spread out over several years. That's not that many...

In conclusion, Marc Cereuil and his colleagues point to the outstanding abilities of Christophe Profit. For them, he has successfully transposed his top-class skills and put them to use as a guide. For Michel he's a *"gentleman and it's his way of doing things. He doesn't question himself, even on the hardest routes."* Vincent Couttet looks back on his active ten-year career as a top-level guide.

He asks with humility how Profit manages to do so many big routes, one after another (by 2008 he had completed ten ascents of the north face of the Eiger, some of them with clients).

Although increasingly rare, one or two grandes courses are still handed out in the tour de rôle each year. They might also have been taken on by some of the other great technical climbers, such as François Marsigny, Thierry Renault and Alain Ghersen who naturally also appear on this list. These days there are only around 30 guides capable of guiding these kinds of routes. The Dumas, Potards, Bellevilles and Herrys, the next generation of high-level mountaineers and guides, will no doubt have their own ideas on these great long routes, where human adventure, desires, emotion and dreams meet technical ability.

Fête des guides 2004

1. Hervé Thivierge
2. Jean Raphoz
3. Serge Kœning
4. Olivier Larios
5. Nicolas Terray
6. Pierre Leroux
7. Lionel Wilbault
8. Jean-Louis Verdier
9. Michel Thivierge
10. Daniel Simond
11. Jean Villard
12. Florence Simond
13. Eric Thiolière
14. Christophe Jacquemoud
15. Vincent Ravanel
16. Victor Schmidt
17. David Ravanel
18. Franck Tresamini
19. Cyril Vion
20. Jean-Marc Vaillant
21. Blaise Verien
22. Marc Roman
23. Roland Ravanel
24. Marc Ravanel
25. Edmond Maresca
26. Jérôme Ruby
27. Jean-François Reymond
28. Jean-Noël Rossier
29. Gilles Ravanel
30. Christian Vallet
31. Bernard Prud'Homme
32. Thierry Ravanel
33. Roger Ravanel
34. Sylviane Tavernier
35. Nicole Hanoteau
36. Patrice Richard
37. Philippe Robe
38. Daniel Semblanet
39. Serge Tresamini
40. Pierre Schropff
41. Sylvain Ravanel
42. Emmanuel Schmutz
43. Michel Schneider
44. Raymond Vesin
45. André Braconnay
46. Camille Devouassoud
47. Eric Favret
48. Gérard Burnet
49. Claire Thiolière
50. Thierry Renault
51. Gilbert Pareau
52. Fernand Pareau
53. Jacques Pourré
54. Suzanne Mollard
55. Lionel Pouzadoux
56. Georges Payot
57. Franco Obert
58. Marc Gaïani
59. Nicolas Poncet
60. Béatrice Minster
61. Vincent Couttet
62. Eve Narcy
63. Nicolas Potard
64. Pierre Ravanel
65. Gilles Claret-Tournier
66. Christophe Profit
67. Pierrick Simond
68. Pierre-Alain Morand
69. François Marsigny
70. Laurent Langoisseur
71. Carole Falconnet
72. Eric Mathieu
73. Jean-Philippe Monet
74. Alexandre Ravanel
75. Frédéric Mathieu
76. Paul Parizet
77. Jean-Marc Ravanel
78. Christian Mollier
79. Bernard Moullier
80. Gérard Pétrignet
81. Armel Faron
82. Jacques Mottin
83. Jean-Marie Olianti
84. Daniel Méot
85. Serge Obert
86. Lionel Pernollet
87. Philippe Galan
88. Corinne Jouin
89. René Patty
90. Guy Peters
91. Pierre Perret
92. Elie Hanoteau
93. Alain Ghersen
94. Frédéric Gentet
95. Raoul Bossoney
96. Franck Astori
97. Christian Dufour
98. Michel Félisaz
99. Olivier Michaud
100. Françoise Mantel
101. Philippe Grospellier
102. Isabelle Frendo
103. Jean-Michel Guignier
104. Denis Etienne
105. Jean-Marie Germain
106. Emmanuel Méot
107. Didier Lavigne
108. Denis Leroy
109. Claude Gex
110. Guy Poncet
111. Frédéric Folliguet
112. Richard Maffioli
113. Jean-Paul Demarchi
114. Gilbert Chappaz
115. Roland Bozon
116. Paul Claret-Tournier
117. Christophe Cretin
118. Gaby Dufour
119. Nicolas Fagou
120. Alain Cretton
121. Jean-Jacques Franchino
122. Olivier Greber
123. Sylvain Frendo
124. René Ghilini
125. Christophe Ducastel
126. Jacques Cuenot
127. Roland Couttet
128. Fernand Audibert
129. Vincent Lameyre
130. Daniel Audibert
131. Francis Bozon
132. Norbert Bozon
133. Jean-François Collignon
134. Pascal Dufour
135. Didier Chenevoy
136. Martial Dumas
137. Jean-Philippe Couttet
138. Bernadette Ducoulombier
139. Armand Comte
140. Christophe Dat
141. Raymond Ducroz
142. Jean-Franck Charlet
143. Philippe Chillet
144. Manu Bozon
145. Fabienne Ravanel
146. Jean-Luc Burnet
147. Louis Folliguet
148. Lionel Bonano
149. Christophe Boloyan
150. Nicolas Grospellier
151. Jean-Louis Le Garrec
152. Jean-Christophe Bêche
153. Stéphane Berger
154. Jean Afanassieff
155. Philippe Bruere
156. Frédéric Devouassoux
157. Edmond Cachat
158. Frédéric Charlet
159. Claude Jaccoux
160. Claude Jacot
161. Jean-Paul Chatelet
162. Alain Payot
163. Kim Bodin
164. Yann Delevaux
165. Sam Beaugey
166. Marc Cereuil
167. Michel Balmat
168. Laurent Collignon
169. Eric Bertolino
170. Mike Cooper
171. Michel Arizzi
172. Frédéric Cambe
173. Jean-Paul Balmat
174. Frédéric Ancey
175. Jean-Pierre Albinoni
176. Eric Bellin
177. François-Eric Cormier
178. Patrick Ancey
179. Jérôme Arpin
180. Claude Ancey
181. Jean-Claude Charlet
182. Jean Blanchard
     caché derrière
     Stéphane Berger

168 166 164 182
69 162 160 151
167 163 159 158 157 156 155 180
165 161 154 153 152 149 148
133 135 137 138 139 140 142 145 146 147
134 136 141 144
123 143 117 116 115 114
121 120 119 118
103 121 107 108 109 112 113
104 105 106 110 111 72
37 85 82 81 79 76 75 71
86 84 83 60 61 80 78 77 73 70
54 56 57 58 62 63 65 74 68
35 59 64 66 69
36 33 32 31 30 29 27 67
34 13 28 26 25
10 12 15 17 24
11 14 16 18 23 22
19 20 21

Sylvain Frendo nears the top of the spur on the Aiguille du Midi first climbed by his grandfather.

THE COMPAGNIE TODAY

THE CHAMONIX GUIDES HAVE BEEN A PRESENCE IN THE MOUNTAINS
FOR OVER TWO CENTURIES.
HOW CAN THEY RECONCILE TRADITIONS AND THE DEMANDS
OF MODERN LIFE AT THIS THE BEGINNING OF THE 21ST CENTURY?

Can we still talk of the Compagnie as a single entity with a single voice? The numerous incidents and events throughout its history as well as its diverse collection of characters show that the Compagnie breaks down into its individual components: the guides themselves, with their distinctive personalities, stories and backgrounds and approaches to the mountains.

One thing is certain; the present always has its roots in the past. In a past that has shaped bodies and minds, and attitudes and characters.

The Compagnie has become part of the mountain lexicon. Yet what does it actually represent beyond a collection of idealised notions? The Compagnie today is first and foremost its guides and mountain leaders (accompagnateurs): around 160 guides, 40 accompagnateurs and 44 honorary guides living in Servoz, Les Houches, Chamonix and Argentière (not including the 'renforts prioritaires' or priority replacement guides).

Their distinctive knitted socks, knee-length knickerbockers and hemp ropes are quickly put back in storage after the 15 August festival and the guides set out again for the mountains.

The balcony overlooking the Mer de Glace,
wouldn't have deterred the 'pirates'.

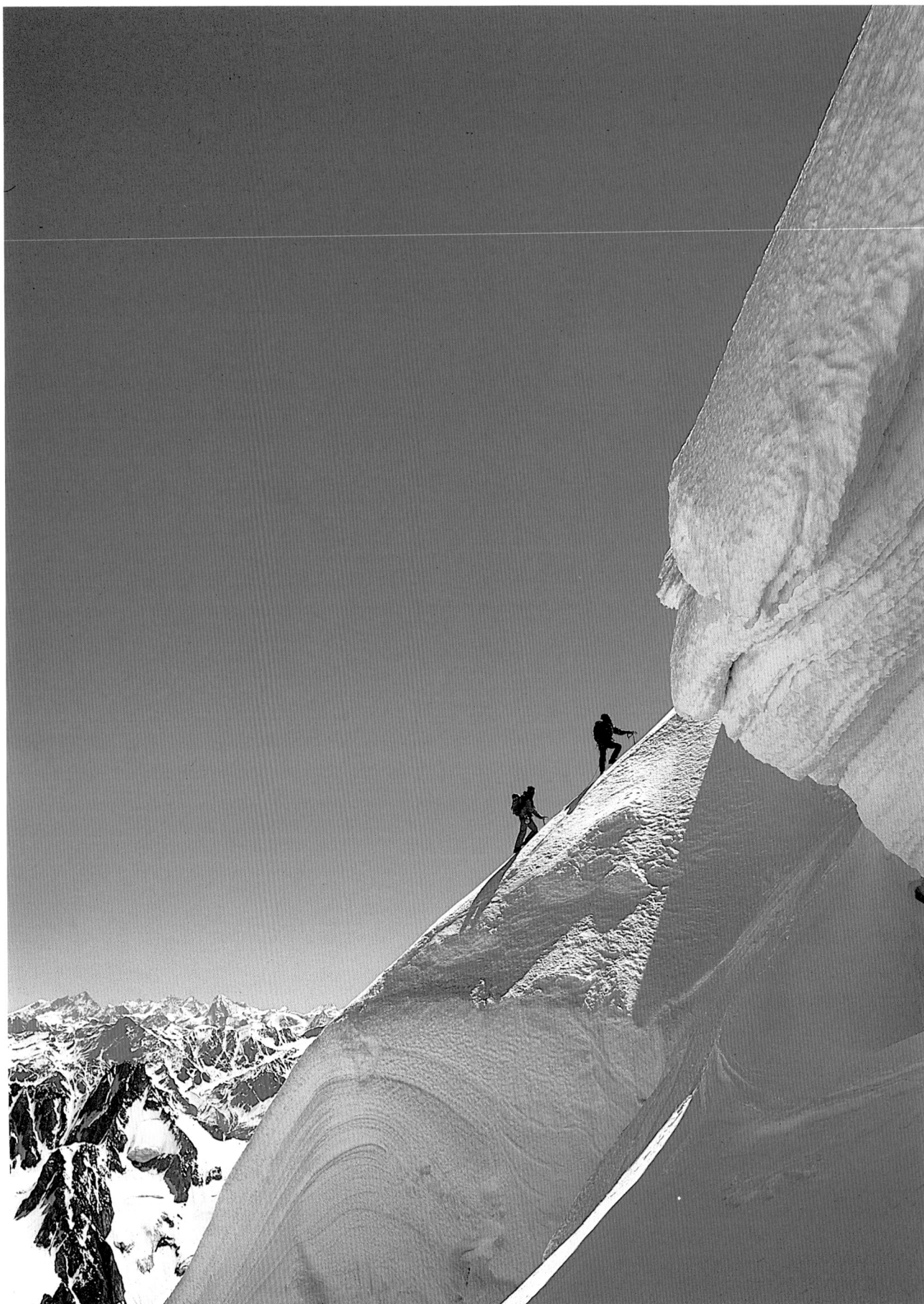

On the snowy dome of the Aiguille Verte, just above the Couturier couloir. This Chamonix classic is a particular favourite among the guides.

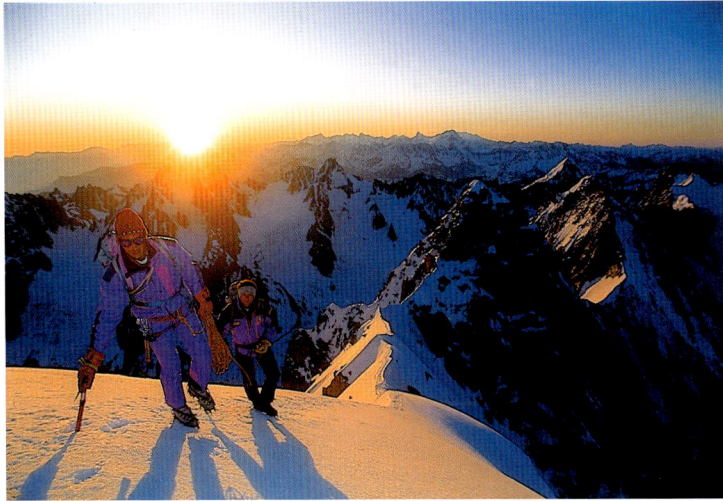

On the Aiguille Verte.
Arriving at
the Grande Rocheuse
is almost always
an intense moment.

GUIDES' STORIES

The seasons come and go at the same unchanging rhythm, and the guides go up to the huts, take their turns with the *tour de rôle*, organise the yearly *fête des guides* and stories are passed on from guide to guide.

Here they tell their stories in their own words. First to speak is Claude Ancey (who took part in the rescue of Desmaison on the Grandes Jorasses in 1967). *"One day in 1967 I left the Grands Montets at one in the morning with a client to do the Couloir Couturier on the Verte. It was a beautiful, cold and very dark night. We couldn't make out the terrain. It was the first time I had been in the area at that time of night. I reached the bergschrund where the climbing starts and I counted the number of couloirs to cross to get to the Couturier. We finally came to the big couloir and got started on it straight away. It took crampons well (we didn't have front points back then and the axes weren't like they are today!). We made quick progress and my client was fit. The day was dawning, the sun reddening the clouds in the distance. Looking up I saw seracs above me. I was a bit surprised as that wasn't how I imagined the couloir would be. I didn't say anything to my client and we carried on to the summit. We were alone, happy to be there and to have done such a great route in six hours. When we descended via the Whymper [couloir] and were in the Couvercle [hut] by midday. I met Joseph Burnet there* who asked me where I'd been. I told him the story and he said 'you just did the Couloir Cordier!' It was only the third guided ascent. And I'd done a great route, by mistake..."

On hearing this, I was really pleased, as was my client, especially as he had hired me to help him train in preparation for the guides' exam."

Another fascinating subject is danger. Obviously, we could place the guides on some kind of pedestal and make fearless heroes of them, but we would be forgetting that they too are men, sometimes fallible in the face of adversity. That said they are well used to tricky situations, as Lionel Wibault's experience in a sudden storm while climbing in the heart of the Dolomites attests. *"Suddenly the sky was filled with a ghastly beauty... A storm was brewing and I realised just how vulnerable we were. In one more pitch I would be on the summit of the Torre Delago, in the Dolomites' Vajolet range, but it felt like the pitch would never end. The wind had really got up and merely looking up at the inky black sky that was starting to envelop me was enough to spur me on.*

My client was climbing as fast as he could behind me, buoyed up and encouraged to cover the final metres of the proud spire of limestone.

On the summit we sorted out the rope without saying

Lionel Wibault.

a word. Expecting the storm to arrive at any minute and for of fear of being propelled into space, I quickly fitted an auto-block.

My only thought was to get off our lightening conductor. The ropes flew horizontally as we threw them down the notch that was our escape route.

Then came the first drops of rain, lashing our faces head-on.

I left my companion with some trepidation, swallowed up by the void as I grasped at my auto-block that was thankfully working fine.

After a few easy swings to find a stance, the impressive rappel came to an end.

All at once the wind blew stronger through the notch of rock and I had a devil of a time hauling my partner in next to me. Suddenly a ferocious storm broke. One more rappel and we would finally be under shelter."

The hands of a guide are like the hull of a boat; whatever the weather and the difficulty, you know they'll hold.

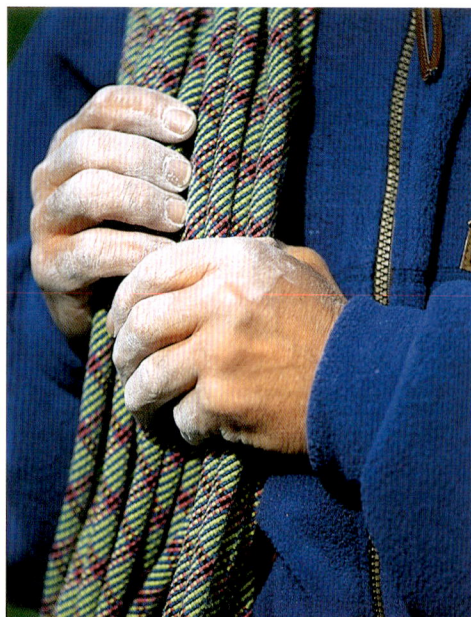

The great Forbes Arête on the Chardonnet.

Relations between guides and clients are not always idyllic. Gilles Ravanel recalled the feeling a guide gets when faced by a particularly clumsy client. *"There are things, possessions, people that nobody likes to share. And the village of Argentière gazes covetously at its mountains; the Verte and the Chardonnet belong to it. Concessions, however, must be made with the Verte: its fame, grandeur and routes, as varied as they are numerous, make it too seductive. She is lusted after like a flighty lover, and like a beautiful woman she sometimes evades the grasp of the Argentière guides...*

The Chardonnet is less glamorous, more intimate and loyal, she is the Argentéraux's own. Generation after generation of local guides have stood on its elegant summit and it is a popular request at the small Argentière guides' office.

That is how, almost 35 years ago, the famous 'tour de role' gave me a certain gentleman, Mr X, for a Forbes Arête on the Chardonnet, a beautiful route that isn't especially difficult. A short meeting with my client immediately had my young guide's self worried. Mr X didn't know the range but had climbed in the Oisans and he was confident the Chardonnet would be a walk in the park.

We made our arrangements and I met my strapping lad in the hut. We were up at two in the morning and, after a bite to eat, we were off. We were on our way. It looked like it was going to be a beautiful day; the snow in the comfortable track was frozen to a perfect consistency and crunched under our crampons. We had only just set off when a team led by one of my colleagues caught us up and overtook us. Laconic and to the point, my colleague exclaimed, in the local Savoyard dialect that was incomprehensible to the fellow with me: 'Mé pour té, me semblave ton monchu l'est un bocon sarpé! [Your client looks pretty incompetent to me!]'

Bah! What would Alain know? The light from his tiny torch was so weak he couldn't really see him. Mr X had done lots of great routes... He just wasn't very fast on the walk in, that's all. We'd catch up on the hard sections.

The teams heading for the Chardonnet were far in front of us now. We had barely started on the Forbes Arête itself when my monchu took a huge swing on the north face and it was only by chance or some kind of miracle that I managed to hold him. A fall like that would dampen anyone's enthusiasm... But not him. He had barely caught up with me, when he was assuring me 'it was nothing' and he would be more careful. Seriously shaken, I reconciled myself to the precautionary measures I would have to take with Mr X, considerations that were extremely useful and which my companion severely tested. I lost count of the number of slips and slides and pratfalls – which certainly didn't form part of Armand Charlet's technique – my client notched up.

The Mer de Glace face on the Grépon, a journey across Chamonix Granite. The difficult sections on this great route are not too difficult. This photo shows one of the superb grade V pitches.

Gilles Ravanel in the Dolomites with a client.
He learnt from experience which clients he could take where.

We got back to the hut three or four hours after the other teams. Anger and a feeling of humiliation (a pro getting back at that time, what a disgrace, what kind of guide would they think I was?!) got the better of me. I lost my patience and vented my spleen at him. I nevertheless managed to control my grumpiness and said almost politely: 'Sir, I will leave you to rest up and follow the path back down alone and if you plan to do any more routes, you should find someone else as it's over between you and me!'

That same evening, the head-guide at the time, who looked after the guides like a father, summoned me to see him and gave me a right earful. My client had passed by the office to pay his bill and said he was surprised at my dissatisfaction. He thought the climb had gone very well and he couldn't understand why I had got upset. Thankfully, my version of events tipped the scales in my favour and I received the penance-free absolution of André, the head-guide.

The reason I remember this incident so clearly is not because of my client's uncommon clumsiness, nor the yarn he spun me about all the routes in the Dauphiné he claimed to have done, rather it was the accuracy of my colleague's judgement, he had got the measure of my would-be climber in the space of a few seconds and in the feeble light of a headtorch."

The curious alchemy of the high-mountain environment:
crevasses, seracs, bad weather, altitude, avalanches...

Big ski tours, such as this one in the Swiss Bernina, are one of the guides' main sources of income.
It is also one of their most dangerous activities as the snow has a myriad of uncomfortable secrets and surprises.

Open the doors to the mountains as one opens the doors to a garden.
Gaston Rébuffat's poetic notion is still applicable today.
These skiers on the Grand Envers variation on the Vallée Blanche
are trying it out for themselves.

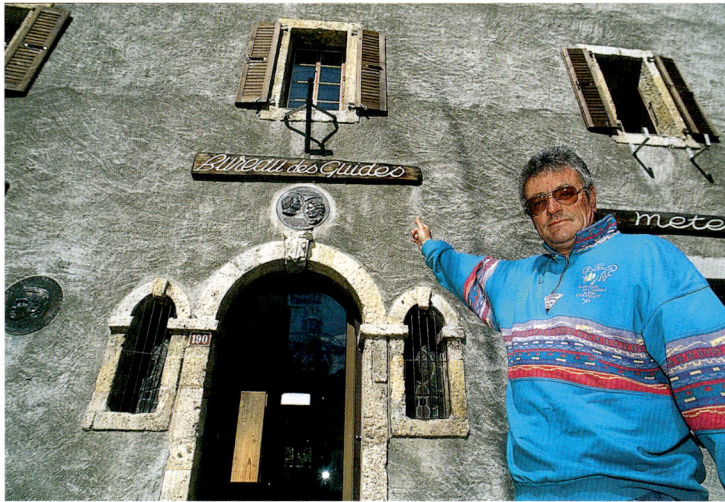

Set in the heart of the town, the guides' office is one of the most authentically Chamoniard places in the valley. Jean-Paul Demarchi invites you to step inside.

THE COMPAGNIE DES GUIDES, A DEFINING IMAGE OF CHAMONIX

Is it these stories, their personalities and the mountains that have shaped this group of men? Their reputation extends beyond the modest community of climbers. Mention Chamonix to almost anyone and he or she will reply, *"Ah yes, the Chamonix guides!"*

Brest is famous for its fishermen, Paris has its nightlife and Chamonix its guides. Its renown crosses frontiers, and former president of the guides and director of the Chamonix Tourist Office Bernard Prud'homme gives a great example: *"On our way home from Greenland, [the sailor] Jean-Louis Etienne and I gave a conference at the UN building in New York. In the semicircular chamber where the problems of the world are discussed everyone had heard of the Chamonix guides"*.

Its history extends beyond the confines of old Europe. It is perhaps Chamonix's reputation as the third most visited natural site in the world, after Niagara Falls and Mount Fuji, that has allowed its reputation to spread. Yet the two remain indelibly linked. The Compagnie also belongs to a collective imagination to which almost everyone subscribes. There has been no usurpation, the Compagnie's reputation continues to attract a whole group of people who love the mountains and who will one day walk through the door of the guides' office.

Yet what is it that brings people to these guides? I asked a few of their potential clients who were asking the price of being guided up the Mont Blanc du Tacul. It was the first time Mr and Mrs Vanier of Aix-en-Provence had been on holiday to Chamonix and they explained it as follows: *"We don't really know much about the mountains but for us it had to be the Compagnie des Guides. We were a bit surprised by the size of the town and the number of guides but we have been given a lot of information. On the other hand, we found the rate for one route a bit pricey, we're not going to do dozens of them…!"*

Once again the unconscious had a role to play in the decision-making process. Apart from the rolling clientele that the personnel of the Compagnie will guide for a single route, why do the more traditional clients come back year after year? Beyond ascents of Mont Blanc (these clients generally try for the summit before turning to other challenges elsewhere), some clients stay with the same guide for years and there comes a stage where these relationships are no longer simply commercial ones and are more often genuine friendships.

Jacques Hauser is a retired physicist in his 60s who has spent many years climbing with Jean-Pierre Albinoni. He has always climbed with guides from the Compagnie: *"I put a lot of trust in those guides, they have an insight and a knowledge of*

One doesn't necessarily have to climb up the great north faces or legendary rock routes to witness the beauty of a land waking up. Jean Villard and Vincent Ravanel reach the summit of the Mont Blanc du Tacul as the day is dawning over the surrounding peaks.

the place, and I can't ignore the magic that surrounds their reputation. Although I've done a good 20 routes with just my son, I still need the guides as they help us to avoid the mountains' traps and pitfalls and in a way my guide is my life insurance." Hauser has done over 150 routes, from the Drus to the Noire de Peuterey, with Jean-Pierre Albinoni and other guides from the Compagnie. Over the years they have established a real rapport, which is evidenced by the fact that Hauser is the godfather to Albinoni's daughter.

René Basdevant is another good example. A director of a multinational drug company, he has climbed with four guides over his climbing career and has notched up a long list of impressive routes, which currently stands at around 200. He has abiding memories of the years he climbed with Marcel Burnet and he, the man who runs a multinational, has no hesitation in favourably comparing Burnet's qualities with those of a managing director. *"In 1962, when I first started mountaineering, we naturally went straight to the Compagnie as there were no independent guides at that stage. The Compagnie had a prestigious reputation for technical prowess and I have been sharing those moments of beauty, emotion and silence as I arrive on the summit with my guide ever since."*

Even if the Compagnie has lost those famous clients who would hire guides for practically the whole summer season, it still has its loyal customers who will remain with it for the rest of their lives. It has also attracted a different kind of clientele by adapting to the changing climate.

Fifteen to seventeen thousand people go through the guides' office each year, two thirds of them in the summer months.

Demand has obviously changed, especially over the past few years, and the Compagnie has evolved as it has always done in the past. It has added rafting, canyoning and even the organisation of seminars with 'incentive-building' workshops to its repertoire of activities. Mont Blanc remains the most popular route in the summer and guides try to sell week-long courses so that they can properly prepare their would-be summiteers. This one mountain alone accounts for 500 to 600 of their customers.

Apart from Mont Blanc, requests are shared among group and private bookings. There are over a dozen guides that specialise in introductory rock climbing on the local crags while introductory ice climbing days have gone down (the Bossons glacier is no longer accessible, leaving only the Mer de Glace). Classic rock climbing routes such as those on the Aiguille Verte and other long routes are organised directly between the guide and client. Yet even in this area there have been

Although clearly visible from the valley floor, the Midi-Plan ridge used to be considered a far-off objective.
The building of the cable car in 1955 considerably changed matters
and now it is one of the most popular routes in the massif.

changes. The traverse of the Aiguilles Dorées, the Ravanel-Mummery traverse and the Barbet Spur on the Aiguille d'Argentière, highly prized 20 years ago, are hardly ever climbed these days. On the other hand, rock routes in the Aiguilles Rouges have become more popular thanks to a flowering in interest in technical climbs where the aim is not necessarily to reach a summit.

Guides too have evolved and you only have to compare the physiques of the peasant-guides of yesterday with the top-class athletes of today to see this. Modern guides tend to be more wiry and less stocky, are perhaps less concerned with long approaches, and are the first to steer their clients towards new and different terrain. If the guide prefers jaunts up the crack lines on the Blaitière, his or her client will soon happily discover the pleasures of granite climbing and may never sample the delights of the more far-flung corners of the massif.

The long, prestigious routes such as the Walker Spur on the Grandes Jorasses and the Frêney Pillar are the preserve around of 20 guides. The main activities of today's guides centre around easy and middling routes.

Contrary to what many people might suppose, not all the Compagnie's members are full-time guides. Of its 160 members, only half of them work full-time as guides. Just like their predecessors who also worked as farmers, carpenters and foresters, most of today's guides have more than one job. Notable examples include the filmmakers Denis Ducroz and Jean Afanassieff, the architect Paul Parizet, the former teacher Christian Mollier who now instructs at ENSA along with François Marsigny, and the painter Lionel Wibault. The majority of the others also work as hoteliers, restaurateurs, shopkeepers and ski instructors.

The summer season is the key working period for the guides and has to last them the whole year and then only if the conditions are good, while other kinds of customers are always around. The Compagnie has gone from being a simple association to a company and has developed it potential, offering its professionals multiple possibilities that are sometimes very different from their original training but well adapted to current demand.

Although getting there might have its difficulties, at heart they all want their clients to discover and love their mountains. Eric Favret, the current president, thinks that there might even be a kind of atavism at work here: *"I'm descended from the Payots on my mother's side. There hadn't been guides on that side for two generations. I think on a certain level it's quite visceral as I go to some places that I don't know and I get the feeling I've been there before".*

Eric is from Taconnaz and was one of the first Les Houches guides to join the Compagnie. *"In Chamonix you are brought up steeped in an atmosphere of the mountains and the guides. But it's not the same here. Until not very long ago people in Les Houches still lived off the land."* You only have to go a few kilometres and the whole mentality changes. As well as the Chamoniards, and since Frison-Roche and the other pioneering guides, it attracts more and more people and the Compagnie receives dozens of applications each year. It's not just the work that attracts them, they are also drawn to the prestige that the Compagnie represents.

And if it stands accused of being outmoded, it should be noted that almost all of the great mountaineers that France has produced have tried their luck with the Compagnie at one stage or another. Most were accepted thanks to their impressive list of routes while others owe their membership more to their people skills. Today over 50% of its members are not from the valley. However, once these Chamoniards by adoption join the Compagnie's ranks they often become its best ambassadors.

Thierry Renault is a good example of this: *"I read about Chamonix in "Premier de Cordée" [First on the Rope]. And straightaway I was struck by the characters such as Ravanel Le Rouge, and I thought that guides were almost fictional characters. It took a meeting with Fernand Audibert for me to realise* that the Compagnie guides weren't the product of a novelist's imagination. I quickly saw Chamonix as a welcoming place for me and I naturally applied [to join the Compagnie], as most of my friends were in it. There are several reasons as to why I was accepted: there were fewer Chamoniard applicants at the time when I applied, I got on well with the guides and I had various skills. So, I was taken on as a replacement guide, then as a trainee and finally as a full member. The Compagnie is a great school for humility, as you learn to live among a diverse range of wonderful and surprising men."*

What Thierry Renault intuitively called 'humility' shines through on 15 August. All the guides are placed on a pedestal but none of them are singled out for special attention. On that day the Compagnie tries to place all its guides on an equal footing, recognising the fact that it needs the guides who work on the standard routes as much as those specialising in extreme routes. However, there is one person who stands out and has difficulty blending in with all the other guides and it's not her fault that she is the only female member.

Sylviane Tavernier is descended from Ravanels and hails from Servoz, she is also a former French cross-country ski champion and is a high-level mountaineer. (She will shortly be joined by Karine Ruby, the Olympic snowboard champion.) Tavernier still remembers her first day: *"I didn't dare put a skirt on the first time I went along for the*

The Tour of Mont Blanc 'junior version'. This is a great way for children to explore the massif and its seven surrounding valleys at their own pace.

Snowshoe or raquettes walks are becoming increasingly popular.

tour de rôle. When my name was called out the head guide hesitated before giving me my ticket, and he must have wondered if I was a client who had wandered in by mistake… Or perhaps he realised he was bringing a tradition to an end."

Sylviane Tavernier would bring a feminine touch to this world of men. It also took a bit of time for the clients to adjust. "I remember one client I had on the Tacul, who kept asking 'you will hold me if I fall, won't you?' I explained our technique to him to try and reassure him but he didn't seem convinced. I ended up finding a safe place and tripping him up. He fell about two metres into a crevasse and I said, 'so, am I holding you?' He regularly comes into the mountains with me now!"

We have, since the start of this account, combined the notion of the Compagnie with that of the guide. Yet we could also add the 'pirates', muleteers, porters and accompagnateurs en moyenne montagne (known in the US and the UK as mountain leaders). Gilbert Mugnier together with the three other accompagnateurs who fought for their integration into the Compagnie have a great deal to be proud of, as they now form an integral part of the institution.

They now annually guide over 5000 hikers and trekkers along paths and trails across the globe. There are also dozens of groups that set off for the Tour of Mont Blanc, hikes around the Dents Blanches and the Grand Capucin as well as tours to Morocco and Nepal and numerous other destinations. And even American clients are requesting this Chamonix-style organisation.

Another reason the accompagnateurs can be proud is the development of snowshoeing, in which they played a vital role. And not only have they created a successful product but they can also dovetail their work with that of the guides, by joining them for trips to the Combe Maudite for example.

Then there are the other activities, such as canyoning and mountain biking, which respond to the changing demands of clients.

Far from being a dinosaur, the Compagnie is working hard to keep up with the evolution of mountain sports.

The organisation has also been involved in the reconstruction, renovation and management of certain huts over the past few years. These include the Cosmiques hut, which is financed in part by the guides. Each member has invested 1000 € (returned when he or she retires) in these tools that form part of their trade. Then there's the Charpoua hut, the old building full of history that no one is particularly interested in any more at the foot of the Drus. The Requin, on the Vallée Blanche, is also in need of repairs.

These show the Compagnie and the guides rolling

The 'salle du Tour de Rôle', where the turn taking ceremony continues, is one of the last places in the valley closed to non-guides. Nobody is allowed to film or photograph the ceremony and the guides themselves foster the aura of mystery surrounding the enigmatic ritual...

up their sleeves and getting back to basics. There have been other initiatives as well, such as a brand of clothing and the development and testing of products in collaboration with Rossignol.

We cannot discuss the Compagnie without mentioning the relief fund. This more than anything else represents the Chamoniard identity and its sense of solidarity.

It is more than a symbol and has been the cement that binds the Compagnie together ever since its creation at the inception of the Compagnie itself. The festival on 15 August is organised for the benefit of the relief fund and is the most important festival in Chamonix. Traditionally, the celebrations start in Les Houches on 13 August. On 14 August the guides and their friends meet in front of the church in Argentière before going on to the cemetery. That evening, there is the show at Les Gaillands, which includes fireworks and concerts. And finally on the 15 August there is the great ceremony. Each guide is individually called up to take his or her place on the steps in front of the church in Chamonix. This is followed by a speech from the president and a tribute to an old guide and the distribution of medals bearing the picture of the guide honoured. The first to be remembered in this way was Michel Croz in 1963.

There are also awards for particularly loyal clients, as some have been going into the moun-tains with the same guides for more than 30 years. After this the local priest blesses the guides' ice axes and ropes. This is followed by the singing of mountain songs by members of the guides' choir before mass is held.

There is then a celebratory drink at which the Chamoniards are joined by guides from Valtournenche, Cervinia, Courmayeur, the Oisans and the Vanoise as well as representatives from the PGHM, EHM, ENSA and the CAF. The celebration is also attended by ministers of state, mayors, members of parliament and even a prime minister has been known to show his support for the guides. The festival finishes in the afternoon with a selection of sporting and aerial performances.

All these celebrations serve to bring money into the relief fund's coffers and the fête des guides is its principal source of income. Some families 30 years after the death of loved one are still given financial and emotional support.

In 1996, with Operation Euro, the Compagnie was able to donate two vehicles to a rural home help association. No other guides' company or independent association can boast such generosity.

Sitting between the past and the present and between a question of overriding passion and that of business, Chamonix's Compagnie des Guides has found a happy equilibrium.

The ritual of receiving one's guide badge is the final confirmation of an attachment to a place and a profession, and to a way of life and a set of traditions.

The symbolism is even more powerful if the man presenting you with your badge is also your grandfather. In this picture, taken in 1996, Frédéric Ancey is awarded his badge by his grandfather Alfred Payot, former President of the Compagnie and grandson of Frédéric Payot.

It is still admired at the beginning of the 21st century because the men who set it up created a legend. By standing by its code of ethics, its high working standards and by calling upon its roots, the Compagnie gives a depth to the job of guide and accompagnateur that few other institutions can claim. Xavier Chappaz, its president and driving force for some 13 years, sums up the Compagnie with the following metaphor: *"Rather than being a straight line, the Compagnie is a beautiful series of curves. It has taken the time to smooth out its angularities and occasionally turns back to contemplate the route it has taken...*

It has to be said that on a daily basis our guides accomplish great feats and display great commitment. This is no less profound or rich when it involves taking men and women, who are not necessarily great mountaineers, to quite ordinary peaks. These clients will have what they will later describe as one of the best days of their lives. The guide is the man or woman who made it possible. It is, therefore, a special community of people who made, make up and continue to shape the Compagnie. It was quite a rogue's gallery of adventurers and rebels who were prepared to take on not only those mountain faces deemed unclimbable but also the traditions of the valley floor. It has to be remembered that in order to build up these age-old traditions, it took innovations of an uncommonly strong nature. The principle behind the tour de rôle is one of an equal right to work and it

is still in force today. Another founding tenet is that of solidarity and the system of mutual insurance, upon which the Compagnie is based. Perhaps this remote valley, far from anywhere, was a good place to experiment with a great modern idea, that of social security. At an age few institutions even attain, the Compagnie is far from being a dying star. It is buoyed up by its current talent and by it founding principles of commitment, equality and solidarity, which it inherited from its past and which make up the essence of a guide. If it can make sense of its traditions and use its past in the way others have made use of theirs in bygone eras to innovate and move forward, then its future is assured.

It is unsurprising it has become a reference point but it needs to stay relevant in a society that is moving and changing at an extremely rapid pace."

Finally, the Edouard Cupelins, Michel Payots, Joseph Ravanels, Georges Charlets, Léon Balmats and Marcel Burnets have left quite a legacy in their wake, one which many mountain lovers would love to take up. And as Benoît Couttet put it so succinctly in Yves Letz's report that appeared in Progrès magazine in 1950: *"It was the old guides who made the Compagnie and the youngsters merely have to follow. It's quite something the Compagnie!"* Something that continues to inspire people to this day...

Heart and soul of the Compagnie, Xavier Chappaz was its president for thirteen years. He is second from right, with a new batch of guides.

*Climbing hard routes on solo or with a partner,
boarding and skiing extreme slopes,
exploring the great mountains of the world,
taking clients up great rock routes or simply
to test their personal limits and abilities,
what might future chapters of this history have to tell us?...*

I would like to thank all those who believed in the project:

Jean-Pierre Albinoni, Fernand Audibert, Jean-Paul Balmat, Marie-France Balmat, François Bellin,
Léon Bellin, Philippe Bellin, René Bozon, André Braconnay, Claudine Burnet,
Gérard and Claudie Burnet, Chantal Carmoin, Gilbert Chappaz, Xavier Chappaz, Jean-Claude Charlet,
Jean-Franck Charlet, Marcel Charlet, Marc Cereuil, Antoine Chandelier, Gilbert Claret-Tournier,
Gilles Claret-Tournier, Léa Claret-Tournier, Claude and Camille Clérico, Armand Comte,
James Couttet, Mme Léon Couttet, M. and Mme Raymond Couttet, Raymond Couttet, Vincent Couttet,
Fernande Demarchi, Jean-Paul Demarchi, Jean-Pierre Devouassoux, Jocelyne Devouassoud,
Régis Devouassoux, André Ducroz, Louis Folliguet, Eric Fournier, Jean-Paul Fréchin,
Roger Frison-Roche, Alain Ghersen, René Ghilini, Maurice Gicquel, Elie Hanoteau, Claude Jaccoux,
Maurice Jaun, Jean-Claude Lachenal, Richard Maffioli, François Marsigny, M. and Mme Mazars,
Béatrice Minster, Christian Mollier, Michèle Morgan, Marius Nikolli, Fernand Pareau, Alfred Payot,
Georges Payot, Lionel Pernollet, Guy Peters, Maurice Pichon, Marie-Thérèse Plovier-Chapelle,
Catherine Poletti, Guy Poncet, Christophe Profit, David Ravanel, Gilles Ravanel, Roger Ravanel,
Roland Ravanel, Vincent Ravanel, Françoise Rébuffat, Thierry Renault, Gilbert and Volga Rhem,
Thérèse Robache, Doug Scott, Pierre Semblanet, Claude Simoncini, René Simond, Roger Simond,
Mme Ulysse Simond, Joseph Tairraz, Pierre Tairraz, Hervé Thivierge, Jean Villard,
the staff at the library at ENSA.

BIBLIOGRAPHY

- Ballu Yves, A la conquête du Mont-Blanc - Découvertes Gallimard, 1986.
- Ballu Yves, Gaston Rébuffat, Une vie pour la montagne - Editions Hoëbeke, 1996.
- Baud-Bovy Daniel, Le Mont-Blanc de près et de loin - Editeurs Gratier, Rey et Cie, 1903.
- Bettembourg Georges, La Mort blanche - Editions Acla, 1983.
- Bourget Jacques, Gérard Devouassoux, Le souffle de la montagne - Editions Solar, 1975.
- Canac Roger, Des cristaux et des hommes - Editions Glénat, 1997.
- Charlet Armand, Vocations alpines - Editions Victor Attinger, 1949.
- Chaubet Daniel, Histoire de la Compagnie des Guides de Chamonix - Editions la Fontaine, 1994.
- Cunningham Carus Dunlop, Pioneers of the Alps - Sampson Low, Marston, Searle, and Rivington, 1887.
- D'Angevillle Henriette, Mon excursion au Mont-Blanc - Editions Arthaud, 1987.
- D'Arve Stephen, Histoire du Mont-Blanc et de la vallée de Chamonix - Editions la Fontaine de Siloé, 1994.
- Debardieux Bernard, Chamonix-Mont Blanc, Les coulisses de l'aménagement, PUG, 1990.
- De Chatellus Alain, De l'Eiger à l'Iharen - Editions J.Susse, 1947.
- Didier Richard, Ailes de Mouches et Tricounis, récits d'Armand Couttet - Editions Jean Vitiano, 1946.
- Frison-Roche Roger, Jouty Sylvain, Histoire de l'Alpinisme - Editions Arthaud, 1996.
- Frison-Roche Roger, Le versant du soleil - Editions Flammarion, 1981.
- Frison-Roche Roger, Mémoires d'Aventure - AGEP, 1991
- Frison-Roche Roger, Premier de Cordée - Editions Arthaud, 1940.
- Ghilini rené, Le vagabond du vide - Editions Flammarion, 1982.
- Isselin Henri, Les Aiguilles de Chamonix - Editions Arthaud, 1961.
- Lachenal Louis, Carnets du vertige - Editions Guérin, 1996.
- Leroux Pierre, Guide - Editions Arthaud, 1988.
- Loux Françoise, Guides de Montagne, Mémoires et Passions - Editions Didier Richard, 1988.
- Mollier Christian, Du glacier du Mont-Blanc au glacier des Bossons, la glace et les hommes, 1993.
- Mollier Christian, Everest 74, le rendez-vous du ciel - Editions Flammarion, 1975.
- Payot Paul, Au royaume du Mont-Blanc - Editions La Fontaine de Siloé, 1996.
- Rébuffat Gaston, Les cent plus belles courses du massif du Mont-Blanc - Editions Denoel, 1974.
- Rébuffat Gaston, Etoiles et tempêtes - Editions Grands Vents, 1976.
- Rébuffat Gaston, La montagne est mon domaine - Editions Hoëbeke, 1995.
- Rébuffat Gaston, Pierre Tairraz, Splendeurs des cimes - Editions Grands Vents, 1976.
- Rousset Paul-Louis, Mémoires d'en Haut, 1996.
- Scott Doug, Himalayan Climber: A Lifetime's Quest to the World's Greater Ranges - Hodder & Stoughton, 1992.
- Smith Albert, A hand-book of Mr Albert Smith's ascent of Mont Blanc - Albert Smith, 1852.
- Terray Lionel, Les conquérants de l'inutile - Editions Guérin, 1995.
- Vivian Robert, L'épopée Vallot au Mont-Blanc - Editions Denoel, 1986.
- Whymper Edward, Scrambles amongst the Alps in the years 1860-69 - Murray, 1871.

Collected works:
- Chamonix : Une vallée, des hommes - Edimontagne 1978.
- Les Alpinistes célèbres - Editions Mazenod, 1958.

Other sources:
- Archives of the Compagnie des Guides de Chamonix.
- Archives of the Mairie de Chamonix.
- Archives of Les Amis du Vieux Chamonix.
- Archives of the Alpine Museum, Chamonix.
- Archives of the ENSA library, Chamonix.
- Archives of the Alpine Club library, London.
- Archives of the département of Haute Savoie.
- Collection Payot.
- Archives Nationales, Paris.

Photo-engraving, design and layout by Atelier Esope, Chamonix
Traduction : Cleere Josephine
© May 2009

ISBN : 9-782953-19-0

MARIO COLONEL

Mario is a long-term contributor to France's *Montagnes Magazine* and has worked with specialist mountain publications across the world, his articles and images frequently appearing in leading journals and magazines. He also works with the American photographic agency Aurora.

A mountain lover and accomplished alpinist, Mario is also the author of a number of books and divides his time between the Himalayas and the Alps. He maintains a particularly close affinity with the Chamonix valley.

For more information on his work visit: www.mario-colonel.com

By the same author:

- *Courses Neige et Glace, Massif du Mont Blanc, Editions Franck Mercier.*
- *Voyage au cœur du Mont-Blanc (with Pierre Tairraz), Editions Franck Mercier.*
- *Trekking autour des grands sommets, Editions Glénat (Special mention, Passy Mountain Literature Festival).*
- *Compagnie des guides de Chamonix, une belle histoire, Editions du Grépon, 1997 (Pays du Mont Blanc prize, Passy Mountain Literature Festival).*
- *Sentiers de grandes randonnées, Editions Glénat, 1998.*
- *Le Mont Blanc, Editions Castor et Pollux, 1999.*
- *Mont Blanc Eternel (text by Roger Frison-Roche), Editions Arthaud, 2000 (Special mention, Passy Mountain Literature Festival).*
- *Abécédaire du Mont Blanc, Editions Flammarion, 2001.*
- *Le Tour du Cervin, la plus belle randonnée des Alpes, Editions Arthaud, 2002.*
- *Chemins du ciel, les plus belles courses d'arêtes des Alpes, Editions Arthaud, 2003.*
- *Les plus beaux raids à skis, Editions Arthaud, 2004.*
- *Cévennes, Editions Alcide, 2006.*
- *Mont Blanc, Editions Mario Colonel (Special mention, Passy Mountain Literature Festival).*